Sheffield Hallam University
Learning and Information Services
Adsetts Centre, City Campus
Sheffield S1 1WB

102 029 881 2

THE ARCHITECTURE OF
EMERGENCE

D1332760

THE ARCHITECTURE OF
EMERGENCE

THE EVOLUTION OF FORM IN NATURE AND CIVILISATION

Michael Weinstock

A John Wiley and Sons, Ltd, Publication

Credits for all black and white drawings
All drawings by Michael Weinstock with Evan Greenberg and Karola Dierichs, and Maria Brewster, Christina Doumpioti, Moritz Fleischmann, Gabriel Sanchiz Garin, Andres Harris, Kostis Karatzas, Tamara Lavrovskaya, Revano Satria, Feng Shuai, Kyle Schertzing and Wang Ying.

WL
720.1
WE

SHEFFIELD HALLAM UNIVERSITY
LEARNING AND INFORMATION SERVICES

This edition first published 2010
© 2010 John Wiley & Sons Ltd

Registered office
John Wiley & Sons Ltd, The Atrium, Southern Gate, Chichester, West Sussex, PO19 8SQ, United Kingdom

For details of our global editorial offices, for customer services and for information about how to apply for permission to reuse the copyright material in this book please see our website at www.wiley.com.

The right of the author to be identified as the author of this work has been asserted in accordance with the Copyright, Designs and Patents Act 1988.

All rights reserved. No part of this publication may be reproduced, stored in a retrieval system, or transmitted, in any form or by any means, electronic, mechanical, photocopying, recording or otherwise, except as permitted by the UK Copyright, Designs and Patents Act 1988, without the prior permission of the publisher.

Wiley also publishes its books in a variety of electronic formats. Some content that appears in print may not be available in electronic books.

Designations used by companies to distinguish their products are often claimed as trademarks. All brand names and product names used in this book are trade names, service marks, trademarks or registered trademarks of their respective owners. The publisher is not associated with any product or vendor mentioned in this book. This publication is designed to provide accurate and authoritative information in regard to the subject matter covered. It is sold on the understanding that the publisher is not engaged in rendering professional services. If professional advice or other expert assistance is required, the services of a competent professional should be sought.

Executive Commissioning Editor: Helen Castle
Project Editor: Miriam Swift
Assistant Editor: Calver Lezama

ISBN   978-0-470-06632-4 (hb)
         978-0-470-06633-1 (pb)

Cover design, page design and layouts by Artmedia, London
Printed and bound in Spain by Grafos S.A.

To Diane

Acknowledgements

Thanks to all my friends and colleagues at the Architectural Association whose company I have enjoyed for so many years, and particularly to the students whose passion and commitment is a continual source of inspiration.

CONTENTS

Preface

The study of the changes that occur to the forms of the world has been a lifelong fascination for me. I spent my youth sailing the oceans in wooden sailing ships, where an understanding of the patterns and processes of the climate are of vital interest. Clouds and storms, winds and currents, shape daily life at sea, and the constant working of the ship and its sails and rigging manifest the forces of the atmosphere and oceans close to hand. The mathematics of navigation: looking through the sextant to bring the noon sun down to the horizon, and the sequence of calculations that follow, the pencil marks and rulings calculating distance and drift on intricate charts to plot position on the ocean surface, speak of the vastness and complexity of the physical world in relation to one human body. The forms of sailing ships and the way in which they work in relation to the forces of the ocean and atmosphere, the long history of their development from simple rafts to the barques and clippers of the great days of sail, and the even longer history of the instruments and mathematics of time and the movements of the sun and stars in relation to the earth, without which the navigation is not possible, were a preface to my architectural studies.

It has long been the tradition in the Western education of architects to think of architecture as a professional domain with a history predicated on a succession of emperors and monuments, kings and cathedrals. In this tradition man and the works of man are separate from nature. However, the word architecture has a much wider meaning in science and industry, generally referring to the organisation and internal infrastructure of a natural or culturally produced object. In this book I use the term in the simplest way, to refer to the arrangement of material in three dimensions and through time. All the forms of the world have architecture: from the smallest molecule to the tectonic plates of continents, from the simplest cultural artefacts such as stone tools and bone calendars to the largest megacity, and all are subject to change over time.

Forms come into being, persist through varying periods of time until they collapse and their materials are reorganised and new forms emerge. All the forms and systems of the climate, the oceans, the mountains and rivers, deltas and deserts, emerged from the complex processes of systems through which energy and material flow in fluctuating patterns. All the forms of life emerged within those systems, evolving all the variations of differing species as the forms of the climate and land changed. Life emerged and flourished, proliferated and speciated in response to those changes. Mankind is one species among all the others, a variant of the living forms of nature. The human form evolved, as other living forms, in response to changes in the climate, the surface of the earth and to changes in other living forms. Human culture evolved as a means of transmitting ecologically contextualised information down through time, encoding knowledge of how to live, how to gain food and fuel and how to shelter from the forces of the climate. Biological and cultural evolutions are distinct from each other but closely coupled.

All the forms of civilisation have arisen from the processes of cultural systems that are inextricably entwined with the processes of the climate and the ecological systems of life on the surface of the earth. Energy, information and materials flow through all the forms of life, through humans and all their works. As with all natural forms, the forms produced by human culture have emerged, evolved, spread and persisted through time, collapsed and new forms have emerged from their reorganisation. Over time humans have proliferated across the face of the earth until all the forms on the surface of the earth have been modified, to greater or lesser extent, by their works. All the forms of the world, of nature and civilisation, interact with each other as the environment of any form is comprised of the other forms. Energy, information and material flow between the forms of the world at multiple scales of space and time, and it is the fluctuations in these flows that induce change.

This book presents an outline of my research and studies in Emergence at the Architectural Association in London: analysis from the life sciences together with the complex systems of the physical world and from anthropology, archaeology and the evolution of human culture. Emergence requires the recognition of all the forms of the world not as singular and fixed bodies, but as complex energy and material systems that have a lifespan, exist as part of the environment of other active systems, and as one iteration of an endless series that proceeds by evolutionary development. In the natural world change is normal, but its intricate choreography is now further accelerated and perturbed by human activities. Global climate change is upon us; its effects will be local and regional – more energy trapped in weather systems produces emergent behaviour and consequences that are not entirely predictable. So too, the emergent behaviour of local economies and cultures, now connected and interlinked globally, is in the process of substantial reconfiguration. The cultural and physical parameters of the changes to all the forms of the world are becoming clearer, and it is evident that causality is dynamic, comprised of multi-scaled patterns of self-organisation in the flow of energy, information and material across all spatial dimensions, and all temporal scales, including human generations. To study form is to study change.

Michael Weinstock, July 2009

1.1 Boiling Water
The rising bubbles of steam in boiling water exhibit some of the
characteristics of emergence – a large number of simple
components, in this case water molecules, and heat energy from
the environment. It is possible to predict exactly when pure water
will boil (at 100° Celsius at the standard atmospheric pressure of
101325 pascals) but it is not possible to predict the position or
form of any individual bubble of steam.

Nature and Civilisation

Humans and all other living beings emerge from, and exist within, the dynamic processes and phenomena of the natural world, and they have had and continue to have a profound effect upon it. All forms of nature and all forms of civilisation have 'architecture', an arrangement of material in space and over time that determines their shape, size, behaviour and duration, and how they come into being. Energy, information and material flow through all the forms of the world, and human forms and culture have coevolved and developed within those flows.

We are accustomed to think of 'nature'[1] as all that is wild and untouched, landscapes of forests, grasslands, shorelines and seas, separate from, and unsullied by, the activities of mankind. In this enduring image the world turns, the seasons come and go, and life is abundant. Man is different, set apart from the wild, with a life that is ordered by culture and technology. This inherited image is ancient, a cultural legacy that derives from creation myths and religious concepts of paradise. Paradise was conceived as a walled orchard garden or an enclosed hunting park, an enclosure of wild nature, but protected from the worst dangers of the wild. Nature, created by God, was innocent, beautiful and divine, and sin entered the world only through human corruption. That concept persists today in the distinction that is commonly made between the purity of virgin nature and the depredations of technology. An alternative but equally persistent concept is that mankind was created for the perfection of nature; and that the natural world is there for the benefit of man, and in dominating the natural world so it is sanctified.

The understanding that human beings, together with their artefacts, are part of nature, has a much shorter history of only 400 years or so. The construction of a systematic study of a 'natural history' was first proposed by Francis Bacon in 1620, and is one of the earliest projects of science. His proposed study of nature included 'things artificial', the works of mankind as a manipulation of nature. 'Natural History' should be split into three interrelated domains; the study of ordinary or usual nature, of deviant nature, and of nature manipulated by man. Nature produces the 'history of generations' or species that develop in the ordinary course, or nature is forced from the ordinary course by the perversity of matter and produces monsters, or nature is constrained and moulded by mankind to produce the artificial. Furthermore, the three regimes were not to be treated separately, but could be subjected to the same inductive methodology of enquiry. 'For why should not the history of the monsters in the several species be joined with the history of the species themselves? And things artificial again may sometimes be rightly joined with the species, though sometimes they will be better kept separate.'[2] The concept of nature as a system that unfolds over time according to rules, and that mankind exists within that system, is the extension of Bacon's 'natural history'. Paul-Henri Thiry D'Holbach's Le *Système de la nature*, published in France in 1770, posits nature as following 'only necessary and immutable laws', an immense system in which 'Man is the work of Nature: he exists in Nature'. The logical extension of that understanding to include human activities is that the construction of tools, artefacts and dwellings is a natural behaviour, and that such natural behaviour was developed and evolved over time. 'Nature sends man naked and destitute into this world which is to be his abode: he quickly learns to cover his nakedness – to shelter himself from the inclemencies of the weather, first with artlessly constructed huts, and the skins of the beasts of the forest; by degrees he mends their appearance, renders them more convenient: he establishes manufactories to supply his immediate wants; he digs clay, gold, and other fossils from the bowels of the earth; converts them into bricks for his house, into vessels for his use, gradually improves their shape, and augments their beauty'.[3]

All organisms must feed, and do so by gathering from their environment; root systems and photosynthesis for plants, grazing of plants by herbivores, predation by carnivores on smaller animals; and humans do so by hunting, fishing and agriculture. Accepting that *Homo sapiens* is one species among others has the logical implication that the activities of humans, their artefacts and constructions, are not any more unnatural than the collective behaviour of the many social species that produce constructions, such as wasps, bees and termites, or the nests of birds. In this view, the struggle for survival produces activities in all living things; some behaviour is better suited for survival and the species survive and flourish, other behaviours are less successful and the species become extinct. Humans are the work of nature, and all the works of man, their material practices, constructions and artefacts, evolve and develop over time as part of nature. However, that does not mean that human activities are necessarily beneficial to other living forms, and indeed there is more than sufficient evidence to suggest that humans have extensively modified the ecological and climatic systems of the world to the detriment of other species.

1.2 Eroded Mountain
The morphology of the surface of the earth emerges from the interacting processes of the molten interior and the exposure of the surface to the continuous processes of erosion. These processes are produced by the climate, and changes to the climate change the behaviour, duration and force of each process. Erosion has worn down the entire mountain, exposing the layered rock strata surrounding the remnant core.

The understanding that the earth is very old, that it too has a history of many changes, and that the forms of living creatures were different in the past because of those changes, began to be developed in the 18th century. The recognition that changes to the form of organisms, and that the environment plays some part in that change, came in the same century. The first systematic examination of fossil evidence, right at the beginning of the 19th century by the French naturalist Georges Cuvier, contains methodical and detailed studies of the shapes of fossil mammoth bones found in Europe and Siberia that demonstrated their differences from living elephant species.[4] This comparative morphological study of vertebrate palaeontology established that there is a common skeletal plan for all vertebrate species, and that species that had existed in the past are now extinct. Cuvier stated that life began in the sea, that life on land followed, and that reptiles had existed before mammals. Once it was posited that the past was different to the present, it became possible to consider that the earth had experienced a series of geological ages, and that each age had its own characteristic landscapes and organisms. The gradual acceptance of these ideas, and the subsequent development of the sciences and disciplines founded on them, has begun to unfold the complexity of the relations of the physical world to the life within it. From the long perspective of geological time, it is clear that 'nature' has no normal or fixed state, but is a continuing series of changing landscapes and climates, and that living organisms change and develop accordingly.

The landscapes of the world have been as much shaped by the history of human activities as by climatic effects such as glaciers, and by geological processes of uplift, erosion and deposition. There is no singular 'natural landscape' to be found, no ideal state of nature that can be reconstructed or modelled. The difficulty of hypothesising a landscape with little or no human influence is evident, but a much greater difficulty arises when climatic variations are considered. Large fluctuations in temperature, between the rapid cooling of ice ages and prolonged periods of high temperatures, have occurred in the history of the earth, each producing significantly different plants and animal species in each climatic condition. The surface of the earth, the shape and form of the land itself, has been subject to continuous change, and the chemical composition of the atmosphere has been changed not just by geological events such as volcanoes but by the biological processes of living things. Human activities have played a significant role in shaping the ecology of all the natural systems of the world, of the living species and of the physical systems of the land, the oceans and atmosphere.

A systematic exegesis must proceed from the understanding that nature is the domain of all living things, and of the dynamic processes and phenomena of the physical world within which they exist, and upon which they in turn have such a profound effect. It must include an account of the way that humans and all other living things come into being and change their behaviour and form, of the physics of the climate, and the material and energy of which all things are made. All the forms of nature and of civilisation have an architecture, an arrangement of material in space and over time that determines their shape, size and duration, how they come into being and their behaviour.

NATURAL FORMS

The forms of nature – living forms such as plants or animals, and non-living forms such as river deltas, hurricanes or desert sand dunes, have an intricate relationship. They interact with each other and with their local environment, and in doing so they modify that environment, which in turn may change sufficiently to induce further reciprocal modifications. Natural forms have the capacity to change significantly and to generate new forms, structures and properties from existing ones. There are many complicated and interlinked processes involved,

1.3 Eroded Canyon
'Slot' canyons are eroded by seasonal flash floods after thunderstorms. The water penetrates cracks in the sandstone and over many thousands of years forms canyons that may be up to 50 metres deep. The water carries particles of sand at high velocity and so abrades the surface. Localised turbulence and eddy patterns in the flow of water produce complex geometries in the eroded canyons.

with significant variations of spatial scale and of time. The formation of a snowflake and a hurricane, for example, are both dependent on energy (temperature) and humidity, but their differing sizes are separated by eight orders of magnitude.[5] Geological processes are also energy critical, for example, the movement of tectonic plates and the raising of mountain ranges, the release of strain energy by earthquakes and the eruption of volcanoes are all powered by the flow of internal heat from the earth's core to the cooler outer surface. Energy is also the most significant factor in the relationships between living organisms and the physical world. All living things require energy to grow, to maintain themselves, and to propagate themselves into the future.

Non-living forms, the forms of the land, the forms of clouds, snow and storms, dunes and rivers, are not permanent static things but dynamic three-dimensional patterns produced by the continuous physical processes of the natural world, and are constantly being broken down and renewed. Living forms, the forms of grass and trees, fish, reptiles, birds and mammals, are also subject to change but are persistent over time, organised by their internal biological processes and by exchanges with their environment. So a biological form persists through long generations, never exactly the same from one generation to the next, and over extended periods responds to the external changes of its environment. Form, in this way of thinking, is something like the wave that appears downstream of the pier of a bridge in a fast flowing river, consistent in the sense that it remains in approximately the same place and with approximately the same geometry but also constantly subject to small changes as the velocity and volume of the river fluctuates. We can say that all forms emerge from the dynamic processes by which natural systems, both living and non-living, produce organised arrangements of material in space and time.

The complex interrelations of the many phenomena that emerge in nature, each consisting of millions of parts or elements, each with its own processes which in turn affect other processes, suggest that the classical methods of analysis, the breaking down of a whole into constituent parts, will not completely suffice. Fossil evidence indicates that the history of biological evolution is a sequence, from simple cell organisms to the higher complexity of plants and animals. Organisms of increasing complexity spontaneously appear, each new level of complexity emerging from a preceding simpler organisation: from molecules to single cell organisms, from small multicellular organisms to plants, and to animals including humans. Each new level of complexity

1.4 Coral

The complex three-dimensional structure of brain coral (*Diploria labyrinthiformis*), like all other biological structures, is assembled by the multiple repetition of simple elements and small local variations of geometry. Corals are colonies of thousands of simple organisms, polyps, linked by a common gastrovascular system through which they share food, water and wastes. They adapt to different environments by the evolution of unique morphologies – brain corals usually form hemispherical mounds, and are slower growing than branching coral.

produces forms and behaviour that are different from the level below. This tendency towards increasing complexity raises a general question about the study of biological forms or organisms. The emergence of the species of lobsters or scorpions, and their morphology and behaviour cannot be predicted by the study of a simple tube-worm, although they both evolved from the tube-worm. This is also true of individual organisms, for example, investigating the cells of a leaf separately and in isolation will help to understand leaf cells, but that ignores how changes in one group of cells can affect other cell arrangements and behaviour, such as phototropism or the transpiration of water and gases from the whole tree. There is a similar, though lesser difficulty, in studying the forms of non-living nature – a study of the shapes of individual sand grains is helpful, but is not sufficient to predict the varied morphology of sand dunes, or how some dunes migrate across the desert and maintain a consistent form while doing so. Natural forms are not created by a single force or event, nor by the simple coexistence of many parts; it is the interactions of each part to its immediate surroundings that initiates processes that over time produce coherent forms.

CIVILISATION

The origin of the word 'civilisation' suggests that it is associated with living in cities.[6] Cities are the largest and most complex material forms constructed by humans, and have a relatively short history of six millennia or so. The term 'civilisation' was traditionally a collective term for groups of cities bound together into states and empires that had definitive boundaries in time and geography, for example, 'Greek civilisation' or 'Mayan civilisation'. The first criterion in archaeology and the social sciences for defining civilisations is large and densely populated cities with monumental architecture. Monuments are the most static and enduring constructions of cities, but a chronology of monumental architecture and emperors, of cathedrals and kings, will not serve to unfold the complex interactions of the systems of nature and of civilisation. Other conventional criteria included a complex social organisation with a ruling elite at the top of a stratified society, written language and mathematics; all of which were used as diagnostic symptoms of what was or was not civilised. The purpose of proliferating criteria is unclear, as the definition was used only to separate out what was uncivilised – the 'primitive'. A similar attitude is now found in the commonly used term 'prehistory' to exclude all human practices, artefacts, constructions and social groupings prior to the emergence of cities.

Cities are dynamic forms, constructed spatial and material arrays that are reworked and rebuilt over time, decaying, collapsing and expanding in irregular episodes of growth and incorporation. A city is comprised of dwellings, and the pattern of their arrangement coevolves with the systems for the movement of food, material, water and manufactured artefacts. The anthropologist Claude Lévi-Strauss described the city as 'a congregation of animals who enclose their biological history within its boundaries and at the same time through their every conscious action mould and shape it. By both its development and its form, it belongs simultaneously to biological procreation, organic evolution and aesthetic creation. It is at one and the same time an object of nature and a subject of culture; an individual and a group; something lived and something dreamed; the supreme human achievement.'[7]

Civilisation is the common heritage of all humanity,[8] the sum total of all the material, ecological and social products of human activities over time. Culture is the evolved system of transmitting increasingly complex social and ecologically contextualised information down through the generations, the means by which each generation is bound into society and through which they contribute to it. The systems that humans have constructed have tended to increase in complexity over time, a process that began over 130,000 years ago in east Africa with the emergence of anatomically modern humans, and that has been accelerated in the recent past. The coevolution of cities and citizens cannot be separated from the turbulent dynamics that characterise the complex relations of city forms to the ecological system within which they arose. From this perspective, civilisation is the product of culture, and is advanced through the evolutionary trajectory of human forms and their increasing human ability to extract energy from nature, to manipulate the materials of nature, and the accumulation and propagation of information.

THE EVOLUTION OF LIVING FORMS

The convergence of biological taxonomies and geological studies of land formations and fossils accelerated in the 19th century. *The Origin of Species* was first published in 1859, in it Charles Darwin argued that just as humans breed living organisms by 'unnatural' selection, organising systematic changes in them, so wild organisms themselves are changed by the struggle for life. He described the process of natural selection as 'the war of nature' involving predators, parasites and environmental pressures such as food supply, temperature and water. Famine and death remove the 'less improved forms', so that only successful organisms survive the fierce competition and have greater breeding success. Their offspring in turn have even greater reproductive success, and so on down the generations. The 'higher animals' or most complex biological forms developed from very simple beginnings, and natural selection was the means by which each species became more perfectly fitted to its environment. 'There is grandeur in this view of life, with its several powers, having been originally breathed into a few forms or into one; and that, whilst this planet has gone cycling on according to the fixed law of gravity, from so simple a beginning endless forms most beautiful and most wonderful have been, and are being, evolved.'[9]

Living organisms can be regarded as systems, and these systems acquire their complex forms and patterns of behaviour through the interactions, in space and over time, of their components. The dynamics of the development of biological forms, the accounts of growth and form, of morphogenesis, have become much more central to evolutionary theory than in Darwin's thesis. Darwin's arguments had an alignment with the then current theory of competitive struggle in capitalism[10] and the concepts of mechanisms in industry. Theories of morphogenesis, the creation of forms that evolve in space and over time, are now inextricably entwined with the mathematics of information theory, with physics and chemistry, and with organisation and geometry. The alignment with concepts and technologies of economics and industry remains consistent today.

The convergent lines of thought between biology and mathematics were initiated early in the 20th century, particularly by the work of Alfred North Whitehead and Wentworth D'Arcy Thompson. D'Arcy Thompson, zoologist and mathematician, regarded the material forms of living things as a diagram of the forces that have acted on them.[11] Living things are made of physical material and are subject to the same forces as non-living material, and so physics and geometry are as significant as natural selection. His observations of the homologies between skulls, pelvises and the body plans of different species suggested a new mode of analysis, a mathematisation of biology. Morphological measurements are specific to species, and at times to individuals within a species, and so are various, but there are underlying relations that do not vary – the 'homologies'. Homology has two distinct but related meanings: to biologists it means organs or body parts that have the same evolutionary origin but quite different functions, and to mathematicians it is a classification of geometric figures according to their properties. Form can be described by mathematical data, by mapping points in three-dimensional coordinate space, by dimensions, angles and curvature radii. D'Arcy Thompson's comparison of related forms within a genus proceeds by recognising in one form a deformation of another. Forms are related if one can be deformed into another by Cartesian transformation of coordinates. Comparative analysis reveals what is missing in any singular description of a form, no matter how precise, and that is the morphogenetic tendency between forms. In this argument genetic information does not need to fully specify the geometry of a form, as the natural forces of the environment and mathematical principles will determine the specific geometry during growth and development.

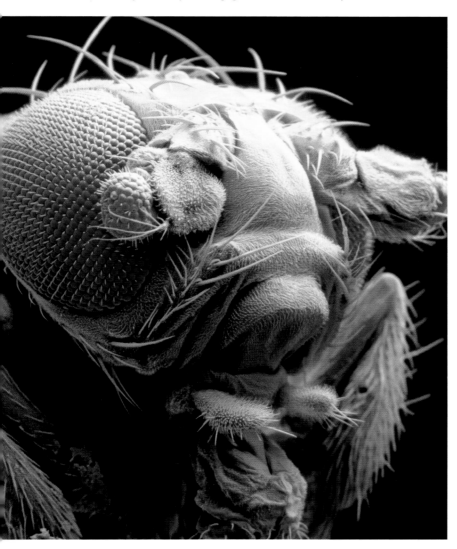

1.5 Mutation
The head of a mutant fruit fly *Drosophila melanogaster*. This mutant has two small perfectly formed eyes in place of antennae, seen here between the large red compound eyes. The mutation is produced by modifying the expression of a single gene during the early development of the fly embryo.

At around the same time, the mathematician and philosopher Alfred North Whitehead[12] argued that process rather than substance was the fundamental constituent of the world, and that nature consists of patterns of activity interacting with each other. Organisms are bundles of relationships that maintain themselves by adjusting their own behaviour in anticipation of changes to the patterns of activity all around them. Anticipation and response make up the dynamic of life. The union of these two groups of ideas is very interesting – form and behaviour emerge from process. It is process that produces, elaborates and maintains the form or structure of biological forms and that process consists of a complex series of exchanges between the organism and its environment. Furthermore, the organism has a capacity for maintaining its continuity and integrity by changing aspects of its behaviour. Forms are related by morphogenetic tendencies, and there is also the suggestion that some, if not all, of these characteristics are amenable to being modelled mathematically.

EVOLUTION AND THE FORMS OF CIVILISATION

Darwin argued that all the species of the world were the offspring of common parents, descended from an 'ancient progenitor', and that 'all past and present organic beings constitute one grand natural system'. The evolutionary development over time of all the species of life was driven by mutation and natural selection.[13] The question arises 'is the development of human culture over time similar to, or comparable to, the evolution of species and the forms of living beings?' The emergence of anatomically modern humans from the ancestral great apes was coupled to an increase in cognitive capacity, to the manufacturing and refinement of artefacts such as stone tools and weapons, personal jewellery and painted images, notched bone 'calendars' and to the building of increasingly complex dwellings. The transmission of knowledge by spoken, graphical and numerical languages constitutes a system of information transmission that is distinct from, but entwined with, the biological system of transmission, the genome. The biological evolution of humans was coupled to the development of a material culture that extended their ecological range and through which they modified their environment.[14] The emergence of the biological form of anatomically modern humans cannot be separated from the development of human culture; they have always been and continue to be interlocked in a coevolutionary process. The development of a larger brain and enhanced cognition is strongly coupled to the evolutionary development of material technology that extends and enhances individual and collective human metabolism. Humans have three times the cranial capacity of the great apes,[15]

1.6 Primate Skulls

X-rays of the skulls of a gorilla (*Gorilla gorilla*, left), chimpanzee (*Pan troglodytes*, centre) and human (*Homo sapiens*, right), all part of the closely related primate group Hominidae. More than 98 per cent of the genome is common to gorilla, chimpanzee and human. The genetic information is not a description of the biological form, but codes the process of generating the form. Significant differences of form are produced by very small differences in the sequence of specific sections of the genome rather than by large 'coding' differences.

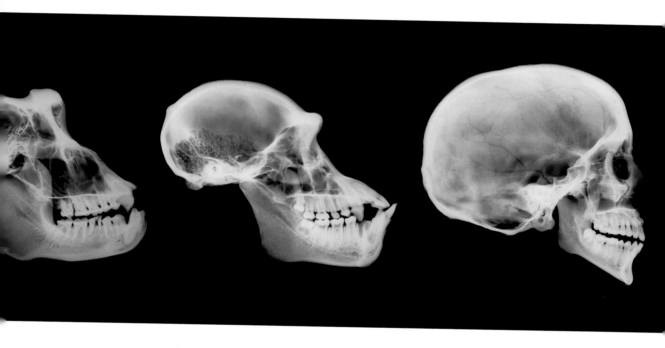

and positive feedback operated between the increase in brain size and the increase in complexity of culture, so that each acted to accelerate the development of the other. Bigger brains enabled a more complex culture, and in turn more complex culture enhanced the ecological 'fitness' of the group and so positively modified the regime of natural selection in favour of bigger brains. Cultural information has been and continues to be transmitted down through the generations. That information is manifested in the social structures and activities of humans, and in the forms of artefacts and buildings they construct. There is a development over time of artefacts and buildings, from the ancient pit dwellings of the first anatomically modern humans to the cities of the ancient world, and on to the built forms and 'megacities' of the contemporary world. It is clear that culture is inherited by descendants, there is descent with modification in artefacts, and the forms of buildings and even cities can be grouped into morphological taxonomies in a similar manner to the grouping of species.

The evolution of language has been intensively studied, and its association with biological evolution begins with Darwin. In *The Origin of Species*, Darwin presents the use of a branching diagram or tree for classifying the origin and subsequent evolution of diversity in the species. He thought that all the differing dialects and languages of the world, extinct and modern, had evolved from a single original language, 'a genealogical arrangement of the races of man would afford the best classification of the various languages now spoken throughout the world'.[16] Human language emerges from the set of vocalised sounds that many social species, including the ancestral apes, use to assert identity and membership of a group. For example, male dolphins and whales produce complex 'songs' for courtship, and for marking the boundaries of their territories.[17] The ability to produce and learn sets of sounds is genetically conserved, as 'vocal learning' maintains social cohesion and organisation. Over time, it provides the instrument for the development and elaboration of an extensive set of arbitrary sounds from which the first spoken languages emerged.[18] The human development of spoken language from vocalised sounds is thought to have taken more than one million years, as it required morphological modifications to the skull and internal reorganisation of the brain.[19] Geneticist LL Cavalli-Sforza, whose studies in

1.7 Mammoth Bones Used in Construction of Dwellings
Some 35,000 years ago in Kostenki, Ukraine, there were more than 50 large settlements with dwellings constructed over excavations in the earth. Excavating into the ground provides good insulation and pit dwellings had clear thermodynamic advantages, smoothing out the external fluctuating temperatures and significantly reducing the load on both the individual and group metabolic processes of humans in winter. Analysis of archaeological finds suggests that mammoths and other megafauna were driven to extinction by human predation combined with the indirect ecological stress to their habitats induced by humans. Climate change may also have contributed.

1.8 Information
A 5,000 year old clay tablet marked with cuneiform script, made with the cut end of reeds. The reed styluses were pressed into wet clay balls or tablets, and recorded transactions, measurements of field area and quantities of grain. The increase in the flow of energy and materials through cities in Mesopotamia accelerated the evolutionary development of systems of notation and mathematical calculation. The first forms of systematic writing emerged simultaneously in Mesopotamia, Egypt and China about 5,000 years ago, at the same time as cities.

linguistics and genetics have revealed strong correlations between the geographical pattern of variations in languages and the human genome, estimates that spoken language is likely to have evolved close to present day complexity only 100,000 years ago.[20] The original language of the small founding population of anatomically modern humans in Africa had evolved variations and split into the major language families by 40,000 years ago.

Human culture has evolved, but it is also clear that there are significant differences between the evolution of human culture and the evolution of biological forms. Humans have had a profound impact on nature, and that suggests the first significant difference between biological and cultural evolution. Whereas biological evolution has adapted all other living species to their environments, the evolution of human culture has adapted environments to the human species. It follows that the criteria for 'fitness' in the regime of selection are quite different. Other differences include the modes of inheriting information. Biological information, the genome, is transmitted 'vertically' down through time from one generation to the next. Cultural information is transmitted not only vertically, but also horizontally, between neighbours of the same generation, so that it diffuses between social groups that are spatially separate but contiguous. Transmission may also be oblique, between different generations in neighbouring locations. This means that when compared with biological evolution cultural evolution can be extremely rapid .

Continuous contact between two or more distinct groups or societies will bring about a process of change known to anthropologists as 'acculturation'. The changes will reflect something of the character of that contact. For example, peaceful contact will result in the emergence of a new variant, in which the beliefs and practices of both societies merge and hybridise, while political, economic or military domination will usually result in one society completely absorbing the other's cultural patterns by a process of selection and modification. Changes or variations of cultural forms occur both by mutation or 'copy errors', and by the recombination of existing information into new sequences and patterns. Information transmission has been an essential characteristic of human culture since anatomically modern humans evolved from the great apes. Information concerning the making of artefacts and constructions has been accelerated exponentially several times, by the sequential emergence of spoken language and trading networks, graphical arts and mathematical notation, written language, accounting systems and agriculture, cities and marine craft, the printing of books and maps, and more recently by telephony, computers and the Internet. Culture is a system of 'descent with modification'; in which ecological and social forces determine which variant forms of information and artefacts survive, are proliferated and transmitted down through the generations.

FORM AND BEHAVIOUR
Form and behaviour have an intricate relationship. The form of an organism or city affects its behaviour in the environment, and a particular behaviour will produce different results in different environments, or if performed by different forms in the same environment. Most plant and animal forms have a limited climatic ecological range within which they can flourish. The culturally produced forms of settlements and cities exhibit rather different relations between form and behaviour. They are not static objects so much as collective forms that humans operate and maintain by a complex series of exchanges with

environments that are extensively modified by human actions. For example, an agricultural settlement that emerged and developed in cool northern latitudes had a cycle of planting, cultivation and harvesting that modified the local ecology over a large territory, which extended far beyond the buildings and walls. Social practices and structures developed in relation to that cycle. The forms and materials of buildings and houses, the spatial arrangement of the town and of its associated land were, in varying degrees, produced by activities that were highly specific to that context. If the settlement were to be transplanted to the hot arid climate of the lower latitudes, the buildings would need some modification and the timing of the agricultural cycles and the species of plants, would have to be changed if the inhabitants were to avoid starvation. In principle, however, the system has proven to be adaptable to a wide range of ecological systems and climates.

Mathematical descriptions of behaviour are found in the elaboration of Whitehead's 'anticipation and response' by Norbert Wiener, who developed the first systematic description of responsive behaviour in machines and animals.[21] Wiener argued that the only significant difference between controlling anti-aircraft fire and biological systems was the degree of complexity. He had developed new programs for ballistics guidance, in which information about the speed and trajectory of a target is input to a control system so that anti-aircraft guns could be aimed at the point where a target would be. The control system could record and analyse the data from a series of such experiences, and subsequently modify its movements. Cybernetics organises the mathematics of responsive behaviour into a general theory of how machines, organisms and systems of all kinds maintain themselves over time. It utilises digital and numerical processes, in which pieces of information interact, and the transmission of information is optimised.[22] Cyberneticists regard 'feedback' as a kind of 'steering' device that regulates behaviour, using information from the environment to measure the actual performance against a desired or optimal performance.

Work in thermodynamics by Ilya Prigogine extended this (and the second law of thermodynamics), by setting up a rigorous and well-grounded study of pattern formation and self-organisation that is still of use in the experimental study and theoretical analysis of biological and non-biological systems.[23] He argued that all biological organisms and many non-living systems are maintained by the flow of energy through the system. A very small proportion of the sunlight that falls on the surface of the earth is transformed into biological form, and most

1.9 Branching
The anatomical organisation of trees has evolved a fully integrated morphology that simultaneously optimises the transportation network for fluids, structural stability and support for the leaf array above. The structural properties of the trunk and branching network emerge from the differentiated pattern of growth interacting with the metabolic imperative of maximising the surface area for photosynthesis. Metabolic scaling characteristics emerge from the geometry of branching networks in the vascular system of trees and in both the cardiovascular and respiratory systems of all mammals.

ecosystems fix approximately 2 per cent of the available sunlight. Solar energy drives evaporation from ocean and lake surfaces, the dynamics of the weather, and transpiration from plants. Energy enters the ecological system as light, is transformed into chemical energy in organic molecules by photosynthesis in plants, and is converted into heat energy by herbivores that feed on the plants, and then by carnivores that feed on the herbivores or other carnivores. Other organisms process dead organic matter, and release a great deal of heat energy during their processes. Once organic compounds are decomposed to their inorganic form they can be taken up by plants once again. Matter is recycled but energy is not. Energy in biological systems is dissipated, lost to the system as heat; once lost it cannot be recycled. All natural and cultural systems rapidly terminate without a constant supply of energy.

The pattern of energy flow through living forms, and through all the forms of human culture, the networks of cities and states, is subject to many fluctuations and perturbations. The flow is modified by 'feedbacks', but occasionally there is such an amplification or inhibition that the system must change, must reorganise or collapse. A new order emerges from the turbulence of the system that has collapsed. The reorganisation often creates a more complex structure, with a higher flow of energy through it, and is in turn more susceptible to fluctuations and subsequent collapse or change through reorganisation. The tendency of living systems and of cultural systems to ever increasing complexity, and of each reorganisation to be produced subsequent to the collapse, suggests that the evolutionary development of all forms is regulated by the dynamics of energy flow.[24] An increase in complexity is always coupled to an increase in the flow of energy through the system, and systems that collapse and revert to a simpler organisation are coupled to a reduced flow of energy. Nearly all systems tend to increase in complexity over time.

THE DYNAMICS OF ORGANISATION

What is common to the study of all the systems of nature and civilisation is the analysis of organisation. Early in the last century, a decade or so after the publications of Whitehead and D'Arcy Thompson, the embryologist Joseph Needham suggested that nature has 'integrative levels' and he argued that hierarchical levels of organisation are exhibited at every scale of the universe – 'the existence of levels of organization in the universe, successive forms of order in a scale of complexity and organisation'.[25] Evolution, J Huxley argued is 'a continuous process from star-dust to human society' and that this was not always the gradual and uniform process that Darwin had suggested but that 'now and again there is a sudden rapid passage to a totally new and more comprehensive type of order or organisation, with quite new emergent properties, and involving quite new methods of further evolution'.[26] Complexity[27] theory formalises the mathematical structure of the process of systems within which hierarchical organisation arises. It focuses on the effects produced by the collective behaviour of many simple units that interact with each other, such as atoms, molecules and cells. The complex is heterogeneous, with many varied parts that have multiple connections between them, and the different parts behave differently, although they are not independent. Complexity increases when the variety and dependency of parts increases. The process of increasing variety is called differentiation and the process of increasing the number or strength of connections is called integration. Biological and cultural evolution produce both differentiation and integration at many 'scales' or levels. Each level interacts with other levels, and hierarchical orders are to be found within all complex systems, from the anatomical form and metabolism of an individual organism, to the distribution of species and ecological systems, to the pattern of settlements and cities distributed across a region.

It has been argued that organisms and the ecological systems within which they exist have evolved from the interactions of elements that combine into a variety of 'assemblies'.[28] Some 'assemblies' survive and go on to become integrated into more complex 'wholes' that evolve through natural selection. Others collapse back into dispersed elements that then undergo further evolution. The process repeats, so that a 'whole' system at one level may be incorporated as a component of a system at a higher level.[29] Further, natural evolution is not a single system but the collective processes of multiple systems that interact and coevolve with each other, so that each individual system is only partially autonomous. The consequence of multiple interactions at many different levels of hierarchy that coevolve across many spatial scales is that the higher level system is organised from within. Self-organisation occurs at the level of a whole ecological system, in the patterns of distribution of the many different species that live within an ecological system, and in the forms of the individual organisms that exist within it.

Self-organised forms are also produced by the collective behaviour of individual organisms. The social or group dynamics of many species, such as flocks of birds and schools of fish, produce what appears to be an overall coherent form or array, without any leader or central directing intelligence. Insects such as bees and termites produce complex built artefacts that exhibit highly organised regulation of the temperature and humidity within their nests without any central planning or instructions. Coherent behaviour of the whole group arises from the repetition of a few very simple actions by many different individuals, each individual acting in response to stimuli from their immediate neighbours and from their close environment. Each individual has its own metabolism, but the energy and material transactions of each individual contribute to a coherent pattern that is conserved and developed over time. There is no central controlling intelligence that directs the construction of the nest, as there are no individuals with a capacity for processing information, nor any systems for the flow of information. The metabolic performance of the whole group and its material construction emerges solely from the interactions between individuals, and the response of individuals to stimuli from their immediate environment.[30] Each individual has a slightly different threshold at which response to stimuli is triggered, and the degree of response also varies a little from individual to individual. The self-organised construction and the metabolic regulation of material forms emerges from the collective behaviour of individuals.

EMERGENCE

Although the word 'emergence' is most commonly understood in everyday language as a perceptual term, a synonym for 'appearance', in the sciences the word refers to the production of forms and their behaviour, by systems that have an irreducible complexity. In the simplest commonly used definition, emergence is applied to the properties of a system that cannot be deduced from its components. Properties 'emerge' that are more than the sum of the parts. This is the oldest understanding of the word emergence, perhaps derived from Aristotle,[31] that 'wholes' have distinctive properties that emerge through the processes of successive interactions between different levels of organisation and integration. Considering the processes of nature and of civilisation as systems accentuates the interactions and connectivity of the different parts of the systems, and the interactions between different systems. The properties of the whole are as important in determining the dynamics of a system as the properties of any individual part. This is a very general description, and so it is necessary to delineate the processes of emergence, the principles and dynamics of organisation and interaction that are consistent across the intersecting domains, and to identify the feedback and critical thresholds that drive the emergence of forms in natural and culturally constructed systems.

The central tenet of system theory is that the concepts and processes of complex systems may be understood as independent of the domain of any one particular system. From this point of view it can be said that natural systems and the cultural systems of civilisation are strongly coupled. However, there are, as might be expected, differences as well as similarities between the literatures of the many different fields of study in those two large domains. Some of the differences might be supposed to arise out of the exigencies of working in a particular field – but as the boundaries and professional barriers between disciplines are being increasingly eroded, it is reasonable to expect that the exchanges between disciplines that have characterised the historical development of the concepts and instruments of emergence will continue. A convergence to a singular theoretical consensus is unlikely, however, and would be unwieldy and perhaps even unnecessary. The development of the concepts of emergence, the shared interests and investigations in diverse fields and the exchange of concepts and analytical techniques between them, mirror some of the characteristics common between natural and cultural evolution.

What is it that emerges, what does it emerge from, and how is emergence produced?' The processes of complex systems produce, elaborate and maintain all the forms of natural and cultural systems, and those processes include exchanges of energy and material with their environment. Living forms maintain their continuity and integrity by changing aspects of their behaviour, their geometry and by their iteration over many generations. Living forms exist in varied populations, and where communication between the forms is effective, collective behaviour, intelligence and culture emerges. The processes of development of natural and cultural forms are strongly correlated. All the systems from which form emerges, and the systems within individual complex forms themselves, are maintained by the flow of energy and information through the system. The pattern of flow has constant variations, and is adjusted by negative and positive feedbacks from the environment.

A whole form may be incorporated as a component of a system that has a higher level of organisation and complexity – and what is 'system' for one process can be 'environment' for another process. Life is an emergent phenomenon, both in the development of life from the prebiotic condition that existed at the beginning of the earth's history, and in the development of each individual organism. This can be understood intuitively in relation to our own bodies. The atoms that make up the molecules in our bodies are not living, indeed no atom can be said to be alive.

THE ARCHITECTURE OF EMERGENCE

The material from which human bodies are constructed has an intricate architecture of its own. The geometrical arrangement and bonding of atoms into the intricate structures of molecules, and the arrangement of those molecules into the more complex architecture of proteins, is the beginning of a series of hierarchical structures of ever increasing complexity that eventually exhibit the characteristics of life. Human life is dependent on the processes of all of our constituent parts, yet our parts do not solely determine human behaviour, nor indeed the behaviour of any organism. It does not seem possible to deduce either the anatomical or metabolic organisation of any living form from its atomic or molecular components. The unfolding of the process of evolution, the emergence of diverse species of living forms over extended time, has been constrained and inflected by the relations of each living form to other living forms, and to climatic regimes and the topography of the surface of the earth. In turn, life has an effect on the processes of the atmosphere and oceans, and the geomorphic systems of the surface of the earth.

The form of anatomically modern humans coevolved with their material culture, each accelerating the other through a series of dynamic exchanges in the fluctuating climate and ecological systems within which they emerged. The vectors of energy and material flows determined the spatial patterning and mobility strategies of human territories in varying ecologies, and the migrations and flow of humans out of Africa to cover the surface of the earth. The evolutionary development of language, art and calendars was integrated into informational systems for the transmission of ecologically and socially contextualised knowledge through space and over time. The founding cultural system of civilisation was fully assembled and widely distributed 35,000 years ago.

There has been a debate between proponents of what are sometimes described as 'weak' or 'strong' emergence.[32] In this argument, 'weak' emergence refers to the emergence of forms and behaviour from systems that are entirely determined by the properties of their parts. Their 'emergent' properties cannot be predicted because the only means of doing so would be a one-to-one simulation. Although it might well be impractical to apply the laws of physics to account for the behaviour of every single molecule in an organism or an ecological system, it could, at least in principle, be done. The enormous computational requirements are not considered, or are conceded. The argument is often put forward in this way: the laws of physics operating at the level of atoms and molecules are sufficient to determine the local and the global behaviour of the system, and so there is neither need nor room for any additional laws or organising principles. In this view all the phenomena of 'nature', from the colonies of bacteria to the emergence of cities and states, are produced by 'material processes that are ultimately reducible, however long and tortuous the sequences, to the laws of physics'.[33] 'Strong' emergence refers to the emergence of forms and behaviours from systems with a high level of complexity that cannot be predicted from the cumulative effect of all of the properties of their parts. Protagonists of strong emergence argue that the whole is more than the sum of its parts, and the processes of complex systems are consistent with the underlying laws of physics that operate at the level of atoms and molecules, but they are not ultimately reducible to the properties of atoms and molecules.

There are several recent propositions for taxonomies of emergence, most incorporating both weak and strong forms of emergence, and various subdivisions that lie in-between those two positions. It is not immediately clear what can be gained by making the distinction between strong and weak emergence. It is evident that the fundamental physics of the world determines the behaviour of atoms and molecules, but it is also clear that the interactions that take place at a multitude of scales between components, between assemblies of components and between whole systems and their environments, are critical to the development and evolution of all forms. Neither argument can be proven, at the moment, to completely exclude the other. If all of the systems of nature and civilisation do interact with each other, and if these interactions do have effects on each other, it follows that increased knowledge of the processes of each system can unfold the emergence and evolutionary development of all the variations of forms and their effects upon each other. As entities should not be multiplied beyond necessity,[34] the preferred approach in this text is to explore each system through the dynamic of their exchanges of material, energy and information with the environment within which they exist.

All natural and cultural systems exist within a physical context, an environment that has many other living and non-living forms within it, and so the environment of any one system is composed of other systems. Energy and material exchanges between the environment and the systems of which it is comprised determine the initial conditions from which an individual system arises, and the dynamics of its development over time.[35] The environment acts on all the systems within it, and in turn the flow of energy and material across the boundaries of each system modifies the environment. The exchanges occur on many different scales of dimension and time, so that the interactions between the systems are complex and subject to fluctuations and variations. These fluctuations may be amplified by positive feedback or inhibited by negative feedback from other systems. The structure and organisation of all forms and behaviour in the world, both living and non-living, are connected by, and contingent, upon the flow of energy and materials between them.

The development of a system from simple beginnings to higher levels of complexity is often presented as a series of major transitions or transformations that are triggered when a 'critical threshold' is passed. 'Self-organisation' is also frequently used in connection with the emergence and development of forms over time – in some cases it is simply used as a description of the sudden appearance of order. When an observer does not recognise the process of a natural system, and it is evident that there is no external controlling intelligence

1.10 Abandoned City
The city of Khara-Khoto in Inner Mongolia was abandoned 700 years ago after the Black River was diverted. The regional climate changed and the local ecology collapsed. The outcomes of collapse in urban ecologies can be: complete abandonment and dispersal of the people; a reorganisation into smaller, simpler and dispersed settlements at a lower level of complexity; and the reordering of the system into a more integrated assembly or reorganisation to a higher level of complexity.

directing the processes of the system, then it appears that the emergence of organisation must somehow be generated from within the system. The search for a definitive model of self-organisation has been the focus of intensive studies and mathematical simulations in recent decades. The terms 'self-generated', 'self-assembled' or 'self-replicating', are common synonyms for self-organisation, each term having a slightly different meaning and use in the varying contexts that are defined by different disciplines. What is common between them is the understanding that organisation emerges as the consequence of multiple and complex interactions between the components. No system in nature or civilisation is closed – that is to say there is always a continuous exchange of energy and material across the 'boundary' of the system. Energy and material must be acquired from the physical world and put to work to construct and maintain the system, and so it follows that it cannot be said that any system is solely self-organised from within. The presence or absence of negative and positive feedback is critical to all systems, as are the boundary conditions of the system, and the relations to an environment that lies outside of those boundaries.

If all systems do affect each other, either directly or indirectly, the question arises of how and in what sequence to examine them. Unfolding the relations between the multiple systems of nature and civilisation can begin by tracing the flow of energy and materials across the temporal and dimensional scales at which a system produces forms and behaviour. At a very fine dimensional scale, properties emerge from the interactions between energy and the spatial architecture of matter. For example, the open lattice-like molecular structure of ice is produced by the geometry of the hydrogen bonds between water molecules. The three-dimensional geometry of that structure includes a high proportion of open space, so that ice occupies more volume than water and is less dense, and that is why ice floats in water. If the ice can absorb heat energy, the extra energy will break the hydrogen bonds, and the ice will undergo a phase change from solid to fluid water. A significantly larger absorption of energy will induce a further phase change from a fluid to a gas; water vapour.[36] These changes are reversible by further energy transactions, so when heat energy is shed, water will freeze to ice and the individual molecules of water vapour will condense into the fluid form of water. The solid, fluid and gas each have different forms and properties, but each molecule still consists of two hydrogen atoms and one oxygen atom. Energy determines the change in geometrical patterns of the bonding between the molecules, and different forms and behaviour emerge.

THE ARCHITECTURE OF EMERGENCE

Time is a significant dimension for all systems, for example, in the way in which the sequence of variations of atmospheric pressure and temperature modulate the form and behaviour of storms. Clouds and storms emerge from the complexity of the global climate, a 'metasystem' driven by heat energy that originates from the light of the sun falling on the earth. Its forms are produced by the interaction of the convection cells of the atmosphere with the dynamics of the ocean currents, and the chemical processes and topography of the land. Each of these dynamic systems has its own cycles of changes that operate on varying scales of dimension and time. Some forms emerge and dissipate rapidly over short timescales of hours and days, while others, like the circulation of the deep oceans, act over more than a thousand years. The forms of the atmosphere interact with each other and with their local environment, rising and falling, growing and dissipating with the constant local variations in air pressure, wind and temperature. In doing so they modify their local environment, and that environment in turn may change sufficiently to induce further reciprocal modifications. The forms of clouds and storms are three-dimensional dynamic patterns that are produced by the continuous thermally driven processes of the 'metaclimate' system, and they are constantly being changed, broken down and renewed in a complex series of energy exchanges.

Energy and information produce effects that act upon the architecture of material in space and over time, and the interaction between them is neither exclusively 'bottom up' nor 'top down'. Information passing down through the generations modifies the interaction of living forms with their environment and the materials and energy that they extract from it. As each generation of living forms succeeds its ancestors, information is propagated down through time. Changes or modifications to living forms occur both by mutation, 'copy errors', and by the recombination of existing information into new sequences and patterns. This may be seen in evolution in general, in the emergence of new species and in the emergence of social or collective behaviour and material constructions of insects, animals and humans. It is clear that all non-living natural forms emerge from the interaction of energy and material within complex systems that proceed through time, and that both the living forms of nature and the forms of civilisation emerge from complex processes that are coupled to the transmission of information.

Chapter 2 describes how variations occur in the energy received by the earth from the sun, and how some of that energy is transformed and transported around the world. The exchanges of energy and material between the ocean,

the land, the biosphere and the atmosphere are traced; and the processes that produce the forms of the atmosphere are presented. The global climate is the metasystem, a system of systems, with an intricate choreography of forms and behaviour that modulates the exchange of energy and material of all other systems, and in turn is affected by their processes. The geomorphic processes from which the forms of the land emerge are examined in Chapter 3. The processes of weathering, erosion and deposition are produced by the climate, and variations and changes to the climate change the behaviour, duration and force of each process. In turn, geomorphic processes also contribute to the generation of feedbacks to the climate metasystem through positive and negative feedbacks including changes in the reflectivity of surfaces, the production of 'greenhouse' gases that change the chemical composition of the atmosphere, and the aerosols from desiccated soils and deserts. Chapter 4 explores the emergence of living forms from two strongly coupled processes, operating over maximally differentiated time spans; the rapid process of embryological development from a single cell to an adult form, and the long slow process of the evolution of diverse species of forms over extended time.

1.11 Urbanisation of the World
The world at night indicates the density of urban concentrations, and changes in illumination from 1993 to 2003. The lights are colour-coded. Red lights appeared during that 10 years. Orange and yellow areas are regions of high and low intensity lighting respectively that increased in brightness over the 10 years. Grey areas are unchanged. Pale blue and dark blue areas are of low and high intensity lighting that decreased in brightness. Very dark blue areas present in 1993 had disappeared by 2003. The abundance of red and yellow on the map indicates the pace of recent urbanisation and suggests the overall pattern of high energy flow across the world.

The evolution of the species is constrained by the dynamics of information passing from one generation to the next, the relations of living forms to other living forms, to differing climatic regimes and to the topography of the surface of the earth. In turn, living forms also affect the processes of the atmosphere and oceans and the geomorphic systems of the surface of the earth. Chapter 5 examines the dynamics of plant and animal metabolisms and their relations to the morphology and scale of living forms. The relationships between living organisms and their environment are analysed in terms of the vectors of information, energy and material flows in populations, habitats and ecological systems. An examination is made of how intelligence, social and spatial organisation, and material artefacts emerge from the collective extension of metabolism, reinforced and developed by positive feedbacks acting to modify the regime of natural selection. Collectives continually modify and regulate their exterior environment and over time change their own ecological niche, and so enhance their 'fitness' in that environment.

Chapter 6 traces the coevolution of the anatomically modern human form and material culture, and the migration and flow of humans out of Africa to cover the surface of the earth. An account is presented of the emergence of anatomical and cultural forms of humans in relation to changes in climate and ecological systems, and to the subsequent modifications of local and regional ecologies by human occupation. The development of language, art and calendars, and their integration into complex informational systems for the transmission of ecologically contextualised knowledge over time is examined. The spatial patterning of territories is analysed in terms of the vectors of energy and material flows, and the emergence and proliferation of pit dwellings, settlements and mobility strategies is unfolded. In Chapter 7 an account is presented of the emergence of the dynamic forms of cities and systems of cities, together with an outline of their relations to culture and ecology. The irregular development of the forms of cities and systems of cities, their constant rebuilding over time, and their expansion, decay and collapse is examined in relation to their informational complexity, population, climate and ecology. Chapter 8 traces the evolutionary development of complexity in the flow of information and energy through the extended metabolisms of settlements, cities and systems of cities, and the global system of the contemporary world. The consequences of the increasing acceleration over time of human 'metabolic' activities on the intricate dynamics of ecological systems are related to the evolution of complexity, and to the episodic collapse and reorganisation of cultural and ecological systems.

Chapter 9 reflects on the emergence of forms in nature and civilisation, on the dynamics of the systems within which all the endless variations of forms have evolved, and on the complex interactions and critical thresholds of change that exist between them. An examination is made of the likely changes to climate and ecology, and of the three potential outcomes of collapse and reorganisation of the global system in relation to the future metabolism of cities in changed climatic and ecological environments.

1 Thought to derive from the Latin word *natura*, from *natus*, past participle of *nasci*, to be born.

2 Bacon, Francis, 'Preparative toward a Natural and Experimental History', in *Novum Organum*, 1620. *The New Organum*, (eds) L Jardine and M Silverthorne, Cambridge University Press (Cambridge), 2000.

3 D'Holbach, Paul-Henri Thiry, Le *Système de la nature* (*The System of Nature*), 1770, now available from Project Gutenberg.

4 Cuvier, Georges, *Recherches sur les ossemens fossiles des quadrupèdes* (*Research on the Fossil Bones of Quadrupeds*), 1812, and *Discours sur les révolutions du globe* (*Discourse on the Revolutionary Upheavals on the Surface of the Earth*), 1825. Rudwick, Martin, Georges Cuvier, *Fossil Bones and Geological Catastrophes: new translations and interpretations of the primary texts*, University of Chicago Press (Chicago), 1997.

5 For example, a hurricane of 100 kilometres diameter (10 to the power of 5) and a snowflake of 1.5 millimetres 'diameter' (10 to the *minus* power of 3).

6 Thought to be derived from *civis*, a Latin word meaning a citizen governed by the law of a city.

7 Lévi-Strauss, C, *Tristes Tropiques*, Librairie Plon (Paris), 1955, trans Weightman, J and D Weightman, Jonathan Cape (London), 1973, p 155.

8 Braudel, Fernand, *A History of Civilizations*, Penguin (New York), 1995 – first published as *La grammaire des civilisations*, Les Editions Arthaud (Paris), 1987.

9 Darwin, Charles, *On the Origin of Species by Means of Natural Selection, or the Preservation of Favoured Races in the Struggle for Life*, John Murray, first edition, first issue, 1859. Full text and images available online at http://darwin-online.org.uk/

10 'In an acquisitive hereditary society he stated acquisition and inheritance as the primary means of survival.' West, Geoffrey, *Charles Darwin: A Portrait*, Yale University Press (New Haven), 1938, p 334. And 'The Application of Economics to Biology', Spengler, Oswald, in *The Decline Of The West*, Knopf (New York), 1939, p 373.

11 Thompson, D'Arcy Wentworth, *On Growth And Form* (first published 1917), Cambridge University Press (Cambridge), 1961.

12 Whitehead, Alfred North, *The Concept of Nature*, Cambridge University Press (Cambridge), 1920.

13 Darwin, *On the Origin of Species,* (Chapter X111). Full text and images available online at http://darwin-online.org.uk/

14 Vrba, ES, 'Environment and Evolution: alternative causes of the temporal distribution of evolutionary events', *South African Journal of Science,* vol 81, 1985, pp 229–36; and Vrba, ES, 'Late Pliocene Climatic Events and Hominid Evolution', (ed) FE Grine, in *Evolutionary History of the 'Robust' Australopithecines*, Aldine de Gruyter (New York), 1988, pp 405–26; and Potts, R, 'Evolution and Climate Variability', *Science*, vol 273, no 5277, 1996, pp 922–3; and Potts, R, 'Environmental Hypotheses of Hominin Evolution', *Yearbook of Physical Anthropology*, vol 41, 1998, pp 93–136; and Potts, R, 'Variability Selection in Hominid Evolution', *Evolutionary Anthropology*, vol 7, no 3, 1998, pp 81–96.

15 Lieberman, DE, BM McBratney and G Krovitz, 'The Evolution and Development of Cranial Form in Homo Sapiens', *Proceedings of the National Academy of Sciences* 99, February 2002, pp 1134–9; and Aiello, LC, 'Brains and Guts in Human Evolution: the expensive tissue hypothesis',

Brazilian Journal of Genetics vol 20, 1997, pp 141–8; and Aiello, LC and P Wheeler, 'The Expensive Tissue Hypothesis: the brain and the digestive system in human and primate evolution', *Current Anthropology*, vol 36, 1995, pp 199–221.

16 Darwin, *On the Origin of Species*, pp 267.

17 Tyack, PL, 'Dolphins Whistle a Signature Tune', *Science*, vol 289, 2000, pp 1310–11.

18 Fitch, WT, 'The Evolution of Speech: a comparative review', *Trends in Cognitive Science*, vol 4, 2000, pp 258–67.

19 Tobias, PV and B Campbell, 'The Emergence of Man in Africa and Beyond [and Discussion]', *Philosophical Transactions of the Royal Society of London B*, vol 292, 1981; and Kay, RF, M Cartmill and M Balow, 'The Hypoglossal Canal and the Origin of Human Vocal Behavior', *Proceedings of the National Academy of Sciences*, vol 95, 1988, pp 5417–9.

20 Cavalli-Sforza, LL, P Menozzi and A Piazza, 'Demic Expansions and Human Evolution', *Science*, vol 259, January 1993, pp 639–46; and Cavalli-Sforza, LL, *Genes, People and Languages*, North Point Press (San Francisco), 2000.

21 Wiener, Norbert, *Cybernetics, or Control and Communication in the Animal and the Machine*, MIT Press (Cambridge, MA), 1961.

22 Shannon, CE and W Weaver, *The Mathematical Theory of Communication*, fifth edition, University of Illinois Press (Chicago), 1963.

23 Prigogine, Ilya, *Introduction to Thermodynamics of Irreversible Processes* (first edition, published 1955); third and last edition, John Wiley & Sons (New York), 1968.

24 Any physical system that can be described by mathematical tools or heuristic rules is regarded as a dynamic system. Dynamic System theory classifies systems by the mathematical tool rather the visible form of a system.

25 Needham, Joseph, *Integrative Levels: A Reevaluation of the Idea of Progress*, Clarendon Press (Oxford), 1937.

26 Huxley, JS and TH Huxley, *Evolution and Ethics: 1893–1943*, The Pilot Press (London), 1947.

27 Weaver, Warren, 'Science and Complexity', *American Scientist*, vol 36, 1948, pp 536–44.

28 Heylighen, Francis, 'Self-Organization, Emergence and the Architecture of Complexity', *Proceedings of 1st European Conference on System Science*, 1989.

29 Simon, HA, 'The Architecture of Complexity', *Proceedings of the American Philosophical Society* vol 106, no 6, pp 467–82, reprinted in *The Sciences of the Artificial*, third edition, MIT Press (Cambridge, MA), 1996.

30 Theraulaz, G, J Gautrais, S Camazine, J-L Deneubourg, 'The Formation of Spatial Patterns in Social Insects: From Simple Behaviours to Complex Structures', *Philosophical Transactions: Mathematical, Physical and Engineering Sciences*, vol 361, no 1807, and 'Self-Organization: The Quest for the Origin and Evolution of Structure', 2003, pp 1263–82.

31 'The whole is something over and above its parts, and not just the sum of them all ...' Aristotle, *Metaphysics*, originally published 350 BC.

32 Bedau, Mark, 'Weak Emergence', *Philosophical Perspectives*, vol 11, 1997, pp 375–99 and 'Downward Causation and the Autonomy of Weak Emergence', in Emergences and Downward Causation, *Principia* vol 6, no 1, 2002, pp 5–50.

33 Wilson, EO, *Consilience: The Unity of Knowledge*, Alfred Knopf (New York), 1998, pp 55, 226.

34 The principle is often expressed in Latin as the *lex parsimoniae* or the law of parsimony. It is widely known as Ockham's Razor, associated with the 14th-century philosopher, William of Ockham.

35 Camazine, S, J-L Deneubourg, N Franks, J Sneyd, G Theraulaz and E Bonabeau, *Self-Organization in Biological Systems*, Princeton Studies in Complexity, Princeton University Press (Princeton), 2001.

36 The energy required to convert ice into water is called the *latent heat of fusion*; 80 calories of heat are required to convert one gram of ice into water. A further 600 calories of heat are required for a gram of water to evaporate into the air. This is called the *latent heat of vaporisation*.

Precession

Current Position

Winter

Summer

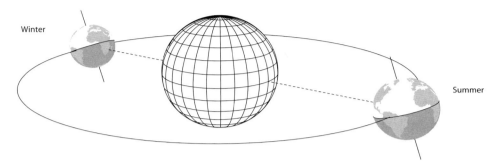

5,750 years from now

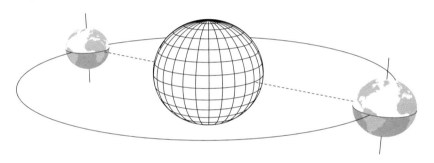

11,000 years from now

Summer

Winter

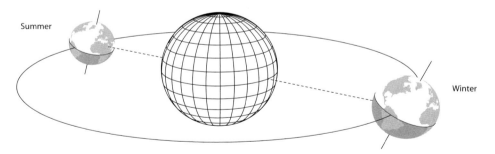

2.1 Milankovitch Cycles
The subtle variations in the movements of the earth relative to
the sun produce oscillations and irregularities in the amount
of energy that falls on the earth. The changing pattern of heat
energy falling on the earth produces changes in the way that
heat is distributed around it by the great circulations of the
ocean and atmosphere. Over the geological timescale, the
climate has oscillated between two states, one of brief warmth
and the other of longer lasting glacial cold.

Climate and the Forms of the Atmosphere

2

Energy falls on the earth from the sun, and some of that energy is transformed and transported around the world. Energy and material between the ocean, the land, the biosphere and the atmosphere are exchanged; and the forms of the global climate emerge from the interaction of those exchanges. Climate is the 'metasystem', a system of systems, and the intricate choreography of its forms and behaviour modulates the exchanges of energy and material between all the other systems, and is in turn affected by them. The metasystem has many critical thresholds with differing scales of distance and time, and is delicately poised so that a small change at one scale may initiate a great and rapid change at another.

Of all of the phenomena of nature, we understand the weather most directly, as the daily and sometimes hourly variations of light, wind and temperature that shape our perception of the world. The weather is local to us, determines the clothes we choose to wear, and has an influence on the way we build our homes and on the way we live in them. We may find delight in the variations of weather, or like Mark Twain castigate its perversity – 'In the spring I have counted one hundred and thirty-six different kinds of weather inside of four-and-twenty hours'.[1] The effects of its variations are visible in gardens and parks, in the prices of food in the markets, and in the sensations and physiological processes of human bodies. The sense of physical well-being in most humans is related to the weather and the seasons, and there is strong evidence of its effects on health. The seasonal changes of the weather give an order to our lives, and even the births of children exhibit a stable seasonal pattern over time. This does vary from region to region, for example in Europe the number of births is highest in the spring, with a smaller peak at the end of the summer, whereas the pattern in America is a low number of births in the spring, increasing through the summer until autumn. The biological explanations of the seasonality of births include theories that link the temporal pattern of births to temperature[2] and rainfall, to cloud cover and hormone levels, and to the range of variation.[3] Weather has significant effects on all plant and animal life, and in turn living things affect the weather.

Collection of weather observations has long been part of marine knowledge and procedure – the hourly record written in the ship's log consisted of close visual observations of the weather, and particularly of natural phenomena that precede change. The shapes and colours of cloud formations were known to give an indication of wind conditions in the atmosphere and of impending changes in weather. A significant step towards converting these subjective observations to measured data was the introduction of the Beaufort scale to measure wind force, which became the standard method of description for the Royal Navy in 1830. The scale is a systematic method for indicating the force of wind by observing its effects on the surface of the sea. Small ripples without crests and 'light airs' denotes Force 1; moderate waves 2 metres high with some foam and spray, and a 'fresh breeze' is Force 5; huge waves more than 14 metres high, a completely white sea with driving foam and spray filling the air, so that visibility is greatly reduced, and hurricane force winds, is Force 12. Each level of the initial scale was also related to the performance of the ship, so that Force 1 was 'just sufficient to give steerage', Force 5 was 'that in which a well conditioned man-of-war could just carry, in chase and full and by, royal topsails', and Force 12 was 'that which no canvas could withstand'. In modified and extended form the Beaufort scale is still in use across the world today.[4]

Sir Francis Beaufort, the Hydrographer of the Admiralty, was the leading 'scientific' naval officer of the time, an expert in the mathematics of surveying shorelines, astronomical observations and the calculation of latitude and longitude, for the making of marine charts. It was Beaufort who appointed Charles Darwin as the naturalist to HMS *Beagle*, in which Darwin visited the Galapagos Islands. The Commander of the *Beagle* was Robert FitzRoy, who was convinced that the weather was not random in its changes, although that is how it appeared to the untrained eye, and that changes in air pressure and temperature had a significant role in the dynamics of storms. On that long voyage[5] he observed that severe storms occurred when cold air from the South Pole collided with warm air from the equatorial and tropical regions, and concluded that high winds were the result of storms, not the cause of them, as was widely thought at the time. FitzRoy later became the first 'Meteorological Statist' of the Board of Trade, responsible for the collection of weather data at sea. Ships' captains were provided with calibrated instruments for measurements and the computation of data for the subsequent compilation of charts for predictions that he called 'forecasting the weather'.[6] FitzRoy developed and distributed the 'storm glass' and several types of barometer, and set up a number of land weather stations linked by telegraph that could make regular reports of the weather at set times. He developed a system of storm warning signals that were displayed in the principal harbours, and published daily weather forecasts soon followed.

Climate is the aggregation of all local weather over the longer periods of seasons and years, a synthesis of all the measured data of local variations over time. To describe weather as changeable or dynamic is to confirm daily experience, and it is not too large a step from there to consider the climate as a complex dynamic system, and to recognise that the many varied forms of atmospheric phenomena such as clouds, typhoons and hurricanes, snow and hail, emerge from the processes of the climatic system. The word climate is derived from the Greek word '*Klima*' meaning the inclination of the sun. Aristotle observed that it is the sun that produces changes, 'Now the sun, moving as it does, sets up processes of change and becoming and decay, and by its agency the finest and sweetest water is every day carried up and is dissolved into vapour and rises to the upper region, where it is condensed again by the cold and so returns to the earth.'[7] This recognition of the sequence of water evaporating from the sea and coming down again as rain did not include ideas of changes to the climate over the longer history of the earth. Natural phenomena were seen to change, but change was considered to be part of a cycle in which the seasons came and went, each with their associated weather in endless repetition.

The energy source that drives the processes of all the systems that contribute to the global climate is the solar radiation that falls on the surface of the earth. The earth is a sphere of some 12,800 kilometres diameter, surrounded by an atmosphere, an envelope of gas that is 40 kilometres thick. The surface of the sphere is irregular, and its atmosphere is a combination of various gases of different density and concentrations that vary over time. The earth and its surrounding gases rotate on a slightly irregular orbit around the sun,[8] it spins rapidly on its own axis,[9] and the axis is not perpendicular to the plane of the orbit but tilted by 23.45°. The tilt of earth's axis is the principal reason for the seasons. On one side of the orbit, the Northern Hemisphere is pointed towards the sun, and the Southern Hemisphere is pointed away from the sun. Six months later, the positions are reversed, with the Southern Hemisphere pointed towards the sun and the Northern Hemisphere pointed away. The tilt of the axis varies over time, the axis moving through a circle, just like the way a spinning top will wobble before it falls over. The energy emitted by the sun is also not

Wind	Symbol	Speed(mph)	Force N	Effect
calm		> 1	0	smoke rises vertically
light air		1-3	1	smoke drifts slightly
light breeze		4-7	2	leaves rustle; wind vane moves
gentle breeze		8-12	3	leaves constant motion light flag extended
moderate breeze		13-18	4	raises dust and papers; small branches stir
fresh breeze		19-24	5	small trees sway
strong breeze		25-31	6	large branches move; use of umbrella difficult
moderate gale		32-38	7	whole trees in motion
fresh gale		39-46	8	twigs broken off trees; difficult to drive a car
strong gale		47-54	9	slight structure damage occurs
whole gale		55-63	10	trees uprooted; severe structural damage
storm		64-73	11	widespread damage
hurricane		above 75	12	devastation

2.2 Beaufort Scale

The Beaufort scale became the standard method of description for the Royal Navy in 1830. The scale is a systematic method for indicating the force of wind by observing its effects on the surface of the sea. Sir Francis Beaufort was the Hydrographer of the Admiralty who appointed Charles Darwin as the naturalist to HMS *Beagle*.

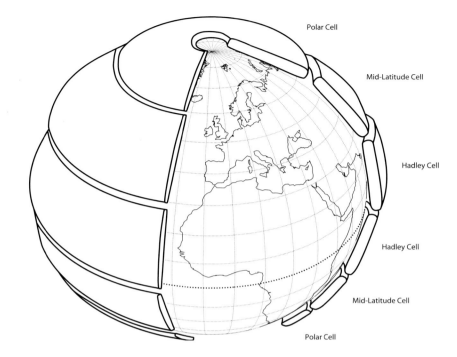

2.3 Atmospheric Cells and Prevailing Winds
Climatic regimes emerge as persistent but variable regional latitudinal patterns
from the interactions of the great circulations of the ocean and atmosphere and
the configuration of the continents. They are strongly correlated with the
Hadley, Ferrel and Polar atmospheric convection cells, and are directly affected
by variations in the atmospheric circulation. The Ferrel and Polar cells are
particularly sensitive to variation, and are so strongly affected by seasonal
variation that they are not clearly defined throughout the year.

constant, but has its own cycle of intensity.[10] The effect of the different cycles
is that the energy that falls on the earth varies in intensity over time on any part
of the surface. In addition to the variations in the intensity of solar energy
falling on the earth and the variations in the composition of the atmosphere,
the system continually receives inputs from the surface below. A large part of
the earth's surface is water, and substantial ocean currents constantly produce
significant variations in the temperature of the water. The mountains, valleys
and plains of the land's surface vary in the way they absorb and reflect solar
energy, and the variations in topography and roughness affect the flow of the
atmosphere across it. Living organisms exist on land and in the seas, and they
too produce variations, affecting the chemistry and moisture content of the
atmosphere. It is clear that the global climate is a metasystem of great
complexity, driven by the outcome of the interaction of contributory systems;

the atmosphere, the oceans, the biosphere (all living things) and the geological processes of the land moderate the 'metaclimate' of the earth. The processes of each system affect the other systems; each acts as a reservoir of energy. Energy and material flow through each of the systems and across their boundaries in to the other systems.

PROCESSES AND PATTERNS OF THE ATMOSPHERE

The driver of the atmospheric system is heat. Heat always flows from hot bodies to cold bodies, never in the reverse direction. This principle, established by Sadi Carnot in 1824,[11] is the basis of what is now known as the Second Law of Thermodynamics. Differences in temperature over distance are required for heat to flow: the heat gradient between one place and another, or the heat gradient between one material and another. Heat is not a fluid, as Carnot thought, but is rather the average velocity of the atoms of any material. When we feel hot, our bodies are registering an increase in the 'excitement' of the atoms that make up our bodies, an increase in their velocities. The highest part of the earth's atmosphere is usually thought of as very cold, even though the individual molecules of gas are very hot, as their constituent atoms are excited by direct solar energy. The overall density of the gas at the top of the atmosphere, however, is very low; consequently as there are so few molecules and so much space between them, any living organism exposed to it would instantly freeze.[12] Light is a form of energy that can travel through the vacuum of space, but as soon as light falls on a material, light energy is converted to heat in the material. So it is convenient to think of heat as a property of a material, and as heat cannot move except through a material, flow is a satisfactory if rather approximate description of the transference of energy process.

The atmosphere receives heat from the sun and from the surface of the earth but loses most of its heat by radiation back into space. Water evaporating from the surface of the earth transports heat up into the atmosphere, and so lowers the surface temperature. Warm air causes water to rise up into the atmosphere as water vapour. Up in the cooler atmosphere it condenses to form rain drops, and so releases that heat. The tiny water droplets aggregate into clouds, and it is the water droplets that reflect light, and give the clouds their characteristic white appearance. The darker the cloud appears, the greater the volume and concentration of water droplets it is carrying. There is an important thermal characteristic of this process – a perpetual heat difference or gradient between the warmer air lower down near the surface of the earth, and the cooler air of the atmosphere. The energy received from the sun is most intense at the equator and least intense at the poles, and so there is another thermal gradient, across the surface of the earth between the equator and the poles.

These two gradients, the vertical gradient from the surface of the earth up into the atmosphere, and the surface gradient from the equator to the poles, set up large circulations of heat in the atmosphere, creating three huge convection cells in each hemisphere. Warm air always rises, as it is less dense than cold air, so the very large convection cells exist permanently, although they are subject to irregularities and perturbations. The global circulation of air works to transfer heat from the equatorial region towards the polar latitudes. The equatorial regions continually receive solar energy and would steadily increase in temperature if the global circulation failed. So too the high polar latitudes that receive very little solar energy would continually cool.

The pressure differences in the atmosphere, measured and analysed by FitzRoy's barometers and computations, are a consequence of local areas of heated air, which as they rise from the surface create an area of lower air pressure beneath them. Air flows from surrounding areas of higher pressure into the newly created areas of lower pressure. The larger the difference in pressures, the stronger the force[13] of the wind; the distance between the area of high pressure and the area of low pressure also determines the velocity of the wind. Large differences in pressure that are relatively close to each other produce higher accelerations of the air; smaller pressure differences separated by larger distances will produce 'light airs' or gentle winds. On a weather chart, lines called isobars are plotted to connect places of equal air pressure; the spacing of the isobars indicates the pressure gradient. Pressure differences generate winds that move directly in a straight line from high to low pressure, but as the air begins to flow, the earth rotates under it, so that the wind appears to follow a curved trajectory. Wind appears to be deflected to the right in the Northern Hemisphere, and to the left in the Southern Hemisphere.[14] The effect is zero at the equator. The smoothness or roughness of the topography of the earth's surface also has an effect on the global circulation pattern of the atmosphere. Mountains, hills and valleys are 'rougher' than the flat plains or open ocean, and increase the friction between the flowing air and the surface. This slows the flow of air locally, causing a mass of air to accumulate behind the deceleration, and that increases the air pressure.

George Hadley proposed that there were two great convection cells in which warm air was thought to rise from the equator to sink at the poles; one in each hemisphere and counter-rotating in respect to each other.[15] It is now observed that there are three main cells in each hemisphere, the Hadley cell which circulates between the equator and latitude 30°, the smaller and weaker Ferrel cell that circulates in the opposite direction between latitude 30° and latitude 60°, and the Polar cell that circulates in the opposite direction again (the same direction as the Hadley cell) between latitude 60° and the poles. This pattern of global atmospheric circulation is affected by the rotation of the earth, which tends to distort them, but they do produce consistent patterns of prevailing winds. The Ferrel and Polar cells are seasonally affected and are not clearly defined throughout the year.

In the Hadley cell, hot moist air rising from the heated surface in the equatorial region moves towards the poles, shedding its water content as rain on the way, thus losing heat. Further heat loss by radiation gradually cools the air sufficiently to cause it to sink in the subtropical region around latitude 30–35°. As the now dry air sinks to the surface, it increases the atmospheric pressure under it. Air at the surface cannot rise under the pressure of descending air, and this inhibits widespread evaporation, cloud formation and rain. The increasing pressure also adds heat to the air by friction, further decreasing its relative humidity. All the large deserts of the world, such as the Australian, Kalahari, and the Sahara deserts, are located in two bands that encircle the earth in these latitudes. At sea, these latitudes are known as the 'horse latitudes' and are characterised by light and variable winds. The name is said to derive from becalmed sailing ships that, to lighten the ship and preserve water, jettisoned the horses they were carrying to the New World.

Once the air reaches the surface, the flow diverges outwards across the surface, towards the pole and towards the equator. Towards the equator, the gradient between the high pressure over latitudes 30° north and south and the low pressure over the equator produces an easterly pattern of prevailing winds known as the 'north-east trade winds' and the 'south-east trade winds' respectively. Similarly, towards the poles, the air flows to the lower pressure over latitudes 60° (the boundary of the Ferrel cell), and the Coriolis effect deflects this flow in another consistent pattern of prevailing winds known as the 'westerlies' in both hemispheres. The collision of the 'polar easterlies' with the 'westerlies' in the area between the Ferrel cell and the Polar cell is where the most intense storms occur.

The general circulation of the atmosphere is the largest pattern of the climate metasystem. This pattern is persistent over long periods of time, but is subject to perturbations and variations, so that in any particular location, at any particular time, local weather conditions may be very different from the general circulation. The pattern of the global circulation within the atmosphere is not permanent, and there is ample fossil evidence to show that there have been periods in the geological history of the earth when the general atmospheric circulation was substantially different to the pattern today.

INPUTS FROM BELOW

The process of the climate metasystem is affected by interactions with the surface of the earth, and inputs of energy and material to the atmosphere are received from the surface below. The two most significant material transfers are water and carbon. These transfers are closed systems, as unlike energy that falls constantly on the earth and some of which is radiated back into space, no new water or carbon is added to the earth.

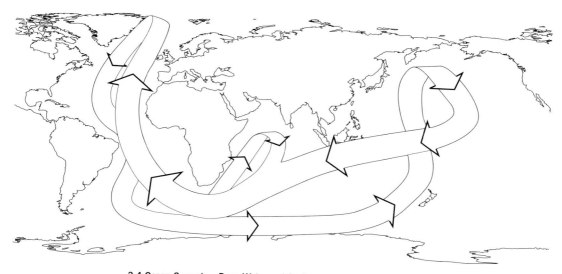

2.4 Ocean Currents – Deep Water and Surface
The forms and behaviour of the climate emerge from the exchanges of energy and material between the ocean, the land, the biosphere and the atmosphere. The exchanges occur on many different scales of dimension and time, so that the interactions between the systems are complex and non-linear, subject to fluctuations and variations. These in turn affect the intensity of local behaviour, the weather, and modify the dynamics of climate change through positive feedback that amplifies change, or through negative feedback that inhibits change.

WATER

Water cycling between the surface and the atmosphere transfers heat from the surface to the atmosphere. Water passes through many systems in unceasing cycles. A single water molecule, for example, may evaporate from the ocean, be carried up into the atmosphere, fall to the land as rain or snow, seep down into the earth and into the rivers, be absorbed into biological organisms including human bodies, and be excreted from them, eventually returning to the ocean or to the atmosphere. All living things contain water, sometimes up to 80 per cent of their body mass, but the water is not held permanently in the organism. Water cycles through organisms, so that they continually ingest water to replace the water that is shed by evaporation from their outer surfaces, and from internal surfaces such as the lungs in mammals. Plants contribute about 15 per cent of the water in the atmosphere through tiny pores or stomata on their leaf surfaces, a process known as transpiration. Water is extracted from the soil by the plant roots, moves up through the plant and into the air. The process of transpiration removes heat from the plant and so transpiration, like evaporation, transports heat from the surface of the earth to the atmosphere above.

Energy is critical to the phase changes of water, the molecules must shed energy to become ice and acquire energy to become a vapour. Ice melts to water when sufficient energy is absorbed[16] to loosen the bonds between the molecules. Water evaporates to vapour with the acquisition of more energy,[17] which breaks the hydrogen bonds that bind water molecules together. That energy remains 'latent' in the water vapour molecules; when the individual molecules combine as the vapour condenses in the atmosphere, the energy is released as heat into the surrounding air. Evaporation also requires the presence of a vertical moisture gradient, a difference between the moisture content at the surface of the liquid water and the lower moisture content of the atmosphere above. Wind helps to maintain the vertical moisture gradient by carrying water molecules away, so the air above the evaporating surface does not become saturated, and water can continue to evaporate.

Most of the earth's water is in the oceans, and most of its gases too are dissolved in the water. The surface layer of the ocean, to a depth of three or four metres, holds as much heat energy as the entire 40 kilometre deep atmosphere. The varying intensities of solar energy that drives the atmospheric circulation also act to differentially warm the oceans. Currents transfer heat from the equatorial region to the poles. Like the global circulation of the atmosphere, the pattern of

THE ARCHITECTURE OF EMERGENCE

the ocean currents is persistent over time, but is subject to variations and perturbations, and there is strong fossil evidence that there have been substantially different patterns of ocean currents in the geological past. Heating of the water in equatorial latitudes and the cooling of the water in the polar latitudes is the principal driver of the system. In the polar latitudes very little solar energy is received from the sun and the surface of the ocean loses heat to the wind, which also carries away the water that does evaporate. Salinity is increased, as only molecules of pure water evaporate. The cold salty water becomes denser and sinks, where it is constrained and directed by the topography of the ocean floor.

The founding text of the science of ocean circulation was published in 1942 by Harald Sverdrup, who described the sinking down of cold, dense water between Iceland and Greenland and the flow southward of the water guided by the topography of the ocean floor.[18] He argued that if there were no winds, there would be a slow surface circulation directed from the equator to the poles, from where it would sink and return, and that this circulation would be modified by the topography of the ocean floor, and by the rotation of the earth. In the absence of winds no currents would be formed, and there would be just a steady state circulation. Winds produce the currents, and from this he argued that the actual circulation of the oceans is determined by the balance of forces between the wind pushing the water and the process of heating and cooling. In his view the transport of water masses by currents would be persistent over very long periods. The flow of ocean currents is now measured in units named after Sverdrup, so that 1 Sv or Sverdrup is a volume flow rate of 106 cubic metres per second.

The circulation of the oceans has always been thought to be slow, but recently carbon dating has made it possible to accurately measure the age of a sample of sea water drawn up from the depths of the ocean.[19] The deep waters of the oceans carry a 'memory' of when they were last on the surface, in the gases that were absorbed from the atmosphere and dissolved in the water. Analysis shows that water taken from the bottom of the North Atlantic sank from the surface of the ocean approximately 600 years ago, and water drawn from the deep Pacific was last on the surface in the southern latitudes more than 1,000 years ago.[20] From the bottom of the Norwegian Sea, cold dense water flows slowly south into the very deep abyss of the Atlantic, all the way to the southern latitudes of the Arctic Ocean basin. It then flows around the southern tip of Africa, and then begins to rise and split into two streams; one flows into the

Indian Ocean, and the other flows along the southern latitudes passing to the south of Australia and into the Pacific, where it slowly rises as it gradually gains heat, becoming warmer and less salty. The now warmer and fresher water from the Pacific flows back, passing north of Australia into the Indian Ocean forcing a vertical circulation or turnover. From there, the water flows as a warmer shallower current back up from the Southern Atlantic to Greenland, where it loses its heat and sinks again so that the cycle continues. This slow circulation of water around the globe, sometimes known as the 'Great Ocean Conveyor',[21] or the 'thermohaline[22] circulation' transports heat energy and dissolved materials around the earth.

Surface currents are faster and shallower than the deep ocean circulation, and are driven by the wind. They generally follow the pattern of differences in atmospheric pressure and the winds driven by the large convection cells (the Hadley, Ferrel and Polar cells) of the atmosphere, and are also influenced by the Coriolis effect. Surface currents are constrained by the land-masses of the continents, so that the boundaries of the large ocean basins cause the currents to conform to a circulation pattern known as a gyre. These are not so much a continuous circular current, but rather four joined currents, so that the two currents aligned approximately north/south flow parallel to the continental land-masses, and the two currents aligned approximately east/west flow across the oceans from one continent towards the other. The western currents[23] carry the heated water from equatorial waters up alongside the western boundaries of the ocean basins to the higher and cooler latitudes, giving up heat to the atmosphere as they do so. These currents are relatively narrow (up to 150 kilometres wide), but rapid flows moving at 50 to 120 kilometres per day, and they are the deepest of the surface currents, affecting the upper 1,000 or so metres of the ocean water. More heat is given up as the lateral currents move across the ocean basins towards the eastern continental boundaries. Cold water currents[24] flow from the high cooler latitudes back down along the eastern boundaries of the ocean basins towards the equator. These currents are broad, and shallow, and move more slowly, typically moving only a few kilometres each day. The two slow, shallow currents[25] that flow westwards on either side of the equator complete the circuit. Gyres rotate clockwise north of the equator and anti-clockwise to the south of the equator, and occur in all ocean basins.

Heat is transported from the equator to the poles by the ocean surface gyres and by the surface winds. As the water circulates, it exchanges both heat and water with the atmosphere – this is what modifies the local weather – the temperature of the air and the rainfall over sea and land areas is affected. Water precipitates out of the atmosphere as rain and snow, with the largest percentage, about 80 per cent, falling on the oceans. Only 20 per cent of the total precipitation falls on the land, and almost all of that will be returned to the atmosphere by the transpiration of plants and by evaporation from the surface. Rivers and ground water aquifers return a small proportion to the oceans. The cycle is completed by water evaporating from the oceans – almost 85 per cent of all water in the atmosphere is evaporated from the surface of the oceans. The transportation of heat energy is the result of the water cycle, which transports twice as much heat as the ocean currents. Heat flows from hot to cool, so that ocean currents are most effective in transporting heat from near the equator to the subtropical latitudes, and heat transport in the atmosphere is most effective in the higher latitudes, from the subtropics to the subpolar regions. As warm ocean water moves from the equatorial regions towards the cooler high latitudes, the atmosphere above it becomes progressively cooler. Air flowing over a warm ocean current will gain heat energy and moisture from the water, and in consequence the warm moist air is more able to form clouds, so that land areas nearby will have increased rainfall. Conversely, air flowing over cold ocean currents will lose some heat energy to the water, and the cooler air is less able to form clouds; consequently nearby coasts will be drier and cooler. These local weather regimes are subject to variation over short periods of time. Changes to weather patterns are driven by oscillations in the input to the atmosphere from the oceans, and this oscillation may occur in quite short cycles of decades, as for example in the 'El Niño-Southern Oscillation' that occurs in the tropical Pacific, but is linked to disturbances to the usual cycles of oceans and atmospheres over a much larger area. Similar oscillation cycles have also been noted in the north Pacific, in the North Atlantic and Arctic Oceans.

CARBON

Carbon is the atom of life. It is the only element that can be organised into the long stable chains that are required for proteins that are essential for all living systems.[26] Like water, each atom of carbon has been through innumerable cycles between the land, the ocean, biological organisms and the atmosphere. There are two principal subsidiary cycles, the geological and the biological, within the general carbon cycle. In the geological cycle carbon is exchanged between the land, the ocean and the atmosphere. Limestone is the most common mineral form, in which one carbon atom is bound to three atoms of oxygen and one atom of calcium. The weather acts on the limestone and breaks down the rock, by physical processes that reduce it to smaller pieces, and by a slow chemical process that dissolves the limestone in the weak carbonic acid that falls in rain, formed from carbon dioxide and water in the atmosphere. Wind-driven erosion removes the products of weathering, exposing fresh rock surfaces so that they are in turn subjected to the process of weathering. Surface water washes the dissolved calcium carbonates down to the oceans, where they eventually precipitate out and fall to the ocean floor, forming layers of sediment. The tectonic plates move, the sediments are pushed down or subducted under the continental land-masses, and in turn, are later raised up as mountains by geological processes, and eventually exposed to the atmosphere again. Intense geothermal activity heats the limestone so that carbon dioxide and oxygen are released, usually through volcanic eruptions. The carbon atom remains bonded to two oxygen atoms to form the molecule carbon dioxide that is released into the atmosphere. Atmospheric carbon dioxide emerges from the interrelated processes of weathering, sedimentation, subduction and volcanism in a cycle that takes hundreds of millions of years. Fossil evidence strongly indicates that atmospheric carbon dioxide and temperature are coupled.[27] Analysis of deep ice core samples indicates that the percentage of carbon dioxide in the atmosphere during the last ice age (20,000 years ago) was about half of what it is today – and geochemical analysis reveals that less than 20 million years ago concentrations were significantly lower than existing concentrations.[28]

The presence of carbon dioxide in the atmosphere is strongly correlated to the cycling of energy between the atmosphere and the surface of the earth. Molecules of carbon dioxide have the capacity to absorb heat energy, so that variations in the atmospheric concentration of carbon dioxide increase or decrease the amount of energy held in the atmosphere or radiated back into space, and consequently the total amount of energy cycled through the global metaclimate system. The structure of the carbon dioxide molecule is arranged so that as it absorbs infrared radiation the molecule vibrates. The vibrating molecule emits the radiation back out to its surroundings, where it will be absorbed by any other gas molecule that can vibrate in a similar manner. Carbon dioxide is not the only gas that has this capacity – water vapour, methane and nitrous oxide act together with carbon dioxide to increase the energy held in the climate system.[29] All these molecules have a similar architecture, each being composed of more than two atoms, bonded in such a way that they can vibrate as they absorb energy from the sun. The other major constituent gases of the atmosphere have only two atoms in each molecule, bonded so tightly together that they cannot vibrate, and so cannot absorb and reradiate energy. Natural processes that capture carbon dioxide and remove it from the atmosphere act to cool the atmosphere and so cool the earth; processes that increase the concentration of carbon dioxide act to warm the atmosphere and so warm the earth.

Living organisms also cycle carbon dioxide and water vapour between the earth's surface and the atmosphere, with land and marine organisms producing and consuming approximately even quantities. The biological cycling of carbon is very rapid, particularly in the ocean where microscopic marine plants that capture carbon by photosynthesis (phytoplankton) are consumed by tiny marine animals (zooplankton) that breathe out carbon dioxide in days or weeks. Carbon dioxide simply diffuses from the atmosphere into the ocean, where it can exist as dissolved carbon dioxide or be fixed by living organisms such as shellfish, algae, plankton and diatoms to produce the calcium carbonate used to make their shells and skeletons, which eventually fall to the ocean floor, and become bound into the sedimentary layers. Only small amounts of carbon from marine organisms settle on the ocean floor but over long periods of time this small but steady removal of carbon dioxide from the atmosphere to ocean floor sediments (about 0.1 per cent of the annual total production from living organisms) has created the largest long-term storage of carbon in the sediments of marine shale. The ocean water holds much more carbon than the atmosphere, for every atom of carbon in the atmosphere there are approximately 50 atoms of carbon dissolved in the ocean.

Marine and land plants absorb solar energy and capture carbon dioxide from the atmosphere by photosynthesis, and produce carbohydrates. Respiration is the reverse of photosynthesis, the energy in the carbohydrates being released by metabolic processes, leaving carbon dioxide and water vapour to be discharged back into the atmosphere. Animals, bacteria and fungi consume and decompose plant organic matter, and in turn release their carbon dioxide and water vapour back into the atmosphere. In the absence of oxygen, respiration releases methane back into the atmosphere. The biological processes of photosynthesis and respiration capture and release very large quantities of carbon every year, up to 1,000 times the volume that moves through the geological cycle. All these processes are temperature sensitive; when conditions are too cold or too dry, photosynthesis and respiration are reduced to almost zero. Carbon is cycled through the biosphere in many processes, each of different duration. Most plants have short seasonal cycles and so store carbon for a brief period, while trees with long lives store carbon for decades and in some case for hundreds of years. Carbon is bound up for thousands of years in soils, in fossil fuels, marine shales and sediments, the cycle between capture and release takes millions of years to complete.

The release of carbon dioxide into the atmosphere from below has had multiple fluctuations over time, modifying the percentage of carbon dioxide in the atmosphere and in consequence modulating its total energy capacity. The overall 'average' temperature of the metaclimate system is affected by the amount of carbon dioxide in the atmosphere – higher amounts of carbon dioxide enable more energy to be absorbed in the atmosphere, and so the temperature rises. Temperature directly affects the speed of the processes that capture or give off carbon dioxide. The chemical weathering of limestone is temperature sensitive too – when the earth is warmer, the process is faster, but in very low temperatures the process is much slower. Similarly, the temperature of the ocean surface regulates the exchange of carbon dioxide between the ocean and the atmosphere, although it is the cooler temperatures that increase the capacity of ocean water to absorb carbon dioxide. Very warm ocean water causes the ocean surface to release carbon dioxide to the atmosphere. The interdependency of temperature and the processes that produce or capture carbon dioxide is subject to 'feedback', and that 'feedback' can either be positive, reinforcing and accelerating the process, or it can be negative, damping or inhibiting the process.

For example, when the atmosphere is increasingly warm, the ocean will be warmed by it and will give up more carbon dioxide (and more water vapour) to the atmosphere, which in turn can then retain more heat energy. Warmer climates and higher concentrations of carbon dioxide in the atmosphere accelerate plant growth, and in consequence increase the capture of carbon dioxide, which will in turn eventually cool the atmosphere. Conversely, cold ocean water absorbs carbon dioxide (and water vapour) more readily than warm water, and the removal of carbon dioxide and water vapour from the atmosphere lowers its capacity for retaining heat. In cooler climates, however, plant growth is comparatively inhibited, so less carbon dioxide is biologically captured and removed from the atmosphere, and this will over time tend to gradually increase the atmospheric concentrations of carbon dioxide, which in turn will enable the atmosphere to retain more heat energy.

THE FORMS OF THE ATMOSPHERE

Clouds are the most visible forms of the atmosphere, what we see is water – either as water, snowflakes or ice crystals. Clouds reflect some of the incoming solar radiation, about 20 per cent, back out into space, and reduce the amount of energy that reaches the surface. They tend to cool the earth by contributing to its albedo, or reflectivity. They also absorb some of the heat energy emitted by the earth's surface, and in turn radiate some of that heat, upwards into the higher atmosphere where it may be absorbed or eventually escape out into space, and downwards towards the surface. The heat that is radiated downward from the clouds warms the atmosphere and the earth's surface below. We experience this effect on our local weather quite directly: winter nights are noticeably warmer when there is cloud cover, and noticeably colder on nights that are clear. As clouds do tend to reflect more solar energy back into space than radiate heat back down to the earth's surface, their net effect on the global metaclimate system is cooling. However, clouds may simultaneously warm some local areas.

If the composition of the atmosphere changes, for example, to a higher percentage of carbon dioxide, nitrous oxide or methane, so more energy can be absorbed by the atmosphere and the whole hydrological cycle will be accelerated. Evaporation will increase and so the amount of clouds in the atmosphere will increase accordingly, with more rain and snow falling on the earth's surface. More heat energy will be retained in the atmosphere, which in turn will warm the surface below – a positive feedback that will continually increase the energy capacity (and the temperature) of the atmosphere. This acceleration will continue until the negative feedback of accelerated biotic carbon dioxide capture and the increased albedo effect of reflection of sunlight back into space act to inhibit the energy increase of the atmosphere and eventually cool the earth.

Clouds may occur at any size, varying in area from hundreds of metres to continent-wide systems. Their forms are constantly changing, so description of the morphology of clouds, like Beaufort's classification of wind force, is based on visual observation rather than measurement. The first classification of the forms[30] preceded the adoption of the Beaufort scale by some 30 years, and this early classification is still in use today. There are three primary forms: cirrus or high detached and wispy clouds; cumulus or low heaps of puffy clouds with a flat base that tend to look a little like a cauliflower; and stratus which are large low sheet-like layers of clouds. Complex or hybrid forms are described by combining the three primary names, for example, stratocumulus is used to describe extended layers of clouds that have some local cumulus features. Further levels of description are achieved by adding a prefix or suffix: altocumulus concerns the height of cloud formation in the atmosphere; cumulonimbus, tall dark storm clouds associated with rapidly rising and sinking air masses, concerns the precipitation of rain or snow. Cumulonimbus clouds produce lightning and thunder, heavy rainfall or hail, storm-force winds and tornadoes. They may extend from a low base of 1,000 metres above sea level up to a height of 12 to 14 kilometres, and they usually have large tops that are anvil shaped, caused by the stronger winds in the upper atmosphere.

The largest storm systems are hurricanes,[31] rotating storms that can be up to 2,000 kilometres across. The distinctive spiral morphology of the hurricane rotates around a calm central region or 'eye' of extremely low air pressure that can be many kilometres in diameter. Hurricanes are large coherent forms that emerge from a cluster of thunderstorms over tropical ocean waters. The process begins when ocean temperatures are in excess of 27° Celsius and when the atmosphere is calm. Warm air rises, carrying large quantities of water vapour and heat, creating an area of low pressure, and air rushes in to replace the rising air. The heat in the warm moist air is released when the water vapour condenses into water droplets in the wall of thunderstorms around the 'eye', and the increasing temperature generates the 'hot towers' of enormous cumulus thunderheads. Some warm air, now dry, will fall back down the inside walls of the 'eye', and this is what makes the 'eye' clear and cloudless. More and more moisture-laden air from the ocean is pulled in and carried upwards in a positive feedback process that increases the area, volume and energy of the storm cells. If this process is located at latitudes of more than 10°, the Coriolis effect induces rotation of the storm cells, so that winds moving towards the centre are diverted into a spiral pattern. The winds converge and collide, driving the warm, moist air upward. At 12 to 14 kilometres above the ocean surface, the strong and steady winds of the troposphere remove the now cooler and drier air exhausted from the top of the hurricane and so help to maintain the continual upwards movement of air and water vapour from the surface. Variation in the high altitude winds, such as wind shear or a change in velocity will inhibit the thermodynamic organisation, but if it is constant the hurricane will continue to grow rapidly, and can change rapidly in intensity, from wind speeds of 120 kilometres per hour (kph) (Category 1) to wind speeds of 250 kph (Category 5) within a single day. The extremely low pressure of the 'eye' draws in water as well as air, and sea level in the 'eye' can be as much as 4 metres above normal sea level, setting off tsunami-scale storm surges. Hurricanes accelerate in size and intensity as long as they can draw energy from warm waters below them, but rarely persist beyond a few days or a week before they dissipate their energy. As storm systems move away from the equatorial region to the higher latitudes, where the Coriolis effect is more pronounced, they intensify, increasing wind speed. The higher latitudes have cooler ocean water however, and this will decrease the temperature gradient between the ocean surface and so the high atmosphere, and the intensity of the hurricane will decrease.

The energy processes that produce the differences in air pressure and temperature of the atmosphere drive all storms. Pressure differences have significant effects horizontally, with big gradients or differences producing winds of greater velocity than small differences, and in a hurricane the pressure

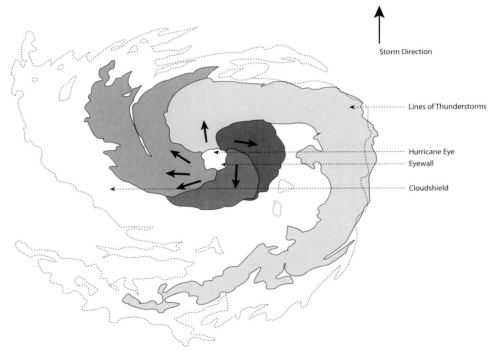

Storm Direction

Lines of Thunderstorms

Hurricane Eye
Eyewall

Cloudshield

2.5 Hurricanes
The largest storm systems are hurricanes, rotating storms that can be up to 2,000 kilometres across. The distinctive spiral morphology of the hurricane rotates around a calm central region or 'eye' of extremely low air pressure that can be many kilometres in diameter. Hurricanes emerge from a cluster of thunderstorms over ocean waters that are in excess of 27° Celsius.

gradient is the difference between the air pressure in the 'eye' and the air pressure outside the hurricane. Temperature differences have significant effects vertically, and in a hurricane the temperature gradient is the difference between the 27°C or warmer ocean and the cold air high in the atmosphere. The balance of these gradients, of the energy and material flows, is short lived, but while they are in balance they organise the dynamics and maintain the morphology of storms, tornadoes and hurricanes. The coherent behaviour of a weather system may persist for days across hundreds of kilometres, reaching up into the high altitude of the troposphere, yet it is composed of individual molecules of air and water. Each molecule is subject only to the forces acting on its immediate surroundings, and each molecule will have a turbulent and very 'local' trajectory through time and space. Coherent forms and behaviour of all weather systems emerge from the massive flow of heat energy[32] across huge distances.

DIFFERENTIATED FEEDBACK AND EMERGENCE OF THE METASYSTEM

The subtle variations in the movements of the earth relative to the sun, the Milankovitch[33] cycles, produce irregularities in the amount of energy that falls on the earth. When considered over long geological time, the metaclimate system has oscillated between two states, one of brief warmth and the other of longer lasting glacial cold. The change from one state to another has not been a gradual and regular ascent or descent in temperature. In each cycle the temperature climbed rapidly from the cold, and then was followed by a very long and irregular fall in temperatures, typically lasting for many thousands of years and punctuated by short-lived spikes of higher temperatures. The analysis of ice cores[34] shows rapid climate changes, and suggests that the climatic cycles between the two modes (periods of approximately 20,000 and 40,000 years, and a very strong cycle of approximately 100,000 years) are all in approximate alignment with the Milankovitch calculations of variations in the earth's relations to the sun.[35]

The bubbles of air trapped in the Vostok ice cores showed that the percentage of carbon dioxide, methane and nitrous oxide in the atmosphere has fluctuated throughout the last 400,000 years, and that there is a pattern to the variations.[36] In each of the cycles the cold glacial periods were terminated by a rapid increase of temperature, of as much as 10°C at the poles and 3°C in the equatorial regions. (This equates to a global average of 5°C.) As the earth moves into an orbital position that increases the solar insolation, the earth is warmed and the release of greenhouse gases from soils and the biosphere is accelerated. The positive feedback of gases amplified the climate change, comparable in scale of effect to the simultaneous change in surface albedo or reflectivity. As the atmosphere warms further and faster, larger areas of highly reflective ice melt, reducing the amount of solar energy reflected back off the ice and exposing darker, more heat absorbing land and water surfaces.

Feedbacks are differentiated over time. Albedo change and the increases in the percentage of greenhouse gases of the atmosphere are 'slow' positive feedbacks, and once they are initiated they persist in their actions over long periods, typically many hundreds to thousands of years. Other feedbacks act on much shorter timescales, and are a direct result of the change to the climate initiated by the slower, longer duration feedbacks. Fast feedbacks act over seasons, years and decades, and generate further changes in the atmosphere by increasing the evaporation of water vapour and cloud cover, by increasing the amount of small airborne particles (aerosols) from dessicated soils, and by reducing the amount of sea ice and snow. Fast feedbacks like these will advance and retreat each year, their effects increasing in the warmer months and lessening in the colder months, but the overall tendency will become more pronounced with each successive year.

Positive feedbacks reinforce each other, the long slow positive feedbacks initiating change and increasing the sensitivity of the metaclimate to the additional actions of multiple positive fast feedbacks. It is difficult to be certain from paleoclimate data or from computational models just exactly how sensitive the metasystem is, but it is clear that the interaction of slow and fast feedbacks produces the potential for large and rapid fluctuations.[37] Positive feedbacks dominate,[38] so that the thermal inertia of the great ice sheets and of the deep ocean circulation, and their slow negative feedback effect on the climate, is eventually overcome by the gradual warming of the atmosphere and ocean. As more heat energy is accumulated in the system, and more fast-acting feedbacks come into effect, the ice melt accelerates until the physical stability of the ice sheets is undermined. Once this critical threshold is reached, rapid disintegration and break up follows, and the subsequent albedo change generates yet more positive feedback, and further accelerates changes in the global climate.

Climatic regimes emerge as persistent but variable regional latitudinal patterns from the interactions of the great circulations of the ocean and atmosphere and the configuration of the continents. They are strongly correlated with the Hadley, Ferrel and Polar atmospheric convection cells, and are directly affected by variations in the atmospheric circulation. The Ferrel and Polar cells are particularly sensitive to variation, and are so strongly affected by seasonal variation that they are not clearly defined throughout the year. They are also sensitive to variations in the temperature and thermohaline circulation of the oceans. The polar regime exhibits the highest potential for rapid change in response to slow and multiple fast feedbacks, and changes in the polar climate act as a further level of feedback on the climatic regimes of the mid latitudes and equatorial regions.

Weather is local. Winds, clouds and storms, rain and snow emerge from the interaction of the behaviour of specific climatic regimes and the topography of the land. The forms of the atmosphere interact with each other and with their immediate local environment, rising and falling, growing and dissipating with the constant local differences in air pressure, wind and temperature. Weather is highly sensitive to variations in air pressure, and to the temperature of the sea, atmosphere and land. The response of the larger metasystem to local changes does vary in spatial dimensions and over time, and the sequence of changes is significant. The question posed by Konrad Lorenz[39] 'does the flap of a butterfly's wings in Brazil set off a tornado in Texas?' is perhaps more powerful as a metaphor than literal truth, but it is evident that quite small and very local differences or perturbations in the atmosphere can provide the initiating change of condition that can lead, through successive positive feedbacks, to the emergence of large coherent forms that dissipate huge quantities of energy, such as storms and hurricanes.

Climate is the metasystem, a system of systems, with an intricate choreography of forms and behaviour that modulates the exchange of energy and material of all other systems, and in turn is affected by their processes. It is evident that the forms and behaviour of the climate emerge from the exchanges of energy and material between the ocean, the land, the biosphere and the atmosphere. The exchanges occur on many different scales of dimension and time, so that the interactions between the systems are complex and non-linear, subject to fluctuations and variations. These in turn affect the intensity of local behaviour, the weather, and modify the dynamics of climate change through positive feedback that amplifies change, or through negative feedback that inhibits change. Each of the contributory systems is also dynamic and complex, with its own internal energy cycles, circulations and feedbacks, and with time signatures and patterns of behaviour that are strongly coupled to the behaviour of the other systems. The processes of all subsidiary systems have an intricate flow of energy and material across their boundaries into the other systems. The interaction of the great convection cells of the atmosphere and the dynamics of the ocean currents, of the metabolic processes of the biosphere and the chemical processes and topography of the land affect each other, and each acts as a reservoir where forms of matter and energy bound together can exist for long periods of time. Some aspects of the energy cycles of the metasystem show dramatic fluctuations on a short timescale of hours and days, while other changes occur over decades or hundreds of years, and some over many thousands of years.

Some 15,000 years ago the ice sheets covered much of what is now Canada, Northern Europe and Asia. Evidence from the most recent ice core samples taken in Greenland demonstrates that the transition to the warmer interglacial period that we now inhabit was abrupt. The episodes of climate change were rapid, coupled to changes in the pattern of the great circulations of the ocean, with a sea level rise of more than 20 metres. Changes to the circulation of the atmosphere took place within a decade or less, and the global temperature increased by as much as 10°C within 20 to 50 years.[40] The metasystem is delicately poised, with many different critical thresholds across multiple scales of distance and time, so that a small stimulus at one scale may drive a great and rapid change at another.

1 Twain, Mark, Speech delivered at the New England Society's Seventy-First Annual Dinner, New York City, 22 December 1876, in *Mark Twain's Speeches*, Harper and Brothers (New York), 1910.
2 Lam, DA and JA Miron, 'Global Patterns of Seasonal Variation in Human Fertility', *Annals of the New York Academy of Sciences,* vol 709, 1994, pp 9–28.
3 Cummings, D, 'The Seasonality of Human Births, Melatonin and Cloud Cover', *Biological Rhythm Research*, vol 33, no 5, 2002, pp 521–9; and Seiver, DA, 'Trend and Variation in the Seasonality of US Fertility, 1947–1976', *Demography*, vol 22, no 1, 1985, pp 89–100; and Werschler, T and S Halli, 'The Seasonality of Births in Canada: a comparison with the northern United States', *Population and Environment*, vol 14, no 1, 1992, pp 85–94.
4 Huler, Scott, *Defining the Wind: the Beaufort scale, and how a 19th-century admiral turned science into poetry*, Crown Publications (New York), 2004.
5 HMS *Beagle* sailed from Plymouth Harbour on 27 December 1831 and returned to Falmouth on 2 October 1836. FitzRoy was awarded the Gold Medal of the Royal Geographical Society in the following year, 1837, and was elected to the Royal Society in 1851 with the support of Darwin. He is widely acknowledged as the founder of what would later become the Meteorological Office, and as the person who did more than any other to provide a scientific method of analysis and prediction for weather.
6 Gribbin, J and M Gribbin, *FitzRoy: the remarkable story of Darwin's captain and the invention of the weather forecast*, Yale University Press (Yale), 2004.
7 Aristotle, *Meteorology*, trans E Weber, available online from Classics Archive, MIT.
8 Earth's orbit varies between nearly circular to slightly ellipsoid. The complete cycle from circular to elongate and back to circular is approximately 100,000 years.
9 A complete cycle of the 'precession' or circular movement of the axis takes 26,000 years.

10 The core temperature of the sun is currently thought to oscillate around 13.6 million Kelvin in cycles of 40,000 years and 100,000 years.

11 Carnot, Sadi, *Réflexions sur la puissance motrice du feu et sur les machines propres à développer cette puissance* (*Reflections on the Motive Power of Fire*), Bachelier (Paris), 1824.

12 Schneider, E and D Sagan, *Into the Cool: energy flow, thermodynamics and life*, University of Chicago Press (Chicago), 2005.

13 Known as the Pressure Gradient Force.

14 This effect is known as the Coriolis effect. It is not a force but an apparent deflection of a moving object in a rotating frame of reference. The effect can be best understood as rotation around a vertical axis. It varies from a maximum at the poles to zero at the equator. It can be demonstrated by standing a pen orthogonally to the surface of a globe – at the poles the pen will have to complete one full rotation around its own axis for each full rotation of the globe, but a pen placed at the equator will not have to rotate on its own axis as the globe turns. The apparent deflection of winds to the right in the Northern Hemisphere and to the left in the Southern Hemisphere can be demonstrated by spinning the globe from west to east. When looking down from above at the North Pole the globe appears to be spinning in a counter-clockwise direction. When looking up at the South Pole it appears to be spinning in a clockwise direction.

15 Hadley, G, 'Concerning the Cause of the General Trade-Winds', *Philosophical Transactions of The Royal Society of London*, 1735.

16 Approximately 80 calories of heat are required to change one gram of ice into water. This is known as the latent heat of melting.

17 Approximately 600 calories of heat must be added to a gram of water for it to evaporate into the air. This is known as the latent heat of vaporisation.

18 Sverdrup, HU, MW Johnson and RH Fleming, *The Oceans, Their Physics, Chemistry, and General Biology*, Prentice Hall (New York), 1942.

19 Carbon dioxide is absorbed from the atmosphere by sea water, and atmospheric carbon dioxide contains a very small amount of the radioactive isotope of carbon, which has an absolutely constant rate of decay.

20 Primeau, F and M Holzer, 'The Ocean's Memory of the Atmosphere: residence-time and ventilation-rate distributions of water masses', *Journal of Physical Oceanography*, vol 36, no 7, 2006, pp 1439–56.

21 Broecker, WS, 'The Great Ocean Conveyor Belt', *Journal of Physical Oceanography*, vol 4, 1991, pp 79–89. Currently viewed as a general schematic of the flow around the globe.

22 Derives from the combination of *thermo* – heat, *saline* – salt.

23 Western currents – in the North Atlantic – the Gulf Stream; in the North Pacific – the Kuroshio; in the South Atlantic – the Brazil; in the South Pacific – the East Australia; and in the Indian Ocean – the Agulhas.

24 Eastern currents – in the North Atlantic – the Canary; in the North Pacific – the California; in the South Atlantic – the Benguela; in the South Pacific – the Peru; and in the Indian Ocean – the West Australia.

25 The North Equatorial and the South Equatorial currents.

26 Levi, Primo, *The Periodic Table*, first published Einaudi Editore SpA (Turin), 1975, trans Michael Joseph Ltd, 1985.

27 Retallack, Gregory, 'Carbon Dioxide and Climate over the past 300 Million Years', *Philosophical Transactions of the Royal Society of London A*, vol 360, 2002, pp 659–74.

28 Pearson, PN and MR Palmer, 'Atmospheric carbon dioxide concentrations over the past 60 million years', *Nature,* vol 406, 2000, pp 695–9.

29 The so-called 'greenhouse' gases.

30 Jean Lamarck, the French Naturalist, is credited with the first classification in 1801, but it is the classification of the English scientist, Luke Howard, in 1803 that is still in use today. Howard was elected as a Fellow of The Royal Society in 1821. A modified version of his classification was

adopted in 1929 by the International Meteorological Commission. The original text is, Howard, Luke, *On the Modification of Clouds*, 1803.

31 Hurricanes are also known in different regions as typhoons or cyclones.

32 It is calculated that an 'average' hurricane produces 2.1×10^{16} cm^3 per day, 1 cubic cm of water weighs 1 gram, so using the latent heat of condensation it is calculated that 5.2×10^{19} joules/day is dissipated by the hurricane, roughly equivalent to 200 times the daily production of electrical power across the world. Calculation by Atlantic Oceanographic and Meteorological Laboratory, Miami, Florida, which maintains online interactive access to various oceanographic and atmospheric datasets (ENVIDS).

33 Milankovitch theorised that the variations of the earth's movements relative to the sun were the cause of the ice ages. Milankovitch, M, *Théorie Mathématique des Phénomènes Thermiques produits par la Radiation Solaire*, Gauthier-Villars (Paris), 1920; and *Mathematische Klimalehre und Astronomische Theorie der Klimaschwankungen*, *Handbuch der Klimalogie Band 1*, Teil A, Bornträger (Berlin), 1930; and *Kanon der Erdbestrahlungen und seine Anwendung auf das Eiszeitenproblem*, published in English as *Canon of Insolation of the Earth and Its Application to the Problem of the Ice Ages* in 1969 by US Department of Commerce and the National Science Foundation.

34 Dowdeswell, JA and JWC White, 'Greenland Ice Core Records and Rapid Climate Change', *Philosophical Transactions of the Royal Society of London A,* vol 352, 15 August 1995, pp 359–74.

35 Hays, JD, J Imbrie and NJ Shackleton, 'Variations in the Earth's Orbit: pacemaker of the ice ages', *Science,* vol 194, no 4270, 1976, pp 1121–32.

36 Neftel, A, H Oeschger, J Schwander, B Stauffer and R Zumbrunn, 'Ice Core Sample Measurements give Atmospheric CO_2 Content During the Past 40,000 Years', *Nature,* vol 295, 1982, pp 220–3; and Petit, JR, J Jouzel, D Raynaud, NI Barkov, J-M Barnola, I Basile, M Benders, J Chappellaz, M Davis, G Delayque, M Delmotte, VM Kotlyakov, M Legrand, VY Lipenkov, C Lorius, L Pépin, C Ritz, E Saltzman and M Stievenard, 'Climate and Atmospheric History of the Past 420,000 Years from the Vostok Ice Core, Antarctica', *Nature,* vol 399, 1999, pp 429–36.

37 Hansen, James, Makiko Sato, Pushker Kharecha, Gary Russell, David Lea and Mark Siddall, 'Climate Change and Trace Gases', *Philosophical Transactions of the Royal Society of London A,* vol 365, 2007, pp 2117–31.

38 Ibid.

39 Title of a lecture by Konrad Lorenz at American Association for the Advancement of Science, 1972.

40 Dowdeswell, JA and JWC White, 'Greenland Ice Core Records and Rapid Climate Change', *Philosophical Transactions of the Royal Society of London A*, vol 352, 15 August 1995, pp 359–71; and prepublication announcement of the findings of the North Greenland Ice Core Project, led by Dorthe Dahl-Jensen of the Centre for Ice and Climate, Niels Bohr Institute of the University of Copenhagen.

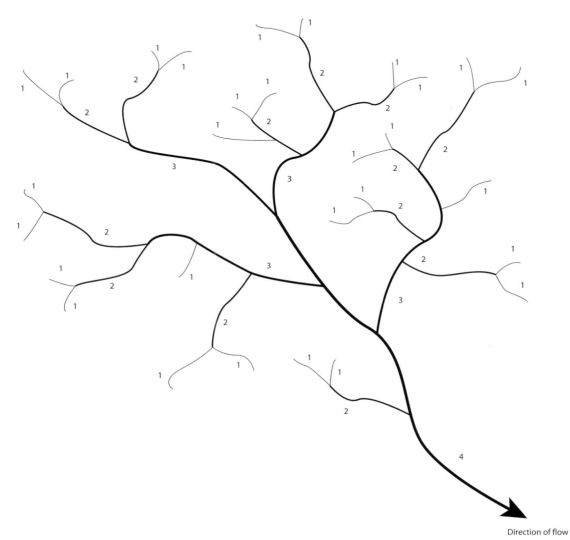

Direction of flow

3.1 Riverine Systems

The topography organises the flow water from water droplets into tiny rills, and from rills into streams and rivers that flow to lakes or the sea. The hierarchical geometry of 'dendritic' river patterns is morphologically similar to other branching networks in natural systems, but only occurs when the general slope of the land surface is consistently gentle or moderate, and the hardness of the surface is uniform. Other patterns occur when topographical and soil conditions are varied.

Surface and the Forms of the Land

The topography of the surface of the earth emerges from the interaction of tectonic forces that act on the land from below, and the weathering and erosional forces that act on it from above. Exchanges of energy and material animate the morphological processes within differing climatic regimes, acting on small particles or grains at a very small scale but producing large forms and complex behaviour over much larger dimensional scales. The forms of the surface develop until they are poised at the critical threshold of change, so that small changes in the flow of energy and material may initiate a rapid change of form. Geomorphological processes generate feedbacks at varying time and dimensional scales that act upon other systems.

We are accustomed to think of the land surface of the earth as unchanging, solid and permanent. These associations are deeply embedded in many languages, and in the culture, values and structures of human societies. The ocean and the atmosphere are visibly fluid, but it is counterintuitive to think of the land as being in a constant state of change. Human lives are brief, and it is the rapidity of our lives in comparison to the long extension of geological time that gives us this perspective. Both the interior of the earth and its surface are in constant motion, with forces in the interior creating new rock material and driving it up to the surface, and other forces breaking down the surface. The general morphology of the land emerges from the interacting processes of the interior, the effects of climate on the surface, and the actions of living forms on the surface. The convection currents of the molten interior induce movements of the tectonic plates, pushing up the land from below, and new surface material oozes out of the deep mid-ocean ridges and from volcanoes. The continuous processes of erosion and deposition produce the topographical features of the surface, the dynamic patterns such as dunes and river deltas. The surface is ground down by glaciers, by chemical weathering, and by wind-driven and coastal erosion, which produces sediment that is carried away by streams and rivers to be deposited on the land and in the sea. These processes are produced by the climate, and changes to the climate change the behaviour, duration and force of each process.

TECTONIC LANDFORMS

The land that exists today has few traces of the original surface of the earth when it was first formed. The world is ancient[1] but it was not until the end of the 18th century that it was recognised that the earth had a long history, and that the surface of the earth had been through many cycles. In 1788 James Hutton published what is now recognised as the founding text[2] of modern geology, in which he argued that the earth was of great antiquity, and during that immense period of time it had been through many slow cycles of change. By the time that Charles Darwin set sail with Robert FitzRoy in the early part of the 19th century, it had long been observed that earthquakes and volcanoes produce large transformations of the surface of the earth, that the wind and rain reduce mountains and erode the land, and that the action of the sea erodes the coast. The idea that the sea and land had changed their relative positions many times was also widely accepted.[3]

In Darwin's account of the voyage of the *Beagle*,[4] his observations of the geology of the mountainous coastlines of South America, and of volcanic islands including the Galapagos, are full of his thoughts and speculations on the processes that might have formed them. He examined many hundreds of miles of both the Atlantic and Pacific southern coasts, and noted the frequency of sea shells embedded in rocks, those lying on the surface at heights of 400 metres above the sea level were always of extinct species. He attributed this to the slow rise of the whole of the southern end of the continent, as the land continued to rise it exposed the sedimentary layer that was once the bottom of the shallow waters of the coast. The sedimentary rock then 'passed through the ordeal of the beach',[5] being subjected to erosion by the sea that exposed the embedded fossil shells. His direct experience of volcanic eruptions and earthquakes, and of the destruction of coastal towns and cities, led him to the conclusion that these were consequences of 'the rending of the strata, necessarily consequent of the tension of the land when being upraised'.[6] His interest in process led him to develop a theory about the formation of volcanic rocks and the crystals embedded in them.[7]

Early in the 20th century it was theorised[8] that the current shape and location of the continents was also not fixed, and that 300 million years ago there had been only one single land-mass that split into smaller pieces that have since then slowly drifted across the surface of the earth. There is now better evidence to support this thesis, which was widely rejected at the time as it was commonly thought that the land and sea floor were simply too rigid to allow any lateral movement. It is evident from a map of the globe that there is a very rough fit of the continents to each other. When allowance is made for changes in sea level by including the continental shelves in the geometry, the fit is much finer. Fossil evidence is supportive too, as fossils of the same organisms are found on different continents. Rocks and coal that are identical in form, age and mineral content are found in South America and Africa, now separated by thousands of kilometres of ocean. Further evidence is the presence in equatorial regions of striations on land surfaces and large deposits of fine sedimentary material produced by glaciers active 300 million years ago. This suggests a single 'supercontinent', located in the Southern Hemisphere, with what is the present day southern part of Africa located over the southern pole. The current configuration of the continents is an instance within a 500 million year cycle of 'supercontinent' formation and break up that proceeds at a few centimetres each year.

Stronger evidence was found in the middle of the 20th century, when the systematic mapping of the sea floor revealed a mid-ocean ridge system that encircles the world, running through the Pacific Ocean, the North and South Atlantic, and between the Indian Ocean and Antarctica. Rocks dredged up from these ridges are younger than rocks further away, suggesting that new rock is being pushed up from below and then being pushed sideways. As the earth has maintained its overall shape of a sphere, this process of new material emerging in mid ocean and spreading across the ocean floor must be balanced by an equal quantity of rock being pulled or driven down below the surface. It follows that the rock deep below the surface is in a plastic state, albeit of the most extremely high viscosity, approximately similar to that of glass. For rock to be plastic requires high temperatures, and fluids that are uniformly heated from below spontaneously generate convection patterns,[9] and so it is thought that there are convection currents within the interior as there are in the atmosphere. The convection cells are driven by heat energy that is generated from within the earth by the decay of radioactive material, with no contribution from above, as solar energy does not penetrate the surface to any depth. The interior of the globe is thought to consist of concentric spheres of rock material, the outer surface layer which is a more or less solid crust, inside which is a deep layer of fluid rock known as the mantle, surrounding a dense inner core of iron. Heat flows from the hot deep interior to the cooler surface, across a substantial gradient from more than

4,000°C to 10°C at the surface. The extreme and irregular viscosity of the material subjected to this heat gradient produces turbulent or non-linear convection. The outer surface layer, the lithosphere, consists of large tectonic plates that float on the more fluid mantle below, and the turbulent convection in the mantle causes the movement of tectonic plates. It is not known if the fluid mantle convects as a whole or in layers,[10] but it is clear that it produces forces that raise, lower or horizontally move different parts of the earth's surface. The tectonic plates move apart by up to 5 centimetres each year, and the fluid magma rises up into the rift in the surface that the movement produces.

In other places the plates collide with each other, and in the collision one plate is pushed below the other, or subducted, and as it moves down the pressure and temperature increase until the rock melts. In turn the increased buoyancy of the melted rock may force a plume of magma up through the surface, transporting enormous quantities of heat. Around the edges of the Pacific Ocean are subduction zones, collectively known as the 'Ring of Fire', where most of the earth's volcanic eruptions and earthquakes occur. Where the rising magma approaches the surface it may develop volcanoes, but most of it remains below the surface as enormous horizontal but shallow layers of very high temperatures. The large gradients of temperature with the surrounding rock set up differential movements that build up stresses in the surface, deforming the rock until it reaches its elastic limit, when it fractures. The sudden release of strain energy travels away from the fracture as earthquake waves.

The largest features of the surface are landforms at a regional scale, the volcanoes, folds of mountain ranges, rift valleys and plains of the continents and ocean basins. They develop and persist over extended geological time, and emerge from the non-linear behaviour of thermal processes deep within the earth.[11]

SURFACE MORPHOLOGY

The interaction of climate and the surface[12] modifies and changes the larger landforms. Water, wind and the processes of living forms are the agents of change, weathering and eroding even the hardest materials, breaking them down into smaller and smaller fragments, and carrying them away and depositing them elsewhere. The developments of detailed surface topography of the more local and transient morphological features of the surface are produced by the actions of water and wind.

In the higher latitudes, when the temperature falls below 0°C, water vapour in the clouds loses heat energy and undergoes a phase change to ice crystals, which grow and fall on the surface as snow. The accumulation of ice crystals into snowflakes is a dynamic process that is dependent on the interrelation of temperature and humidity, producing variant geometries and sizes. The molecular structure of water forms bonds at 120°, so the geometry of snowflakes is hexagonal, with 120° intersections.[13] A snowflake may pass through many different conditions during its fall to earth, and each different condition will change the structural geometry of the snowflake form. Generally, six-sided hexagonal crystals are shaped in high clouds; needles or flat six-sided crystals are shaped in middle height clouds; and a wide variety of six-sided shapes are formed in low clouds. Colder temperatures produce snowflakes with sharper tips on the sides of the crystals, and growth from the centre out to six branches. Smoother forms are usually the result of slow growth in slightly warmer conditions.

GLACIAL LANDFORMS

There have been at least four major ice ages in the earth's past, and many smaller ones. Ice ages are not thought to have a simple cause, but rather a complex interaction of oceanic and atmospheric conditions coinciding with planetary cycles – when the flow of warm water from the equator towards the poles is blocked, and when there is a reduction in the atmospheric concentration of carbon dioxide, and when fluctuations in the energy emitted by the sun coincides with the variations in energy falling on the earth produced by Milankovitch cycles. These conditions reinforce each other in positive feedback loops. The position of the continents in the past was quite different to their present positions, and in consequence the ocean circulation differed considerably too,[14] inhibiting the flow of warm water in the higher latitudes, causing temperatures to fall and ice sheets to begin to form. Once the ice was established, the albedo of the ice provided an additional positive feedback, accelerating the cooling by reflecting more solar energy back into space. When the part of the supercontinent Pangaea was over the South Pole, there was extensive glaciation of what is now South America, Africa, India and Australia.

Snow that accumulates over long periods of time in very low temperatures eventually becomes so dense that it compresses under its own weight and is transformed into dense ice. Ice masses begin to move when the accumulating ice becomes too massive to maintain its rigid shape and it plasticly deforms, becoming a glacier. Glaciers have variant forms with distinct flow characteristics,[15] such as linear glaciers that are constrained to flow in a single direction by topography; or continuous sheets or masses of ice that move out from a central area in all directions; and large flat masses of ice that spread laterally over a level surface. Glaciers scour the land wherever they touch, leaving characteristic deep scratches or striations. The abraded material becomes embedded in the moving ice, increasing the scouring action, and being deposited elsewhere. The abraded material varies in size from huge rocks to fine grains and is known as till, or when deposited as moraine. Ice has shaped much of the landscapes of the middle and high latitudes.

The advance and recession of glaciers has oscillated over time, and they have had a significant effect on much of the landscape we see today. Glaciers now cover almost 10 per cent of the earth's land surface, mostly in the two large ice sheets of Greenland and Antarctica. In the past they have advanced several times to cover a third of the whole surface of the earth, advancing as close to the equator as the tropics. It is thought that the evolution of plants had a significant role in the major periods of glaciation between 300 and 400 million years ago. Trees and seed plants are thought to have first evolved about 400 million years ago, and as they expanded across the surface of the earth they triggered a substantial change to the chemistry of the atmosphere.[16] The photosynthetic process of trees takes carbon dioxide from the atmosphere and releases oxygen, so as large forests first began to appear and spread, there was an accelerating drawing down of carbon dioxide and corresponding increase in the level of oxygen. As the level of carbon dioxide in the atmosphere fell below 300 parts per million, the heat-carrying capacity of the atmosphere was diminished, and the ice sheets began to advance from the poles. The consequent change in albedo provided a positive feedback, and yet further advances of the ice.

When surface temperatures increased, the ice melted and retreated from the oceans and the land, allowing more solar radiation to be absorbed. The retreating ice revealed a modified land surface, scarred and eroded by the force of the moving ice. In mountainous regions the scouring of the sides and bottoms widened and deepened the valley that constrained the glacier, leaving a U-shaped cross section that contrasts sharply with the V-shaped cross section of valleys created by river erosion. Small glaciers feed larger glaciers, as streams feed rivers, and these smaller valleys tend to have their floor high above the level of the main valley floor. Dramatic waterfalls are sometimes seen at these 'hanging valleys'. At the head of the valley, where the snow first accumulated and transformed into glacial ice, circular bowl-shaped depressions 'cirques' are found, and where these 'cirques' have formed in close proximity the land in-between will be ridged or peaked.[17]

Sheet glaciers can accumulate to enormous size, covering whole continents, and can be up to 3,000 metres deep. Because of their great depth they can cover all but the highest mountain features and generate very large forces under them, so that the erosion effects on the land are extensive. Underneath these massive sheets, the ice flow follows the topographic constraints of the surface, and abrades the land, polishing the rock and leaving striations. River valleys that existed prior to the ice are widened and deepened into huge variations of the U-shaped cross section common in mountainous areas, and shallow basins are gouged out, later becoming very large lakes.[18]

The ice will deposit the material abraded from the surface, and there are characteristic forms to the moraines or mounds of material. Continental scale sheet ice often constructs large streamlined hills with long tapered ends orientated in the direction of the ice movement. The water streaming off the melting ice deposits material in front of the glacier to construct other forms, such as plains of material ahead of the glacier, and the conical heaps of sand and gravel[19] often found at the edge of moraines. Water from the melting ice carves long twisting tunnels in the underside of the glacier, and these accumulate beds of sand and gravel that eventually are deposited on the land as long ridges. When sheet ice melts *in situ* the material will settle out as an extensive flat plain studded with randomly disposed large boulders and 'kettle' holes.

Ice also has an effect on the physical weathering of rocks, particularly in polar and very cold regions where the temperature falls to -5°C, with either daily or seasonal warmer periods when temperatures are a few degrees above 0°C. When the temperature is above freezing, water seeps into small crevices in rock and subsequently freezes to ice when the temperature falls. The change in volume (by 9 per cent) shatters the rock and over time the fragments of shattered material accumulate to cover large surface areas. The freeze and thaw cycles then act on the 'regolith' material to produce characteristic surface forms that cover the land in raised net-like patterns of circles and polygons, or strips and steps. The material is organised into these patterns by the sorting of particle sizes by low temperature convection cells within the loose surface material, driven by the cycle of freezing and thawing. The frozen ground 'heaves' the larger fragments upward and horizontally outward.[20] Temperature change, between day and night and between seasons, also contributes to physical weathering. Rock expands as it gets hotter and contracts when it cools, and mineral differences within the rock will cause some areas of the rock to expand more than others, building up stress that eventually will shatter rock. Differential expansion and contraction combined with alternating wetting and drying of the rock encourages the penetration of water molecules between the mineral grains of a rock. The increasing build up of water within the rock exerts a tensional stress on the grains, pulling them apart.

Water carries chemicals in solution and the ions it carries as it moves around the surface enhance weathering processes. Dissolved carbon dioxide, absorbed from the atmosphere in falling rain, produces a weak acid that is effective in breaking down carbonate and silicate forms of calcium and magnesium, and there are other acidic solutions that have comparable effects. The most significant factor is the climatic condition, as chemical weathering also requires heat, and so is most effective in tropical regions that have hot humid climates. The surfaces of limestone landforms, commonly called karst landscapes, are pitted with holes of many sizes and shapes, and within the surface the weak acid weathering forms extensive sets of caverns, usually connected by subterranean water channels, that may cover hundreds of square kilometres.

Plant life also contributes to the fragmentation and weathering of the land. Trees evolved from small shallowly rooted land plants that existed only on thin microbial 'proto' soils of moist lowland habitats, and were consequently limited in their geographical spread, and their effect on the atmosphere and the surface of the land. The evolution of large trees, with their increased reach and deeper penetration of roots, enabled them to spread over previously inhospitable and harsher terrains. It is thought that as the forests spread, the rates of weathering and soil formation were accelerated,[21] changing the processes and patterns of the land surface. Atmospheric circulation was also changed by the transpiration of water, and by the spread of the newly evolved plants and trees across the earth. More water vapour was lifted into the atmosphere above the continental scale forests, and rainfall was increased by the change in surface albedo. During the Devonian period, the amount of carbon dioxide drawn down from the atmosphere by the proliferation of plant life was so substantial that the atmosphere was significantly cooled. A reduction in atmospheric carbon dioxide has the consequence of reducing the heat retained by the atmosphere. It has been argued that the extent of the rapid spread of forests and plants was so vast that it made a significant contribution to global cooling, precipitating the intense glaciation of the ice age at the end of the Devonian period.[22]

RIVERINE LANDFORMS

Water falls onto the surface of the land as rain, and the topography organises the flow water from water droplets into tiny rills, from rills into streams and rivers, and from rivers into lakes and oceans. Water modifies the surface by erosion, removing material as it flows and carrying away dissolved and solid materials to deposit them in lower flatter areas as sediment, and eventually out to lakes and the oceans. The long profile or section of a river emerges over time from: the interaction of the topography; the variations in rainfall and snow melt in the mountains, which determine the velocity and flow volume of the water; the size of the sediment particles carried by the water; and the hardness of the surface material over which it flows. Water flowing downhill has potential energy because of its elevation from the earth's surface, and the energy is proportional to both elevation and mass. When water flows, the potential energy becomes kinetic energy, the energy of motion. The higher the velocity of flow, the more kinetic energy it has, and the greater the volume of water moving at a given speed, the kinetic energy is greater because of the greater mass.

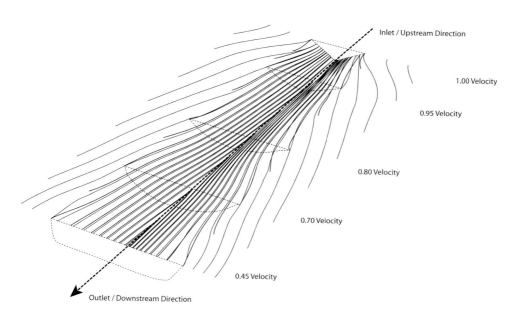

Inlet / Upstream Direction

1.00 Velocity

0.95 Velocity

0.80 Velocity

0.70 Velocity

0.45 Velocity

Outlet / Downstream Direction

3.2 River Profile
The long profile of a river has different channel properties along its length. It has a steep and narrow V-shaped channel where the stream originates and velocity of the water is high. As the profile becomes less steep the velocity decreases, the volume increases and the channel broadens. Close to the mouth of the river the velocity is very low, and the channel has a broad U shape. Material eroded from higher up the river is deposited on the floodplains, which get broader as the river slows.

The long profile has different channel properties along its length, varying cross sections and where the flow occasionally spills over the constraints of the channel when surface water is abundant, level areas or floodplains form alongside the channel. The profile may take thousands of years to develop, gradually reducing topographical irregularities by erosion and deposition. At the headwater in the mountainous area where the stream originates, the profile is steep and velocity of the water is high, providing the mechanical energy for cutting a narrow V-shaped channel. All eroded material is carried away, so that flat areas or floodplains alongside the rapidly flowing water do not develop.

As the long profile becomes less steep the velocity is lower, but the volume is increased. Most of the coarser heavier material such as gravel and sand is deposited onto the floodplain alongside the channel. The channel may split into braids, changing in number and geometry as the water flow varies over time. The angle of the long profile becomes shallower until it is almost flat near the mouth, and here the channel is a broad U shape, with maximum volume of water carrying very fine material. This is deposited in extensive flat floodplains and in bars where the channel has meandered. No matter how large the river, it will never run straight for more than 10 times its average width. When rivers carrying a heavy load of eroded material have a rapid change in elevation,[23] for example, when they emerge from the narrowing constraints of mountainous terrain to a nearly horizontal plain, the channel increases substantially in width with a corresponding drop in velocity, and a great deal of the sediment is deposited by the braided channels. As the water channels shift across the surface, depositing sediment and changing course, a fan-shaped alluvial plain is formed. At the mouth of a river the velocity will decrease further, particularly when flowing into standing water, and the finest material begins to be deposited. Small side channels emerge, diverting flow away from the main river channel, and distributing the sediments over the wider area of the characteristic triangular delta.[24] Variations in the flow or volume of water due to the seasonal weather patterns or longer term climatic changes, and variations in the quantity of sediment modulate the delta over time, but the morphology is also sensitive to the dynamics of the sea or lake into which the river is discharging. Waves, currents and tidal movements modify the configuration of sand-bars and barrier islands in the delta, and so modulate the flow and the channel pattern.

In climatic regions where rainfall is high, most river systems flow across the land surface to the sea, and in drier regions most rivers flow to landlocked lakes. In extremely arid regions there are no surface streams, and most surface water penetrates into the ground or evaporates from broad shallow floods. The geometrical patterns of dendritic[25] river systems and drainage networks are morphologically similar to other branching networks in natural systems. Other network patterns occur less frequently, and are specific to different topographies and tectonic landforms. Dendritic patterns occur when the general slope of the land surface is consistently gentle or moderate, and the hardness of the surface is uniform, whereas parallel patterns emerge on steeper slopes on strongly orientated landforms, and trellis-like patterns emerge on strongly folded hard surfaces.

COASTAL LANDFORMS

It might be thought that the coastline is only the horizontal section of the topographical relief of the earth's surface, the line where the complexity of the land surface forms simply ends and where the ocean begins. That is true in that the horizontal profile of any coast will have at least the same degree of irregularity as any vertical section, but coastal landforms develop very complex morphologies through the coupled processes of erosion and deposition in a high energy zone[26] that is the boundary between the land and the sea. Coasts are highly dynamic energy zones, powered by the energy systems of the climate and they are extremely sensitive to sea level changes. The local climate of each coastline varies according to its latitude and its position in relation to the main ocean and atmospheric circulation systems. Driven by the energy of wave and surface currents of the oceans, erosion cuts away the land, and where the energy level is less, the sediment is deposited as beaches. These coupled processes act along great linear dimensions but over a very limited vertical range. The upper limit of 10 metres or so above mean sea level is determined by the height of waves driven by storms, and by the tide. As wave energy decreases exponentially with depth, the lower limit does not extend more than a few metres below the surface. In-between these vertical limits is the active zone of erosion and deposition. Even a minor change of the sea level will start a new cycle, when the existing surface is either submerged by higher sea levels and becomes part of the active zone, or falling sea levels expose surfaces that were previously deeply submerged below the active zone. Sea level changes according to the climate; current sea level is about 120 metres above the level of 20,000 years ago, during the last extreme 'glaciation' when much of the surface water of the earth existed as ice.[27] In the warmer 'interglacial' climates sea level is estimated to have been between 6 and 30 metres higher than it is now, [28] and if all the ice that exists on the surface of the earth today were to melt, the current sea level would be raised by 70 metres.[29] There have been numerous fluctuations of sea level over geological time, driven by changes to the climate and by tectonic changes to the geometry of the ocean basins that altered the depth of the oceans relative to the continental land-masses. In consequence, coastlines have been through multiple iterations of uplift and submergence.

Each of the continents has a shelf-like boundary rim of land that is submerged in shallow water, known as the continental shelf. The characteristics of the coastal margin vary greatly, but there is a distinct morphological difference between the western and eastern seaboards of the major continents that corresponds with the direction of movement of the tectonic plates. On the western coasts of the continents, which are generally tectonic collision zones, the shelf is narrow and ends with steep falls into the deep ocean. In these areas the coastal beach is narrow and closely bounded inshore by cliffs. Waves undermine the cliffs by hydraulic action, driving air and water into cavities under pressure, and by the abrasive action of sand, gravel and pebbles scoured from beaches. Erosion of these coasts is slow, and the material found on the narrow beaches tends to be stony, with occasional large boulders. As the cliffs are eroded, older beach material is sometimes exposed, including the skeletons and shells of marine organisms that were deposited along more ancient beaches when the sea level was higher.[30] Where coastlines are made of rocks of different hardness, erosion will produce headlands and bays, and the characteristic arches, stacks and caves. Rivers that meet the sea on these coasts can cut large 'valleys' in the continental shelf.

Eastern coasts of the continents tend to be the 'trailing edges' of the tectonic plates, and the submerged continental shelves are very much wider, falling in a more gradual slope to the deep ocean. The inshore landforms of continental eastern shores tend to be broad flat plains. Erosion here is much faster, waves scouring sand and sediment off the coast at the rate of a metre a year, and carry it along the shore, sometimes for hundreds of kilometres, before depositing it.

Seas that are partially encircled by island chains, such as the Gulf of Mexico, are relatively shallow, and also have wide continental shelves, but the inshore landforms of these 'marginal' coasts are more usually small mountains or hills rather than the flat plains of the eastern seaboards. Wave energy is lower in these shallow smaller seas than in the larger oceans. Waves acquire energy by winds moving over the surface of the ocean, and the greater the distance, or 'fetch', of open water the greater the amount of kinetic energy they possess. In the low energy regime of these sheltered coasts, the sediment carried by slow moving rivers will be deposited and large river deltas tend to form.

AEOLIAN LANDFORMS

The wind picks up and carries small particles from loose surface material, and these produce the abrasive action of the wind on land surfaces. Winds blow from areas of high pressure to areas of low pressure as part of the global and regional circulation patterns of the atmosphere and the complexities of the metaclimate system, but close to the surface the local topography affects both the direction and velocity of the wind at varying spatial scales.[31] Wind can also carry particles high into the atmosphere, and in times of prolonged and severe drought loose soil particles are very fine, producing dust storms of continent-wide dimensions. In the 1930s the severe drought that affected large areas of North America, exacerbated by poor agricultural practices, broke down the coherence of the soil and the exposed topsoil was carried eastwards in huge dust storms all the way to the Atlantic. These conditions persisted throughout the decade and the dust storms became known as 'black blizzards'.

Large quantities of very small fine grains are carried by the wind as dust and these 'aerosols' in turn have an effect on the local and regional weather patterns, changing the albedo of the clouds that carry the material.[32] The particles are less than 0.2 millimetres in diameter and are deposited when the wind speed drops, although the very smallest particles are carried into the upper atmosphere and can travel huge distances, eventually falling back to the surface in rainfall. The dust sediments deposited by the wind accumulate over time, filling and covering existing topographical features. The depth of the deposits is a factor of the wind velocity, the fineness of the particles and the distance the material is carried. One of the deepest deposits covers an area of 300,000 square kilometres in northern China, and is estimated to be over 300 metres deep. The fine sediment accumulates to form a loose and highly porous material, known as 'loess',[33] which frequently has thin vertical cavities within it, formed by plants that were buried and subsequently decayed. The Loess Plateau was once a high flat plateau covered with trees and grasses, densely populated as many of the ancient Chinese dynasties constructed capital cities there. Large populations require intensive agriculture and fuel for industry, in this case charcoal. Several cycles of severe droughts, coupled with extensive deforestation that exposed the land surface to yet more drying, destabilised the soil, eliminating the root systems that bound it together. Today it is one of the most intensely eroded landscapes on earth. The angular quartz grains interlock and together with the fine vertical cavities result in the characteristic morphology of low cliffs and short columns. Loess is easily cut and eroded by water, and when saturated it is prone to landslide and collapse. The heavy summer monsoon rains saturate the steep slopes cut by rivers and streams, and the whole region is subject to massive slumps and surface movements. The Yellow River derives its name from the millions of tons of suspended silt that gives the water a yellow colour.[34]

Deserts emerge from the interacting processes of atmospheric circulation and oceanic circulation, and cover almost a third of the land surface area of the earth. The hot deserts of the world lie where cool dry air sinks from the convection circulation of the Hadley cell. As the air sinks, pressure and temperature increase. Light winds flow across the surface and pick up heat. Already dry, the winds dispel what little cloud cover exists, exposing the land to the sun and so increasing its temperature – a thermal dynamic pattern that persists over very long periods of time. The largest desert of this kind is the Sahara, and although rain does occasionally fall, decades may pass between significant rainfalls. Water flowed here 10,000 years ago, and it was a fertile area. Satellite radar imagery reveals a different topography beneath the sand of the Sahara, a topography cut by springs and rivers and with open surface water in large lakes. The absence of water and the lack of vegetation are critical to the development of deserts and their characteristic morphology. The progressive drying and heating effects of the climatic pattern that has persisted for thousands of years have turned the whole of North Africa into an arid desert.

Hot deserts have extreme temperature ranges, as without cloud cover the land surface absorbs heat very rapidly in the day, rising to a maximum of 45–50°C and loses heat rapidly at night, falling to 0°C and on occasions as low as -18°C. Deserts on the western edges of continents where the cold currents of the ocean gyres run parallel to the coast, have a smaller temperature range. The wind patterns of coastal deserts are more complex than in the hot deserts, oscillating between local and regional local wind systems. The temperature of the Atacama Desert, on the coast of Chile, does not rise much above 25°C and rarely falls below 0°C, but it is thought to be the driest of all deserts, with no rainstorms for hundreds of years. In winter months there are frequent fogs that inhibit solar radiation and so decrease temperatures. The temperature in polar deserts rarely climbs above 10°C, and frequently oscillates around 0°C, in rapid freezing and thawing cycles, from which distinctive gravel patterns emerge. They are morphologically distinct from other deserts.

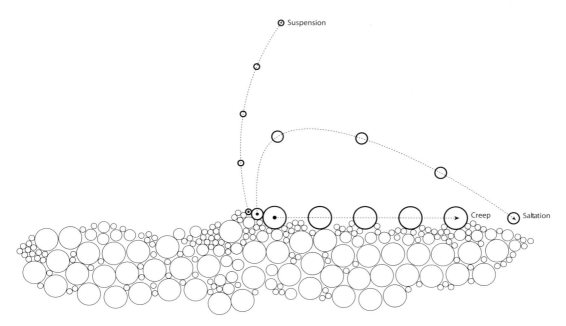

3.3 Saltation
The individual grains of sand are less than one millimetre in size, and are propelled along the surface in short shallow trajectories. The process of transportation (or 'saltation') sorts the grains by size. The larger grains and small pebbles that are too heavy to be transported by the wind gain some lesser momentum from the impact of lighter grains. These heavier granules accumulate in the hollows between dunes, and may accumulate into stable 'granule' ripples of much larger dimensions than fine sand ripples.

Sand is composed of particles that are too heavy to be held in suspension in the air, but are light enough to be moved by the wind. The shape of the particle and its mineral origin are not significant, so that any dry granular material, including snow, develops similar Aeolian forms. The wind sweeps land surfaces clear of loose sand particles, and the suspended particles abrade other surfaces. As wind velocity increases, there is an exponential increase in the quantity of sand transported by the wind, which dissipates much of the wind energy. The wind loses even more velocity by friction when passing over 'rough' surfaces of sand or vegetation, and so the suspended particles are deposited. This process produces patterns and forms that are morphologically differentiated by scale. Windswept and abraded rocky surfaces, large flat sand sheets and dune fields are the characteristic large, regional forms of deserts. The largest patterns are known as 'ergs' or sand seas, irregular accumulations of heavy sand grains and pebbles into vast sand sheets that cover thousands of square kilometres. The dunes that travel across them tend to all have a similar form, and to be similar in size and in orientation. Individual dunes have ripples on their surface, and both dunes and ripples are fluidly active. They are stable in the sense that their geometry is consistent over time, but they are fluid in the sense that they move.

Sand ripples are the smallest pattern, with crests and troughs forming at right angles to the direction of the wind. They appear on slowly accumulating flat areas and on the windward face of sand dunes, and are highly transient, moving rapidly downwind, forming and dispersing and reforming according to the velocity of the wind. In a moderate wind, ripple patterns form within 10 minutes, and move downwind several metres in an hour. The individual grains of sand are less than a millimetre in size, and are propelled along the surface in short shallow trajectories. Trajectories are a metre or so in length, and a little more in height, with the wavelength of the ripples (the distance between crests) rarely exceeding one metre and a few centimetres in height. There is no uniform ratio of height to wavelength, with measured samples in the field varying in the range 1/10[35] to 1/18.[36] The process of transportation (or 'saltation') sorts the grains by size. The larger grains and small pebbles that are too heavy to be transported by the wind gain some lesser momentum from the impact of lighter grains. These heavier granules accumulate in the hollows between dunes, and may accumulate into stable 'granule' ripples of much larger dimensions than fine sand ripples. The growth of granule ripples is very slow, typically taking months to develop rather than the minutes of sand ripples, and they may persist for decades.

Dunes form from accumulations of fine sand, blown by strong steady winds into a mound or ridge. Larger by two orders of magnitude than a ripple, up to 100 metres long, the section of dunes is similar to that of ripples, with a gentle slope on the windward side and a steep 'slip face' on the leeward side. The individual sand grains migrate up the windward side, dropping out of the wind at the crest. The leeward side becomes steadily steeper until it reaches its maximum angle of stability (the 'angle of repose') when it will avalanche or slip and reform the slip face.[37] The process continues and the entire dune migrates downwind. As a dune grows in height, its rate of advance slows, although they may still move a hundred metres in a year in long lasting high energy wind regimes. The movement of very small individual grains through short trajectories maintains the form of the dune and moves the whole form downwind. The relative timescales of the trajectory of a single grain and the movement of a dune differ by up to seven orders of magnitude.

Dunes are morphologically varied in plan (viewed from above), and the relative number and positions of slip faces. Wind direction and the relative abundance and particle size of sand are the factors that determine the variations in form. The most widely recognised form is crescent shaped, with a concave slip face and the horns of the crescent orientated downwind. Linear dunes form in subtropical deserts where sand is less abundant, and the surfaces of the hollows between them are covered in heavier gravel and pebbles. These dunes form parallel to the direction of strong and persistent winds, and may be 100 or more kilometres long. On beaches or floodplains where there is moisture, an abundance of fine sand and winds of low velocity, linear dunes form at right angles to the wind. In climatic regimes that generate winds from several directions over time, other variant forms develop, such as the 'star', a radially symmetrical dune with a high centre (several hundred metres) and three or more slip faces.

As ancient riverine landforms lie beneath the sand seas of the Sahara, so ancient Aeolian forms lie beneath some grasslands and tropical forests. The characteristic pattern of dune fields is recognisable in Colorado and Nebraska,[38] the central part of the Great Plains that is now covered and stabilised by vegetation. Vegetation is very sensitive to changes in water supply and temperature; and particularly so when they are coupled together, when rain becomes increasingly less available and temperatures continue to rise. The vegetation dies off, exposing larger areas of bare surface, so that more heat is absorbed by the surface. A small change to a slightly warmer global climate will induce increases in heatwaves and far lower precipitation in some areas. Once started, the process of warming and drying is self-reinforcing by positive feedback. It is evident that the land surface of large areas of the Great Plains region, and of other stabilised deserts around the world, is close to the threshold at which widespread mobilisation of the sand will begin again. The existing hot deserts will begin to expand, and the ancient hot deserts will be mobilised. Polar and coastal deserts are also sensitive to temperature and moisture change, but with quite different potential effects. There is a latitudinal differentiation in any warming of the climate metasystem, with more rapid and bigger rises in temperature at the highest latitudes. The polar regions are also sensitive to very small changes in climate. The phase change between ice and liquid water is delicately poised in this climatic regime, as the increased energy input from warmer atmospheric temperatures will be absorbed as latent heat. The process is endothermic, so that the temperature of a mixture of ice and water remains at or very close to 0°C during the phase change, and will not rise until the phase change is complete and all the ice has melted. Strong positive feedbacks, including albedo change, will result in rapid non-linear changes to the permafrost land surfaces. As the permafrost thaws, the fine Aeolian deposits on the surface are exposed to erosion. As the land surface becomes warmer and wetter, vegetation will initially increase, and the polar deserts will change to tundra grasslands, and the tundra to forests. This may not be a universal response across all polar areas, as increasing temperatures increase evaporation. Increases in rainfall will not be evenly distributed, and some areas will receive less than others. Where rain does not replace the evaporated water, the surface will begin to dry and the new vegetation will die off. The desertification of the cold dry tundras of parts of Siberia and Alaska will recommence.

CRITICAL THRESHOLDS AND THE EMERGENCE OF FORMS OF THE LAND

The general morphology of the land emerges from the interacting processes of the interior and the surface of the earth. Tectonic forces uplift the land from below and the processes of weathering and erosion act on the land surface, breaking down the surface of tectonic forms into fragments and sediments that are carried away and deposited elsewhere. Surface topography of more local and transient morphological features of the surface is produced by the actions of ice, water and wind. The behaviour of the climate metasystem, the temporal and spatial patterns of temperature, wind and water control and modulate the varying timescales of processes that act on the surface. Those processes are dynamic, subject to variations in intensity, duration and effect. They are not separate from one other but are interrelated by an intricate choreography of exchanges of energy and material. Many areas of the land experience more than one process over the extension of geological time, so that residual forms from a later process may overlay forms from an earlier and quite different process. The ancient river channels and networks that lie under the sand seas of the Sahara are an interesting example. Also, prior conditions are significant in the development over time of a process, and of the forms that emerge from it. Positive feedbacks amplify small local perturbations so that they may in time lead to large changes. In the atmosphere it is very local perturbations that provide initiating changes that can lead, through successive positive feedbacks, to large storms. Geomorphic systems behave in the same way but over longer time periods. For example, local changes to the rainfall pattern over a small area of land, will initiate changes to rills and streams that through successive feedbacks can lead to changes to patterns of sediment deposition far downstream, and ultimately to changes to the river network.

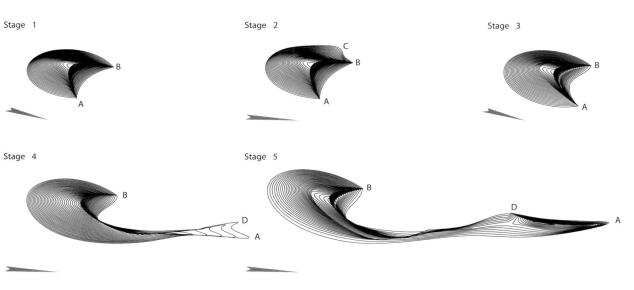

Stage 1

Stage 2

Stage 3

Stage 4

Stage 5

3.4 Dune Formation
(1) The typical crescentic dune forms under steady wind. (2) If, however, the wind direction changes, one horn is extended in the new axis of the wind, whereas the other recedes and a new, slightly receded bulge forms. (3) If the wind returns to its main direction, this new extended horn is still more prone to extending than the receded one and forms a sand attractor. (4) If the wind again blows from the secondary axis, this tongue is encouraged to grow. If it reaches a point that allows it to move out of the wind shadow of the original crescentic dune, it receives the sand stream flowing to the leeside and the critical moment of transformation from crescentic to linear formation is reached. (5) If the two directions prevail, the process is iterated so that eventually a great chain develops.

It follows that the morphological development of the land is more than a simple sequence of tectonic and climatic cycles, each with their associated set of forms, with a final destination of a steady state or equilibrium. Glacial, riverine, coastal and Aeolian processes are systems that cannot be separated from their immediate physical environment: the tectonic formation of the land that has determined variations and differences in elevation and variations in hardness of material, and the climatic regime that determines temperature, wind and precipitation. Nor can they be separated from their own trajectory through time. Long-lasting and large morphological changes may be a disproportionate or non-linear response to very small local changes, as the forms of the land tend to be sensitively poised close to the threshold of change.

When a form exists that is close to the threshold of change, there may be more than one variable that will precipitate the change. The stability of a slope, for example, is a balance between the resistance of the grains of sand, or soil, or snow, and the force of gravity that generates a shear stress that pulls them down the slope. When the shear stress becomes greater than the frictional resistance and the cohesion of the particles, a mass of material will slump or flow until the steepness of the slope is sufficiently reduced to a stable angle. For dry grains, the stable angle or angle of repose is determined by the friction between the grains, which depending on the size of grains is between about 30° and 37°. As mass accumulates, for example by 'saltating' sand grains, or by fresh snowfall higher up the slope, the slope will be in a state of 'self-organised criticality',[39] poised at the threshold of change. The addition of a single grain may cause a few grains to slide down the slope, or it may be that there will be no change at all, or it may precipitate collapse over a larger area. Over time, all of these events will occur, with the small changes being the most frequent, and the large catastrophic changes the least frequent.

The infiltration of water into a sand or soil slope will also precipitate a change, as the surface tension between the water and the solid increases the resistance so that the slope can be steeper and remain stable. As the slope absorbs more and more water, however, all friction will be lost, and the material will suddenly behave like a fluid, and slump or collapse. The flow varies in spatial scale, and may be locally contained by the surrounding topography or may develop into a much larger mud flow, mixed with large debris into a slurry of increasing mass, volume and velocity that will flow over large areas. The transfer of energy by vibration will also reduce friction between the grains, as in snowpack avalanches, earthquakes and tremors, with similar results. Avalanches of snow may start wherever a slope exceeds 30°, accelerating and accumulating mass rapidly, and travel very long distances.

Some landforms develop until they are poised at the critical threshold of stability,[40] held there by the balance between forces (energy) and resistance (material). Critical thresholds are the point at which a geomorphic system changes from one state to another, driven by energy or material variations, resulting in a change in form. A canonical example is the dramatic change in river forms in the semi-arid region of the south-western USA at the end of the 19th century. The change in form was rapid, only a few years in some rivers, from wide shallow valleys with trees, shrubs and grasses to deeply cut steep sided 'arroyos', bare of all plant life.[41] 'Arroyos' may be hundreds of kilometres long, 20 or so metres deep with vertical sides and 50 metre wide flat floors. Fast positive feedbacks drove the transition through the critical threshold. There is a high variability of rainfall in semi-arid regions, with dry periods interspersed with wet. A general increase in rainfall over the region was recorded, not steady rain, but intense downpours over very local areas interspersed by prolonged hot dry periods. Variability of seasonal and annual patterns was intensified, so that in very wet periods the volume and velocity (the force or kinetic energy) of the rivers increased, accelerating local erosion, weakening the root systems of plants (decreasing the resistance), and deepening the channel. In the drier periods the weakened plants died off (further decreasing the resistance), destabilising the riverbanks and floodplain. Repetitive but differentiated cycles, each slightly different with varying velocities in different stream branches of the river, cause the channel to shift laterally across the floor of the deepening 'arroyos' in each cycle.

There is a slow negative feedback that over many centuries will eventually fill in the incised channels. The very high load of eroded material carried by the rivers absorbs energy and reduces the velocity and the force and thus slows erosion. Plant growth starts again, further reducing the velocity and increasing the resistance to erosion, thus increasing the deposition of eroded material.

The processes from which topography emerges are forces that act on small particles or grains and local flow of material over very small spatial areas, but produce very large forms and complex behaviour over much larger dimensional scales. In turn they generate successive feedbacks, differentiated over time and spatial dimension, which act on other systems. Geomorphic systems are dynamic, complex and nonlinear.[42] The regional and latitudinal patterns of the climate metasystem generate differentiated regimes of temperature, precipitation and wind, with a range of variation and perturbations in each regime. The processes of weathering, erosion and deposition are produced by the climate, and variations and changes to the climate change the behaviour, duration and force of each process. In turn, geomorphic processes also contribute to the generation of climate feedbacks; positive feedbacks of surface albedo change and increase in the percentage of greenhouse gases and more ephemeral feedbacks such as the aerosols from dessicated soils and deserts. Many landforms are poised at the critical threshold of change, so that small differences to the ratio or balance between force and resistance, energy and material, will precipitate a rapid change of form.

1 Currently thought to be approximately 4,500 million years old, and some of its surface rocks are thought to be 3,500 million years old. Age is estimated by measurements based on the radioactive decay of very long-lived natural isotopes of potassium, thorium and uranium in the rock. Radiometric dating is quite different to the radiocarbon (the shorter lived C-14 isotope) method widely used for dating organic materials.

2 Hutton, James, *Theory of the Earth; or, an investigation of the laws observable in the composition, dissolution and restoration of land upon the globe*, 1788.

3 Le Roy, L, *Of the Interchangeable Course or Variety of Things in the Whole World* (London), 1594. Le Roy did not propose any mechanisms, but did state that land and sea could change places and that mountains could be reduced to plains.

4 Darwin, Charles, *Journal Of Researches Into The Natural History and Geology Of The Countries Visited During The Voyage of HMS Beagle Round The World 1832–1836* (first published 1859 in London by H Colburn), reprinted as *The Voyage of the Beagle*, Everyman (London), 1906.

5 Ibid.

6 Darwin, *The Voyage of HMS Beagle*.

7 Pearson, PN, 'Charles Darwin on the Origin and Diversity of Igneous Rocks', *Earth Sciences History*, vol 15, 1996, pp 49–67.

8 Wegener, Alfred, *The Origin of Continents and Oceans*, 1915.

9 Known as Bénard Cells. There are many hundreds of scientific papers on Bénard Cells and the Rayleigh numbers that are useful to predict the onset of convection patterns and instabilities in them. A good general account is given by Ball, Philip, 'On the Boil', in *The Self-Made Tapestry: pattern formation in nature*, Oxford University Press (New York), 1999.

10 Albarede, Francis and Rob van der Hilst, 'Zoned Mantle Convection', *Philosophical Transactions of the Royal Society of London A*, vol 360, 2002, pp 2507–20; and Machetal, P and P Weber, 'Intermittent Layered Convection in a Model Mantle with an Endothermic Phase Change at 670 km', *Nature*, vol 350, 1991, pp 55–7.

11 White, RS, 'The Lithosphere Under Stress', *Philosophical Transactions of the Royal Society of London A*, vol 357, no 1753, 1999, pp 901–15.

12 Büdel, J, *Climatic Geomorphology*, Princeton University Press (Princeton), 1982, first published as *Klima-geomorphologie*, Gebrüder Bornträger (Berlin), 1977.

13 0 to -4°C: small hexagonal plates; -4 to -10°C: needles and hollow columns; -10 to -21°C: sectored plates, hexagons with indentations, large dendrites; below -21°C: ice crystal formation is increasingly inhibited.

14 Elliot, M, L Labeyrie and J Duplessy, 'Changes in North Atlantic Deep-Water Formation Associated with the Dansgaard-Oeschger Temperature Oscillations (60–10 ka)', *Quarternary Science Review*, vol 21, 2002, pp 1153–65; and Ganopolski, Andrey, 'Glacial Integrative Modelling', *Philosophical Transactions of the Royal Society* of London A, vol 361, 2003, pp 1871–84.

15 Meier, M, 'Flow of Blue Glacier, Olympic Mountains, Washington, USA', *Journal of Glaciology*, vol 13, 1974, pp 213–26.

16 Algeo, TJ, RA Berner, JB Maynard and SE Scheckler, 'Late Devonian Oceanic Anoxic Events and Biotic Crises: "rooted" in the evolution of vascular land plants', *Geological Society of America Today*, vol 5, no 45, 1995, pp 64–6.

17 Pyramidal peaks are left when three or more 'cirque glaciers' erode away a mountain from the sides. These peaks are called horns, as in the Matterhorn in the Switzerland.

18 The Great Lakes of North America are glacial erosion features of sheet ice.

19 Known as Kames, formed when the meltwater carrying sediment runs into a depression or crevasses in the land surface.

20 Krantz, WB, KJ Gleason and N Caine, 'Patterned Ground', *Scientific American*, vol 259, 1988, pp 68–76.

21 Algeo, TJ and SE Scheckler, 'Terrestrial-Marine Teleconnections in the Devonian: links between the evolution of land plants, weathering processes, and marine anoxic events', *Philosophical Transactions of The Royal Philosophical Society of London B*, vol 353, 1998, pp 113–30.

22 Algeo, TJ, RA Berner, JB Maynard and SE Scheckler, 'Late Devonian Oceanic Anoxic Events and Biotic Crises: "rooted" in the evolution of vascular land plants', *Geological Society of America Today*, vol 5, no 45, 1995, pp 64–6; and Algeo, TJ, SE Scheckler and JB Maynard, 'Effects of Early Vascular Land Plants on Terrestrial Weathering Processes and Global Geochemical Fluxes during the Middle and Late Devonian', in *Plants Invade the Land: evolutionary and environmental perspectives*, (eds) Gensel, PG and D Edwards, Columbia University Press (New York), 1998.

23 Schumm, SA and HR Khan, 'Experimental Study of Channel Patterns', *Geological Society America Bulletin*, vol 83, no 6, 1972, pp 1755–70, explores the relationship between slope and sediment load, response of landforms to critical thresholds for erosion and deposition.

24 The Nile has a triangular shaped delta, but other geometries exist such as the 'birds-foot' shape of the Mississippi delta.

25 A branching form or pattern that resembles a tree, commonly used to describe the extensions of the cytoplasm of a neuron, patterns of crystallising minerals, and river patterns. Derived from the Greek 'Dendron' meaning tree.

26 Inman, Douglas L and Scott A Jenkins, 'Energy and Sediment Budgets of the Global Coastal Zone', *Encyclopedia of Coastal Science*, Kluwer Academic Publishers (Dordrecht), 2003.

27 Fairbanks, RG, 'A 17,000-year Glacio-Eustatic Sea Level Record', *Nature* 342, 1989, pp 637–42.

28 Thompson, WG and SL Goldstein, 'Open System Coral Ages Reveal Persistent Suborbital Sea-Level Cycles', *Science*, vol 308, no 5720, 2005, pp 401–4.

29 Alley, RB, P Clark, P Huybrechts and I Joughin, 'Ice-Sheet and Sea-Level Changes', *Science 21*, vol 310, no 5747, 2005, pp 456–60. Now a widely accepted calculation of the combined volumes of the Greenland and Antarctic ice sheets, as summarised in table 11.3, *Some Physical Characteristics of Ice on Earth, Climate Change 2001, The Scientific Basis*, Intergovernmental Panel on Climate Change, 2001.

30 Inman, DL and R Dolan, 'The Outer Banks of North Carolina: budget of sediment and inlet dynamics along a migrating barrier system', *Journal of Coastal Research*, vol 5, no 2, 1989, pp 193–237.

31 Fujita, TT, 'Tornadoes and Downbursts in the Context of Generalized Planetary Scales', *Journal of the Atmospheric Sciences*, vol 30, 1981, pp 1544–63. Fujita proposes that the movements of the atmosphere be divided into scales that decrease by two orders of magnitude from 40,000 kilometres.

32 Joseph, Joachim, Alexander Manes and Dov Ashbel, 'Desert Aerosols Transported by Khamsinic Depressions and Their Climatic Effects', *Journal of Applied Meteorology*, vol 12, no 15, 1973, pp 792–7.

33 Thought to derive from the German word 'Loss' meaning loose.

34 Fang, JQ and ZR Xie, 'Deforestation in Preindustrial China: the Loess Plateau region as an example', *Chemosphere*, vol 29, no 5, 1994, pp 983–9.

35 Bagnold, RA, *The Physics of Blown Sand and Desert Dunes*, Methuen (London), 1941.

36 Sharp, Robert P, 'Wind Ripples', *Journal of Geology*, vol 71, no 5, 1963, pp 617–36.

37 Bagnold, RA, *The Physics of Blown Sand and Desert Dunes*, Methuen (London), 1941.

38 Muhs, D, 'Age and Paleoclimatic Significance of Holocene Sand Dunes in Northeastern Colorado', *Annals of the Association of American Geographers*, vol 75, 1985, pp 566–82.

39 Bak, Per, Chao Tang and Kurt Weisenfeld 'Self-Organized Criticality: an explanation of the 1/f noise', *Physical Review Letters*, vol 59, no 4, 1987. Presents the first argument that unconstrained dynamical systems naturally evolve into a self-organised critical state.

40 Schumm, SA, 'Geomorphic Thresholds: the concept and its applications', *Transactions of the Institute of British Geographers*, New Series vol 4, 1979, pp 485–515.

41 Cooke, RU and RW Reeves, *Arroyos and Environmental Change in the American South-West*, Clarendon (Oxford), 1976.

42 'Complex "nonlinear" dynamics are not (merely) an artifact of models, equations, and experiments, but have been observed and documented in many geomorphic phenomena and are not rare or isolated phenomena.' Phillips, JD, 'Sources of Nonlinear Complexity in Geomorphic Systems', *Progress in Physical Geography*, vol 27, 2003, pp 1–23.

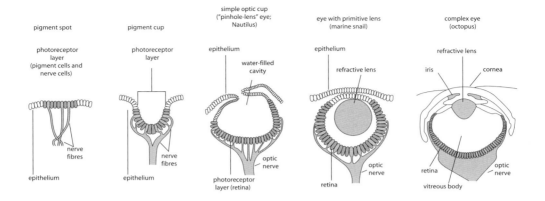

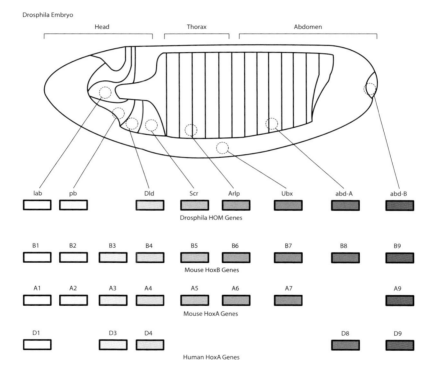

4.1 Evolution and Gene Expression

The emergence of small complex anatomical organisations makes possible the emergence of ever larger and even more complex organisations. Complexity builds over time by a sequence of modifications to existing forms. Regulatory genes produce the initial spatial organisation of the embryo, by accelerating or inhibiting growth in varying sequences and patterns, and so act as differentiated feedbacks on the process of growth. Small variations in the strength of inhibition or acceleration induce a periodicity in the self-organising patterns, that in turn produces yet more complex spatial and anatomical organisations across the range of scales.

Living Forms

4

The forms of all living beings emerge from two interlinked processes with very different time spans; embryological development from a single cell to an adult form, and the evolution of diverse species of forms over extended time. Each cell of every living form carries within it the information for the development of the whole being, and this information is transmitted generation by generation down through time by the genome. The evolutionary development of complex anatomical organisations and all the variations of species have occurred in relation to the differing climatic regimes, topographies and ecological systems of the surface of the earth. In turn, living forms have modified and continue to modify the processes of the atmosphere and oceans, and the geomorphic systems of the surface of the earth.

It is difficult to conceive of an image of nature that does not contain living things, to think of the earth without life, but for almost half of the time the world has existed there was no life at all. Before life emerged, the atmosphere and climate were very different. Over the time since the sun formed, the density of the core has increased, and in consequence, it has become smaller and hotter. Higher temperatures produce faster fusion reactions, and so more light is emitted. When the earth first formed, the sun was much less bright, emitting about 30 per cent less light than it does today. Such a low level of energy falling on the earth, if the atmosphere and the surface of the earth were as they are now, would mean that there could be no liquid water and the oceans and the surface of the earth would be entirely frozen over. Earth would resemble a ball of ice and snow. Yet there is geological evidence suggesting that a billion years later, when the sun was still far fainter than it is today, the oceans had formed and life had emerged.[1] Nor is there is any evidence of glaciers in this early period. It follows that the atmosphere must have been very efficient at retaining heat from the faint young sun, and therefore had a quite different chemical composition to the atmosphere today, with a higher proportion of greenhouse gases. There was no free oxygen at all, and high levels of carbon dioxide and hydrogen in the atmosphere, emitted by the highly active volcanoes of that period,[2] would have raised atmospheric temperatures despite the weaker output from the sun.

The first living forms, Archaea, were marine organisms, each a single cell that fed on carbon dioxide and hydrogen, and excreted methane. It is thought that these bacterial forms emerged from the self-replicating patterns of complex chemical systems in high temperature conditions.[3] These simple unicellular organisms still survive today, wherever there is no oxygen, and temperatures are high, such as the hydrothermal vents known as 'black smokers' at the bottom of the deep ocean, or in the stomachs of animals and in sewage systems. They do not require light for life, as their metabolic process does not involve photosynthesis.[4] Over time the proportion of methane in the atmosphere would have continued to rise, providing a slow positive feedback that drove up atmospheric temperatures even further. Other bacteria capable of using methane as source of energy and carbon developed, and persist today in conditions wherever there is no free oxygen, particularly in soil and peat bogs.

Archaea are robust and survive in extreme conditions, but cannot exist in the presence of oxygen. Geological evidence suggests that the first significant amounts of oxygen in the atmosphere appeared a little more than 2 billion years ago, when another marine organism, cyanobacteria, emerged. They are also unicellular, but use light energy rather than chemical energy for their metabolic processes, and so require shallow warm water as their environment. The first photosynthetic organism, they assembled into small colonies, mats of bacterial filaments that became infiltrated with minerals they had extracted from the sea water, forming the oldest known fossils. Their descendant variant forms are widespread across the earth today, and the marine variant is still producing the small columnar forms of laminated rocks known as stromatolites. In the chemical reactions of photosynthesis, carbon dioxide and water in the presence of light are converted to carbohydrates and oxygen, and the oxygen is excreted.

Over a billion years the numbers of these small colonies increased to such an extent that their excreted oxygen accumulated in the atmosphere. Oxygen reacts with methane in the presence of light, breaking down the methane into water and carbon dioxide. As the chemistry of the atmosphere changed, so its capacity to retain heat energy was reduced. Species dependent on methane died off, and temperatures began to fall. The oxygen content of the atmosphere continued to rise and the methane content to fall. As bacterial life flourished and expanded, more and more carbon was bound up in living form, and subsequently sequestered, further lowering the heat-retaining capacity of the atmosphere. The critical threshold was passed, and the first ice age began. Over time carbon dioxide was released back into the atmosphere by tectonic activity, the atmosphere was able to retain more heat, and temperatures rose sufficiently to cause the ice to retreat. The cycle of 'ice house'/'hot house' oscillations lasted for 500 million years.[5] The emergence of life and the biotic processes of the smallest and simplest of organisms initiated significant changes to the climate, and in consequence to the forms of the surface of the earth.

THE EVOLUTION OF CELLS

A cell is the simplest organisation of life but all living cells have complex internal systems separated into semi-autonomous functional areas. Each cell is enclosed and separated from its surroundings by a surface membrane, and able to dynamically maintain itself by the exchange of energy and material through that surface. Each cell also has within it the genome, an information set or programme for accurate construction of descendants identical to itself. The complex architecture of living forms requires more than the simple coexistence of many cells in close proximity; the spatial organisation of many cells has to enable interactions of each cell to its immediate neighbours, and it is the interaction that initiates the processes that produce hierarchical order and morphological complexity.[6]

The cells in plants, fungi and animals are 'eukaryotic', meaning 'true nuclei' and that is what distinguishes them from other living cells, the 'prokaryote' bacteria, that are simpler in organisation. The most significant early evolutionary development of eukaryotic cells was the incorporation of simpler organisms, such as cyanobacteria, into the interior organisation of the cell, where they became the energy processing system for the host cell. The chloroplasts in plant cells are cyanobacteria, and they produce the carbohydrates used for energy and the production of more cells in all green plants. In animal cells, mitochondria perform a comparable function. The mitochondria and chloroplasts within cells were both once free living independent unicellular organisms, and preserve their own bacterial genome independently of the host cell genome, and have subsequently coevolved with their hosts. The subsequent evolutionary development of more complex organisms was made possible by the intracellular symbiosis of energy producing subsystems into the larger system of the eukaryotic cell.

Charles Darwin argued that all living and extinct beings were the offspring of common parents, descended from an 'ancient progenitor', and that 'all past and present organic beings constitute one grand natural system'. The diversification and proliferation of all living forms of all the species of life, was driven by variation and selection. 'I have called this principle, by which each slight variation, if useful, is preserved, by the term Natural Selection.'[7] In his view variations are random, small modifications or changes in the organism that occur naturally in reproduction through the generations. Random variation produces the raw material of variant forms, and natural selection acts as the force that chooses the forms that survive. Just as humans breed livestock and vegetables by 'unnatural' selection, methodically organising systematic changes in them, so wild organisms themselves are changed by natural selection, a slow, steady, gradual and continuous process of change. Darwin did not, as is sometimes said, assume that selection was the only mechanism of evolutionary change. In the last sentence of the introduction to *The Origin of Species* he wrote: 'I am convinced that Natural Selection has been the most important, but not the exclusive, means of modification'. Darwin never did go so far as to state that complex life forms had evolved from simple cells, although it is clear that he, and his contemporary and ally Thomas Huxley[8] were drawn towards that possibility. 'All the organic beings which have ever lived on this earth have descended from some one primordial form, into which life was first breathed.'[9] What the original form was was not stated, although the concluding sentence of *The Origin of Species*, 'from so simple a beginning endless forms most beautiful and most wonderful have been, and are being, evolved' does suggest that he did not consider that the origin was a complex 'higher' form.

The development of a single being from an embryo to an adult form was then regarded as related to but distinct from the evolutionary 'descent from ancestors'. Darwin stated 'the early cells or units possess the inherent power, independently of any external agent, of producing new structures wholly different in form, position, and function'.[10] His account of the properties of cells included their ability to proliferate by division, and to differentiate themselves to form the various tissues of a body. Stephen Jay Gould published *Ontogeny and Phylogeny*[11] almost a hundred years later, arguing that all changes in form are the result of changes to the timing of the developmental processes relative to each other, and to the rate at which they are carried out. His synthesis of embryological development and evolution focused on changes to the timing and rate of development.

All living forms grow by producing more cells, and genes regulate the timing of growth. Small genetic mutations affect the sequence of cellular growth during development, producing changes in forms, and natural selection acts to preserve or eliminate the changed forms. Changes to the timing of growth, and to the rate of growth, generate changes to the growth of cells, in their locations and orientations, and consequently change the shape, size and functions of the adult form. The history of growth that each individual organism experiences in the development into an adult form, the ontogeny, can be different to that of the ancestor, and that may affect specific parts or the whole of the form. In Gould's synthesis, evolution is regulated by the transmission of genetic information down through the generations, by changes in form during development, and by natural selection.

Life existed solely as unicellular forms for 3 billion years, and then in a relatively short period of 5 million years multicellular organisations developed that were sufficiently complex for animal life, and a great variety of new forms rapidly emerged. It has been argued that since then the evolutionary history of living forms consists of variations on the anatomical organisations evolved in that short period of intense biological innovation.[12] The development of complex cellular organisations requires cells to divide and elongate, groups of cells to grow more in one direction than another, and to differentiate into distinct tissues. These are spatial organisations as well as functional arrangements, and require cells to develop in specific orientations, in precise locations and at specific times.[13] Every reproductive cycle requires the organism to replicate its genetic material, and this process is susceptible to small copying errors, so that offspring are produced that are a little bit different from the parents. Small errors or mutations occur to the genome, and in consequence changes occur in the process of development, resulting in changes in the adult form. Some changes are preserved by natural selection, and over millions of years this results in the evolution of living forms, producing new species with different capacities, better adapted to new circumstances or climates. Every living form emerges from two strongly coupled processes, operating over maximally differentiated time spans: the differential development of cells in the growth of an embryo to an adult form, and the evolution of forms over time.

MUTATION

The mythical monsters of the classical world were imaginary creatures, composed of parts of known animal and human forms. The Sphinx, for example, had the head of a woman, the body of a lion and the wings of a bird. The Minotaur had the body of a man and the head of a bull, and the Centaur had the body of a horse and the head and torso of a man. These monsters were mutations of the human body, deviations from the ideal of harmonious proportion and beauty, beings that united mankind and animals.

Other monsters, like the Chimera, a fire-breathing monster that had the head of a lion, the body of a goat and the tail of a serpent, were composed entirely of animal forms. Cerberus had three dogs' heads, a serpent tail, with many serpents' heads on his back.

There are common characteristics they share, of which the most striking is the fact that they were composed of different parts in order to do more than mortal humans could do. Stronger and more powerful than normal humans, they also were untamed and closer to the more 'natural' animal, and terrible in their appetites and anger. The Sphinx devoured humans who could not answer its riddle;[14] Cerberus, the hound of Hell,[15] tortured souls; the Minotaur was confined in the labyrinth built by Daedalus[16] to hide its monstrosity, and fed on the flesh of virgin youth. The Centaurs killed men and ravished human women and boys,[17] but they were also knowledgeable of human culture – Chiron, the most righteous centaur,[18] taught Achilles medicine and music, hunting and war.

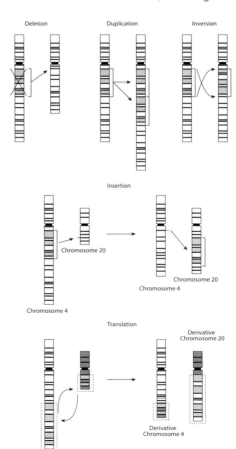

4.2 Mutation
Changes arise in the genome by mutation, which in turn produces changes in the sequence of genes and so changes to the physical form or phenome. It is thought that the regulatory set of genes emerged long before the evolution of physical complex forms, and many of the regulatory genes are similar across species.

Classical monsters were not truly alien but rather mutations of known human or animal forms, parts of existing forms aggregated into systems of differences, and it was the union of differences that produced their excessively natural, superior yet deviant functionality.

Mutations to the forms of animal and human bodies occur naturally. Cyclops mutations, for example, are a frequent occurrence in many species. Fish may become cyclopic if their embryos are thermally or chemically traumatised,[19] pregnant ewes grazing on corn lilies can produce cyclopic lambs, and in humans excessive alcohol or diabetes during pregnancy dramatically increases the chances of the embryo mutating to the cyclopic form. It is a very common mutation,[20] a deviation at the very beginning of the normal development of the embryo. The morphological characteristics of Cyclopia are similar in all species, including humans. The mutation produces an undivided brain, lacking the normal two hemispheres, and a single eye, usually with the nostrils located above the eye.

The construction of a systematic study of all 'the monsters and prodigious products of nature, of every novelty, rarity or abnormality'[21] is one of the earliest projects of science. The study of the different, of the 'errors of nature', of the monstrous and mutated, is an essential part of Bacon's proposition that natural history should be split into three interrelated domains: the study of ordinary or usual nature; of deviant nature and of nature manipulated by man. Nature produces the 'history of generations' or species that develop in the ordinary course, or nature is forced from the ordinary course by the perversity of matter and produces monsters, or nature is constrained and moulded by mankind to produce the artificial. Furthermore, the three regimes were not to be treated separately, but could be subjected to the same inductive methodology of enquiry. 'For why should not the history of the monsters in the several species be joined with the history of the species themselves? And things artificial again may sometimes be rightly joined with the species, though sometimes they will be better kept separate.'[22]

At the end of the 19th century, William Bateson published a substantive account of the mutations in living forms, *Materials for the Study of Variation*.[23] Bateson's interest lay in how living forms come into being, how they are adapted to 'fit the places they have to live in', and in the differences between forms, and particularly in the causes of variation.

Although an admirer of Darwin, he believed that the process of evolution was not one of continuous and gradual modification, but was rather discontinuous. New forms and species could not come into being through a gradual accumulation of small changes, and distinct parts arose or disappeared rapidly. He argued that from distinctive variations, entire new forms could spring up, already perfectly adapted. His argument rests on his analysis of the morphology of living beings, observing that 'the bodies of living things are mostly made up of repeated parts', organised bilaterally or radially in series, and many body parts themselves are also made up of repeated units. The parts are already functional, pre-adapted so to speak, so that morphological changes or variations can occur by changes to the number or order of parts. Another common variation he named 'homeotic', in which one body part is replaced by, or transformed into, a likeness of another part, for example, appendages such as legs and antennae that have similar morphological characteristics. He regarded most differences or variation between forms and species as differences in the arrangement, number and kind of inherited repeated parts, believing that changes are initiated by a change in 'force' during development. He described this force, to much derision at the time, as rhythmic or 'vibratory' harmonic resonances or similar wave-like phenomena, capable of dynamic response to environmental changes. Discontinuity in evolution is suggested by fossil evidence, which suggests long periods of relative stasis punctuated by sudden short periods in which many new species appear.[24] Gould's 'punctuated equilibrium' is perhaps the best known, if not most widely accepted, version of the theory that forms tend to persist unchanged for great lengths of time, and undergo brief but rapid change to produce new species in response to severe changes in their environment.

'Hopeful monsters'[25] was a controversial term used by Richard Goldschmidt to describe an event of mutation that suddenly produces a new species. Goldschmidt proposed that mutations in the genes that regulate the development process of the embryo could produce large effects on the phenotype. Furthermore, these developmental macromutations or 'hopeful monsters' had the potential to succeed as a new species. The idea of developmentally significant mutations producing large effects is widely accepted, but to extend from this to a theoretical proposition of speciation through systemic mutation has little support, as it neglects the role of natural selection and the dynamics of evolving populations. A single hopeful monster cannot constitute a new species, or found one. At least part of Goldschmidt's theory, universally rejected by the prevailing orthodoxy of the time, might get a more sympathetic

THE ARCHITECTURE OF EMERGENCE

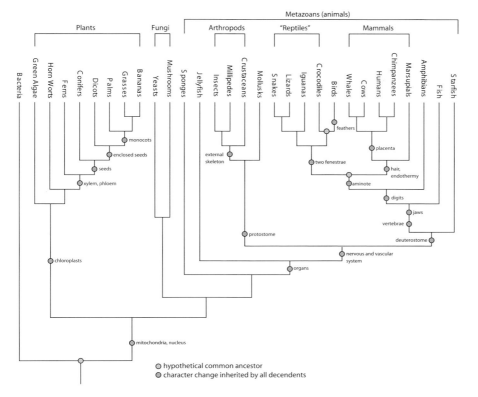

4.3 The Tree of Life

Small changes in the regulatory genes have the potential to produce changes to the size, shape and number of repeating modules in the living form. The emergence of small complex anatomical organisations makes possible the emergence of ever larger and even more complex organisations. Complexity builds over time by a sequence of modifications to existing forms. There is both fossil and genetic evidence that the emergence of the general vertebrate organisation, and its subsequent modification into amphibians, reptiles, birds, and mammals, occurred in this sequence.

hearing today; in particular, his finding of what he called 'rate genes', genes that control the timing of local growth and differentiation processes. The earlier a mutation occurs in the process of embryonic development, the more extensively it will alter the organism; very early mutations produce such profound changes that the fully developed organism is rarely viable. The more complex an organism is, the more extensive the changes will be, and the more likely it is that they will be lethal to the organism. Gould gives an analysis of what might make a monster hopeful[26] – it must be well suited to a previously unexploited environment and be organically fully functional. A mutation that produces two eyes on one side of the head of a fish, such as tuna, is a monster; a mutation to a flatfish that produces two eyes on the upper surface of the head that will enable the fish to see more clearly above is a 'hopeful monster'.

Biological mutations reveal the potential space of morphological variation, the set of available forms of any given species. In evolutionary terms, they are subject to strong negative selection, but are produced in every generation by random mutations or errors early in the internal processes of embryonic development. Mutations will tend to persist only if they offer some advantage over competing forms, or in the relation to the environment.

GROWTH AND DEVELOPMENT

D'Arcy Thompson agreed with Darwin's argument that natural selection is efficient at removing the 'unfit', but in his view all forms are influenced by the physical properties of the natural world, and the form of living things is a diagram of the forces that have acted on them. He did not deny the inheritance of form down through generations, but regarded evolution as an insufficient explanation, 'we tend to neglect these direct physical and mechanical modes of causation altogether, and to see in the characters of a bone merely the results of variation and of heredity'.[27] The physical forces act on living forms and determine the scales, bounding limits and informing geometries of the development of all adult forms. Evolution and differential growth during development produce the material forms of living things. The combination of the internal forces such as chemical activities and the pressure in their cells, and the external forces of the environment such as gravity, climate and the available energy supply determine the characteristics of the field in which they act; the effect of these natural forces is expressed in different ways depending on the size of the organism. 'Cell and tissue, shell and bone, leaf and flower, are so many portions of matter, and it is in obedience to the laws of physics that their particles have been moved, moulded and conformed.'[28] His recognition of growth as the principal means of achieving variation in inherited forms predates Gould's synthesis, but most significantly, D'Arcy Thompson proposed that 'a new system of forces, introduced by altered environment and habits' would, over time, produce adaptive modifications of forms. Living forms, like non-living forms, exist in a field of forces, and alterations in those forces will inevitably produce the response of evolutionary changes to forms. Furthermore, these changes will be systemic, to the whole being rather than to a specific part, 'more or less uniform or graded modifications' over the whole of the body.

All beings begin life as a single fertilised cell, and subsequently develop into the mature adult form. The characteristic organisation and morphology of the adult form, the differentiated arrangement of cells in space, is determined in the process of embryological development. Each cell of every form carries within it the information for the construction and reproduction of the whole being. That information, the genome, is carried in the nucleus of the cell, and is transmitted through time down the generations. As forms that are more complex have emerged, the genome too has become more complex, overlaying and enfolding ancient genetic sequences from simpler forms.[29] The recent mapping of genetic sequences of different beings has revealed that the genome in many living forms is very similar, and in some cases almost identical. It is universally agreed that the genome 'encodes' the construction of the living form, but it remains unclear whether every single gene has a unique and singular function during the development of the embryo. Some genes appear not to be involved at all, and many are involved at different times and at different rates, in quite separate processes.

All living forms also have in common a small subset of the genome that is thought to act on the timing and sequences of growth from a single cell to a completed form,[30] regulating where and when growth starts and stops. Among the regulatory genes is a common sequence, thought to be very ancient and known as the 'homeobox'.

Growth and development occurs in a field of stress induced by the physical forces of the earth. Each individual cell is also a complete material system, with its own internal pressures and is subject to gravitational and thermodynamic stresses from the environment. Biological materials and fluids, like all other materials and fluids, have a tendency to self-organise into differentiated patterns under chemical, thermal and mechanical stress. In some embryos, for example, the first visible manifestation of organisation is the appearance of lines, bands or stripes, or spots on the otherwise undifferentiated surface of the spherical or ellipsoid form. This kind of patterning is a common feature of reaction-diffusion patterns that appear and stabilise when two or more chemicals diffuse through a tissue or across a surface. Alan Turing's seminal paper 'The Chemical Basis of Morphogenesis',[31] argued that these and similar reactions are sufficient to explain the mechanism for which genes in the newly fertilised cell determine the subsequent anatomical organisation of the form. These patterns begin to mark out the axial organisation of the body parts, the spatial position and orientation of the head, torso or thorax, and the limbs. Regulatory genes act in complex spatial and temporal sequences within a field of physical stresses, by initiating or 'expressing' the production of proteins and hormones that accelerate or inhibit the self-organising tendencies of biological materials and cells.[32] They act as differentiated feedbacks on the process of growth.

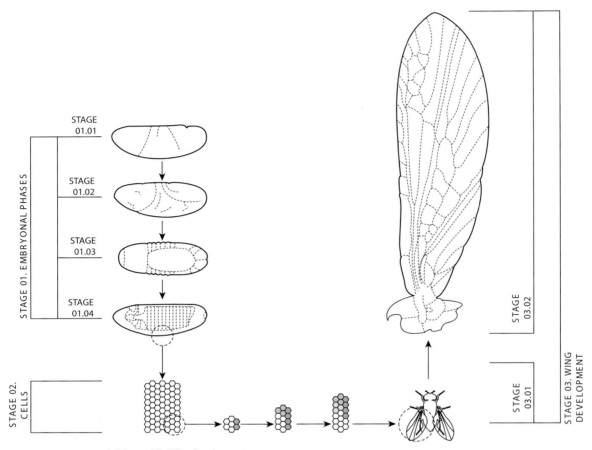

4.4 Drosophila Wing Development
All living forms have in common a small subset of the genome that is thought to act on the timing and sequences of growth from a single cell to a completed form, regulating where and when growth starts and stops. It is these genes in the newly fertilised cell that determine the axial organisation of the body parts, the spatial position and orientation of the head, torso or thorax, and the limbs. Regulatory genes act in complex spatial and temporal sequences within a field of physical stresses, by initiating or 'expressing' the production of proteins and hormones that accelerate or inhibit the self-organising tendencies of biological materials and cells.

PLANTS

The process of development in plants begins with patterning the very early embryo with axes of organisation; the regions that will become the stem and root are patterned as terminal elements of the top to bottom axis.[33] The stem is capable of growth throughout the life of the plant and may develop branches, leaves, and the cones or flowers of its reproductive system. Plant forms adjust season by season to sunlight, temperature and the availability of nutrients. Land-based plants are multicellular organisations, but some unicellular plants aggregate into complex organisations without ever becoming truly multicellular.

Algae are the most ancient of unicellular plants. They reproduce and proliferate by dividing themselves, with the new cells splitting off as independent forms. Many species live independently and they do not aggregate together in any ordered geometries, although in favourable environments they may become very numerous. Unicellular organisms are small, the geometry of the form is usually spherical, ellipsoid or cylindrical. Consequently, they have a high ratio of surface area to their contained volume. This ratio is metabolically useful, as a large surface area maximises the contact with the exterior, and enables them to absorb nutrients rapidly through passive diffusion.[34]

Loose aggregations of unicellular forms offer advantages in marine environments. Each cell remains an individual, able to grow and reproduce independently. Suitable geometrical arrays of individuals can manipulate the local flow of water, enhancing exposure to nutrients and provide enhanced protection from potential predators. An example is the *Hydrodictyon*, or water net algae, that has an aggregate form of a cylindrical net up to 20 centimetres long. The individual cells are also cylindrical, and array themselves in hexagonal or pentagonal patterns to form the net. Each cell produces a new very small cylindrical array of tiny cells within it. The offspring leave the parent cell as a fully formed miniature net that grows rapidly to full size.

Caulerpa algae also aggregate into cylindrical arrays, and a cylinder of any size always has the same ratio of surface area to volume. In aggregation each cell retains its individual capacity for rapid growth and reproduction, the cylindrical geometry maximises surface to surface contact of the cells to each other, and simultaneously provides exposure to the exterior environment so that metabolic activities can be coordinated.

The cylinders or tubes of *Caulerpa* array into elaborate networks that may develop to more than 20 metres long. The morphology of the array may even resemble the stems and leaves of large land-based plants, yet every cell is an independent being.[35] The cells are the largest of any organism on earth, with individual cells of up to a metre long in some species, and can develop features that are functionally analogous to roots.

Land-based multicellular plants develop in a more intense stress field, and require specialised tissues that are developed for structural rigidity and others for the vertical movement of nutrients. The vessels that move fluids and nutrients are known as vascular tissues, and are typically long tubes located in the central axis, where they will experience the lowest tensile, compression or torsional shear stresses. Other tissues surround the vascular bundles, and are developed with higher structural capacity to respond and adapt to environmental stresses and dynamic loadings[36] of gravity and wind pressure. The differentiated distribution of cells, fibres and bundles, according to height and slenderness, produces variable stiffness and elasticity within multicellular plants. Variations in the cross section produce anisotropic properties, and a gradation of values between stiffness and elasticity along the length of the stem that is particularly useful for resisting dynamic and unpredictable loadings.[37]

ANIMALS

In vertebrates, the sequence of development commences with a single cell, the fertilised egg, which divides to produce a spherical cluster of cells. Surface patterning defines the axes of orientation, followed by proliferation of the cells. As numbers increase, a thickened flat plate forms and the edges curl up until they meet, forming a hollow tube. The tube is patterned, one end grows and becomes differentiated into regions and subsequently develops into the brain. The other parts of the tube also become convoluted and subsequently differentiate to become the vertebrate spine and lower limbs. Development generally proceeds from head to tail, and a fully recognisable version of the final form is achieved very rapidly. The duration of the process depends on the final body size, so that a full body plan is evident in mice by day 14 of gestation, and in humans by day 60.

The four-limbed vertebrate organisation is ancient, and the development in all species typically follows the same sequence. Groups of cells accumulate in bud-like protrusions on the sides of the tube, located on specific axial patterns. As they grow, they develop their own axial organisation, and modular differentiation. The tissue develops a spatial template in soft cartilage for the later developing bone cells to occupy. The limbs are constructed in three modules, with the skeletal pattern organisation typically consisting of a single bone in the upper limb, two in the lower limb, and a number of digits in the terminal module. In humans, the arms and legs have a very similar organisation, but in other animals there are more differences in

THE ARCHITECTURE OF EMERGENCE

the organisation of forelimbs and hind limbs. The vertebrate spine also consists of repeated modules, and as with limbs, a great variety of different anatomical organisations can be constructed by variations in the kind, size, order and number of the component units. The finest scale of patterning is produced by the interaction of cells as they differentiate, a process known as lateral inhibition. The cell creates a very local and limited biochemical zone around itself, so that other cells of the same kind are inhibited from developing within that zone. This produces a gap, and when repeated across a dense array of cells, a stable pattern emerges. Small variations in the strength of inhibition induce a periodicity from which more complex patterns and spatial organisations emerge.

Animals and plants that have quite different evolutionary lineages may have striking similarities in the general organisation of their body parts, their anatomical structures, and the processes of their organs.[38] Common organisations and anatomical architectures emerge from the coupling of processes that are strongly differentiated in time and by scale; slow processes acting over multiple generations, and very fast processes acting only in the short period of embryological development.[39] In the first process, some biological forms, structures and metabolic processes are better able than others to withstand the physical stresses of the world, the rigours of the environment and the competitions of life. Natural selection will gradually tend to produce a generalised response of adaptation to specific environmental stresses, and this will occur across many species. Over sufficient time, forms will tend to converge. In the second process, the genome acts on the construction of individual forms. The accumulated complexity of the genome manifests in a general tendency to initiate cellular differentiation along common sequences and pathways. Common sequences of development, in a stress field that all developing organisms share, will tend to lead to generic outcomes.

Furthermore, a large portion of the genome is similar across groups of species; the sequence of development is also similar, as is the molecular chemistry of the biological materials from which living forms are constructed. All materials experience the same physical forces, are subject to the same stresses and react in similar patterns. Small variations in the sequence of inhibition and acceleration, or in the duration of either inhibition or acceleration may produce changes in the development of the embryo at many scales, through the reorganisation and recombination of biological components.

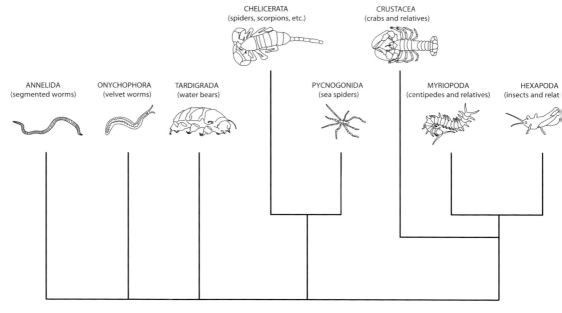

4.5 Arthropoda
The complex morphologies and varied body plans
of arthropoda have all evolved from one simple
common ancestor, the marine tube worm.

SPECIES AND CLIMATE

Darwin thought that climate had a significant role in 'the struggle for life', by reducing the availability of food circumstances and so increasing competition between the species. He also observed 'in going northward, or in ascending a mountain, we far oftener meet with stunted forms, due to the directly injurious action of climate, than we do in proceeding southwards or in descending a mountain. When we reach the Arctic regions, or snow-capped summits, or absolute deserts, the struggle for life is almost exclusively with the elements'.[40] There is a pattern to the number and distribution of species in different climatic regions. There is a gradient, from pole to equator, in the number of species, with the largest number of different species in the latitudes near the equator. Extreme climatic regimes have fewer species, and new species have emerged less often in these regions. Some animals are metabolically inflexible, having a narrow range of suitable temperatures and vegetation, so respond to climatic change by migration to more suitable territories. In the oscillating periods of glaciation initiated by the Milankovitch cycles, hippopotamus are known to have migrated from Africa in to central Europe, and many species from Siberia in to southern Europe. Migration to new latitudes in response to temperature change will expose the migrant species to different topographies and surfaces, to diverse seasonal patterns and types of vegetation, and to new competitors or prey. The combined effect creates a changed 'selective regime'. A different set of forms and behaviour will tend to concentrate in the population through the positive feedback of natural selection. Animals and plants that do not migrate may have a small but significantly wider tolerance of changing conditions, and this too will be positively enhanced over time by natural selection, resulting in living forms that have a greater flexibility and range of conditions in which they can flourish.

Isolation of a territory, such as an offshore island, ensures that migrating species are very rare, but when a rare migration event does occur, it may be followed by a rapid speciation into multiple descendant species. If the original mainland, for example, was a mature ecological system, the indigenous species will be so established, so numerous and widespread that there is simply no available territory or resources for new species. On an island there may be underpopulated or unoccupied territories with less or little competition for resources. The Galapagos is an interesting example, being the site of extensive radiations of plants and animals.[41] As on other island sites, members of the plant family Compositae (including weeds, lettuce and herbaceous flowering plants) have rapidly diversified. Trees generally do not spread easily on islands in ocean climates, as the seeds rarely survive in salty environments and usually fall close to the parent tree. Weeds generally do spread rapidly in all conditions, because the seeds are small, hardy and light, and so become widely dispersed. There were no trees or shrubs on the Galapagos, so Compositae rapidly speciated, and evolved from typical weed form to shrubs, and from shrubs to trees.

The original ancestor of Darwin's finches on the Galapagos Islands was a ground-dwelling, seed-eating bird that is thought to have migrated the 800 miles from Ecuador millions of years ago. One original migrant species diversified into the 13 distinct species that Darwin observed, some species living by eating seeds, and other species by eating insects. Darwin observed that their beaks varied in size and shape, and that appropriate feeding modes matched the variations in form. Finches with slender beaks fed on insects or drank nectar, finches with shorter, stronger beaks cracked open seeds. As the lineage rapidly diversifies, the new species evolves different morphologies and behavioural adaptations.

Speciation, the emergence of new living forms that are distinct from their ancestors, is associated with the occupation of new territories and with changes in climate. The climate metasystem and the surface of the earth have been through many iterations of change, at global, regional and local scales. Local and regional changes may occur at many different time and spatial scales. The effect of these changes is the emergence of new territories with novel combinations of temperature and precipitation, and consequently different regimes of natural selection. New regional climatic zones appear, such as deserts, steppes and tundras; and new physical barriers arise from the dynamics of the climate system, such as rivers, lakes and new coastlines. New species have emerged from small populations that have been separated from the normal territorial range of a numerous and widely distributed ancestor species. It is thought that the emergence of mammals in Africa followed this pattern, with population numbers inducing a wide geographical spread until a widely dispersed and stable population was reached about 1 million years after their origins.[42]

Speciation is thought to have occurred throughout time, but fossil evidence suggests that the pattern of the long history of evolution is far from regular. There have been a few intense speciation events when there was a nearly simultaneous emergence of many new forms of animals and plants. Innovative anatomical architectures tend to have emerged in relatively short periods, each associated with different climatic regimes. The climate metasystem and the geomorphic systems of the earth's surface tend to be delicately poised close to the critical threshold of stability. Significant global climatic changes are strongly coupled to mass extinctions of life. There are known to have been five major mass extinctions, each associated with climate change and different in effect and duration, each followed by mass originations and speciation.

For example, during the Devonian period small plants emerged and diversified into ferns, horsetails and the first trees with extensive root systems, and ultimately extensive forests. The percentage of oxygen increased as the plants proliferated, and carbon dioxide fell. Atmospheric carbon dioxide was increasingly taken up by the global proliferation of plants and the growth of forests, so lowering the heat-retaining capacity of the atmosphere and eventually causing global temperatures to fall. Positive feedback of albedo change, caused by the increase of ice-covered surfaces, accelerated the falls in temperature, further extending ice cover. As temperatures fell and ice cover advanced, the land area available was reduced, and a series of irregular small-scale extinctions gradually reduced the diversity of species.

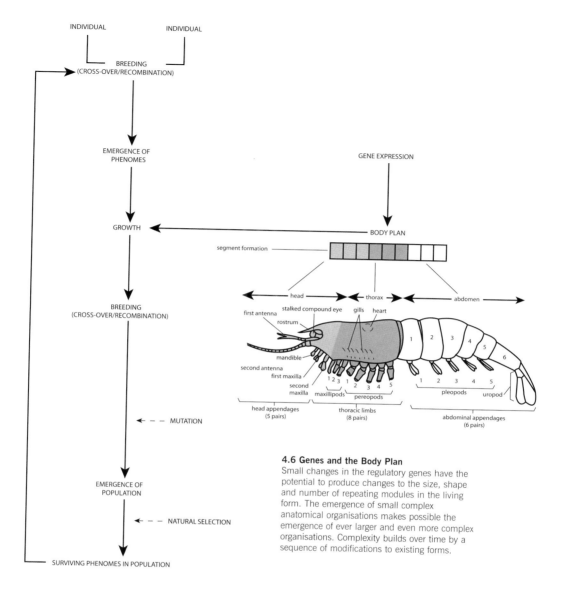

4.6 Genes and the Body Plan
Small changes in the regulatory genes have the potential to produce changes to the size, shape and number of repeating modules in the living form. The emergence of small complex anatomical organisations makes possible the emergence of ever larger and even more complex organisations. Complexity builds over time by a sequence of modifications to existing forms.

What is common between extinction events is the sequence of change that follows the mass extinction. In the immediate aftermath there are few surviving species of plants and animals, but each individual species rapidly proliferates to high numbers. This is followed by the emergence of life forms with new anatomical architectures and metabolisms, usually in one region only. The new forms then spread out in to new territories, and rapidly diversify into multiple descendant species. The emergence of new species creates new relationships between plant and animal species and acts as a positive feedback, creating new food webs or symbiotic resources that offer opportunities when yet more species emerge. As the complexity of interactions between species grows, the rate of speciation slows, and new ecological systems gradually emerge and stabilise.[43] The pattern of speciation and radiation is highly irregular across many scales of space and time. However, it is generally agreed that the emergence of fully mature ecological systems across the world takes millions, rather than thousands, of years. There are differences between the sequence and pattern on the land and in the ocean, which has fewer mass extinction and speciation events. There are no physical barriers in the oceans, although changes in sea level creates or destroys shallow water territories. Changes to the dissolved oxygen in the ocean, and to salinity, are also correlated to extinction events in the ocean.[44]

Mature ecological systems consist of multiple plant and animal species that are widely distributed, with complex interactions between the species, with the climatic regime and with the topography. It follows that there are internal dynamics to the interactions between the species, and consequently fluidity in the overall organisation of the ecological system. The size of the population of any species will vary over time, and this will in turn affect other species, usually by accelerating or inhibiting the relations between predator and prey. A fluctuation in one population may be caused by a local topographical change, by disease, or by the population numbers increasing beyond the capacity of its food resources. This may have no effect on other species, or affect a few species in a contained area, or the effects may cascade through many other species in ever widening circles until the whole ecosystem is affected. Ecological systems, like climatic and geomorphic systems, tend to be poised close to the critical threshold of change, and the internal dynamics of the relations between species is a significant factor in mass extinctions and origination events.[45] A regional climatic change will initiate a local perturbation in the ecological system that, in turn, may accelerate sufficiently to drive the whole system across the critical threshold. Extinction and origination may occur without the external force of a catastrophic event, such as a giant meteor strike.[46]

EMERGENCE AND THE FORMS OF LIFE

What distinguishes the emergence of living forms from the emergence of forms of the atmosphere, and the forms of the earth's surface, is the transmission down through time of the genome. Each cell of every living form carries within it the information for the development of the whole being. The sequential activation of the genes, which 'express' the proteins and hormones needed for the construction of biological materials, is regulated by a small subset of the genome. The differential growth of cells occurs in a field of stresses induced by the physics of the earth and the tendencies of biological materials to self-organise into differentiated patterns. Regulatory genes produce the initial spatial organisation of the embryo, by accelerating or inhibiting growth in varying sequences and patterns, and so act as differentiated feedbacks on the process of growth. Small variations in the strength of inhibition or acceleration induce a periodicity in the self-organising patterns that in turn produces yet more complex spatial and anatomical organisations across the range of scales.

Most living forms have an anatomical and spatial organisation that consists of repeated modules that vary in size, shape and number. The genome too is modular in organisation, consisting of many repeating sequences arrayed in distinct groups, each of which may contain common or multiple sequences that also occur in other groups. Over evolutionary time the genome has grown in size and complexity, but there is no apparent correlation between the size of the genome and the complexity of a living form. It has been observed that large living forms with very large genomes, such as trees in temperate climatic regions, tend to produce variant descendant species less often than other species.

Changes arise in the genome by mutation, which in turn produces changes to physical form or phenome. It is thought that the regulatory set of genes emerged long before the evolution of physical complex forms, and many of the regulatory genes are similar across species. Most mutations are either neutral or harmful to the living form; beneficial mutations are rare. The rate at which mutations occur does vary between species, and even within a single species. Species that reproduce rapidly have shorter generations and so will accumulate more genome mutations over time than species that reproduce slowly. These tend to be small organisms with higher metabolic rates, which may also contribute to the faster mutation rate. Existing regulatory and other genes are repeated and the sequence is shuffled by mutation. The co-option or recruitment of existing genes in to new organisations means that no new molecules are needed, and that repetition and reconfiguration will produce a higher complexity within the genome. Small changes in the regulatory genes have the potential to produce changes to the size, shape and number of repeating modules in the living form. The emergence of small complex anatomical organisations makes possible the emergence of ever larger and even more complex organisations. Complexity builds over time by a sequence of modifications to existing forms. There is both fossil and genetic evidence that the emergence of the general vertebrate organisation, and its subsequent modification into amphibians, reptiles, birds, and mammals, occurred in this sequence.

The emergence of new and diverse species is strongly coupled to the dynamics of climate and the surface of the earth. New regional climatic zones and new physical barriers arise from these dynamics, and these induce migrations, shifts in the range of the species, and isolation from the parent species. Exposure to new and different climatic regimes, topography and ecologies will, over time, produce speciation in new regimes of natural selection. The distribution of speciation over the extended time of evolution is far from even, with short intense speciation events punctuating long periods of little evolutionary change. Intense speciation events follow mass extinctions, with the few surviving species rapidly increasing in numbers and territorial range. New anatomical architectures and metabolisms emerge and radiate out in to new territories; the many new forms of animals and plants further diversify into multiple descendant species. As the complexity of ecological organisation accelerates, speciation slows, and the new ecological systems stabilise.

Energy and material flows between living forms and their physical and chemical environments. Living forms modify the surface of the earth and the climate, and these in turn may change sufficiently to induce further reciprocal modifications in living forms. The topography of the earth emerges from the dynamics of tectonic processes, the processes of erosion and the transportation and deposition of sediments. Living forms may accelerate or inhibit these processes, by the chemistry of biological processes and by physical interaction, such as stabilising surfaces with roots. Plants affect the atmosphere by transpiration of water, by altering albedo and heat transfer and by altering the chemical composition. Climatic regimes in turn modify the patterns of precipitation and the emergence of topographical forms.

In periods of high average global temperature, such as the Late Cretaceous, extensive deciduous forests died back in the hotter lower latitudes and shifted their range towards the high latitudes. The forests changed the albedo of the surface so that more solar radiation was absorbed, providing positive feedbacks to the warming of the land and oceans, and consequently to the atmosphere.[47] All living forms have a specific climatic range for which they have evolved specific anatomical and metabolic organisations. Some species have a broader climatic tolerance than others, but in general terms the range is narrow. All living forms respond to changes in the climatic conditions of their territories by migration, or if they are constrained by geographical barriers, they either speciate into new forms that are able to flourish in the new conditions, or they become extinct. Current studies of the biological response to contemporary climate changes exhibit the contraction of accustomed territories, range shifts and migrations, and species extinctions. This is most evident in polar and mountaintop regions, where it is estimated that ranges have moved 6 kilometres towards the pole each decade, and on mountains 6 metres upwards. Some changes in the genome of affected species has also been observed, which in time may 'modulate the magnitude and dynamics of the range shift'.[48] The average global change in the recent three or four decades is commonly represented to be only half a degree or so, but the dynamic patterns of the climate metasystem determine that climatic regimes change most severely and most rapidly at the poles.

Every living form emerges from two strongly coupled processes, operating over maximally differentiated time spans: the rapid process of embryological development from a single cell to an adult form, and the long slow process of the evolution of diverse species of forms over extended time. The evolution of the species is constrained by: the relations of living forms to other living forms; climatic regimes and the topography of the surface of the earth. In turn, living forms affect the processes of the atmosphere and oceans, and the geomorphic systems of the surface of the earth. Living forms exist in territories and climatic regimes that tend to be poised close to the critical threshold of change. The relations between species in an ecological system are dynamic and non-linear, and have been a significant factor in extinctions and speciation events. The processes of all natural systems have an intricate flow of energy and material between them. The interactions between the processes of the climate metasystem and the geomorphic systems of the surface of the earth produce feedbacks that act on the process of evolution and the diversity and distribution of living forms.

1   Kump, LR, SL Brantley and MA Arthur, 'Chemical Weathering, Atmospheric CO_2, and Climate', *Annual Review of Earth and Planetary Sciences,* vol 28, 2000, pp 61–67; and Kasting, JF and DC Catling, 'Evolution of a Habitable Planet', *Annual Review of Astronomy and Astrophysics*, vol 41, 2003, pp 429–63.
2   Miyakawa, S, H Yamanashi, K Kobayashi, HJ Cleaver and SL Miller, 'Prebiotic Synthesis from *CO* Atmospheres: implications for the origins of life', *Proceedings of the National Academy of Science (USA)*, vol 99, 2002, pp 14628–31.
3   Morowitz, HJ, *Energy Flow in Biology: biological organization as a problem in thermal physics,*

Academic Press (New York), 1968; and Morowitz, HJ, *The Emergence of Everything: how the world became complex*, Oxford University Press (New York), 2002.

4 Russell, MJ and AJ Hall, 'The Emergence of Life from Iron Monosulphide Bubbles at a Submarine Hydrothermal Redox and pH Front', *Journal of the Geological Society of London*, vol 156, 1997, pp 869–88; and Russell, MJ, AJ Hall, AG Cairns-Smith and PS Braterman, 'Submarine Hot Springs and the Origin of Life', *Nature*, vol 336, 1988, pp 117; and Cavalier-Smith, T, 'Cell Evolution and Earth History: stasis and revolution', *Philosophical Transactions of the Royal Society of London B*, vol 361, 2006, pp 969–1006.

5 Schrag, DP, RA Berner, PF Hoffman and GP Halverson, 'On the Initiation of Snowball Earth', *Geochemistry, Geophysics, Geosystems Journal*, vol G3, 2002, p 1036.

6 Harold, FM, *The Way of the Cell: molecules, organisms and the order of life*, Oxford University Press (Oxford), 2001.

7 Darwin, Charles, *On the Origin of Species by Means of Natural Selection*, or the *Preservation of Favoured Races in the Struggle for Life*, John Murray (London), 1859, p 72.

8 Huxley, TH, *Evidence as to Man's Place in Nature*, Williams and Norgate (London), 1863.

9 Ibid, p 420.

10 Darwin, Charles, *The Variation of Animals and Plants Under Domestication*, John Murray (London), 1868.

11 Gould, Stephen Jay, *Ontogeny and Phylogeny*, Belknap Press (Cambridge), 1977.

12 Gould, Stephen Jay, 'The Evolution of Life on Earth', *Scientific American*, vol 271, 1997, pp 85–91.

13 Harold, FM, *The Way of the Cell: molecules, organisms and the order of life*, Oxford University Press (New York), 2001.

14 Borges, Jorge Luis, *The Book of Imaginary Beings*, Jonathan Cape (London), 1970, first published as *El Libro De Los Seres Imaginarios*, Editorial Kier (Buenos Aires), 1967: *The riddle of the Sphinx – 'which animal walks on four legs in the morning, two at noon, and three in the evening?' solved only by Oedipus, who answered that it was a man who crawled as a child, walked when grown, and in old age leans on a staff.*

15 Durling, Robert M and Ronald L Martinez (trans), *The Divine Comedy of Dante Alighieri, Volume 1. Inferno Canto VI*, Oxford University Press (Oxford), 1996.

16 Daedalus was the architect of the Labyrinth, and was later imprisoned in it. He escaped by making wings from wax and eagle feathers for himself and his son Icarus.

17 The carving on the Parthenon, known as the Centauromachy, is of the battle caused by the drunken Centaurs attempting to carry off the bride of the king of the Lapiths on the day of the wedding. See also Ovid, *Metamorphoses XII*, Innes, M (trans), Penguin Classics (London), 1955.

18 Homer, *The Iliad*, XI, 832, trans Fagles, Penguin Books (New York), 1990; see also Alighieri, *Inferno, Canto XII*.

19 Leroi, Armand Marie, *Mutants: on the form, varieties and errors of the human body*, Harper Collins Publishers (London), 2003.

20 Ibid. Cyclopia in humans occurs in 1 in 200 aborted foetuses, and 1 in 16,000 live births.

21 Bacon, Francis, 'Preparative toward a Natural and Experimental History', in *Novum Organum*, 1620. See (eds) Jardine, L and M Silverthorne, *The New Organon*, Cambridge University Press (Cambridge), 2000.

22 Ibid.

23 Bateson, William, *Materials for the Study of Variation Treated with Especial Regard to Discontinuity in the Origin of Species*, Macmillan & Company (London), 1894.

24 Eldredge, N, *Reinventing Darwin*, Weidenfeld & Nicolson 1995; and Gould, Stephen Jay, *The Structure of Evolutionary Theory*, Harvard University Press (Cambridge, MA), 2002.

25 Goldschmidt, Richard, *The Material Basis of Evolution*, Yale University Press (New Haven), 1940.

26 Gould, *The Structure of Evolutionary Theory*.

27 Thompson, D'Arcy Wentworth, *On Growth and Form*, Cambridge University Press (Cambridge), first pub 1917, p 1023.

28 Ibid, p 10.

29 Erwin, D, J Valentine and D Jablonski, 'The Origin of Animal Body Plans', *American Scientist*, vol 85, no 2, 1997, pp 126–137.

30 Carroll, SB, 'Homeotic Genes and the Evolution of Arthropods and Chordates', *Nature*, vol 376, 1995, pp 479–85.

31 Turing, AM, 'The Chemical Basis of Morphogenesis', *Philosophical Transactions of the Royal Society of London B*, vol 237, 1952, pp 37–72.

32 Newman, SA and GB Muller, 'Origination and Innovation in the Vertebrate Limb Skeleton: an epigenetic perspective', *Journal of Experimental Zoology B (Mol Dev Evol)*, vol 288, 2005, pp 304–17.

33 Meyerowitz, EM, 'Genetic Control of Cell Division Patterns in Developing Plants', *The Journal of Cell Biology*, vol 17, 1997, pp 208–12.

34 Nobel, PS, *Biophysical Plant Physiology and Ecology*, Freeman (San Francisco), 1983.

35 Niklas, KJ, 'The Evolution of Plant Body Plans, a Biomechanical Perspective', *Annals of Botany*, vol 85, 2000, pp 411–38.

36 An introduction to some aspects of dynamics in biological systems is presented by Jeronimidis, G, in 'Biodynamics', in (eds) M Hensel, A Menges and M Weinstock, *AD Emergence: Morphogenetic Design Strategies*, vol 74, no 3, 2004, pp 90–95.

37 Weinstock, Michael, 'Self Organisation and the Structural Dynamics of Plants', in (eds) M Hensel, A Menges and M Weinstock, *AD Morphogenetic Design: Techniques and Technologies*, vol 76, no 2, 2006, pp 26–33: an outline of how evolutionary biology has utilised redundancy or excess capacities to adapt to environmental instability, with reference to the integrated morphologies of bamboos and palms.

38 Morphologists refer to the general anatomical architecture as the body plan. Similar or related body plans are generally classified together in groups or 'phyla'. This taxonomy does not normally take into account metabolic processes.

39 Berril, NJ and BC Goodwin, 'The Life of Form: emergent patterns of morphological transformation', *Rivista di Biologia-Biology*, Forum 89, 1996, pp 373–388.

40 Darwin, Charles, *On the Origin of Species.*

41 Wilson, Edward O, *The Diversity of Life*, Norton/Harvard University Press (New York), 1993.

42 Vrba, ES and D DeGusta, 'Do Species Populations Really Start Small? New perspectives from the Late Neogene fossil record of African mammals', *Philosophical Transactions of the Royal Society of London B*, vol 285, 2004, pp 285–93.

43 Solé, RV, JM Montoya and DH Erwin, 'Recovery after Mass Extinction: evolutionary assembly in large-scale biosphere dynamics', *Philosophical Transactions of the Royal Society of London B*, vol 357, 2002, pp 697–707.

44 Jablonski, D, 'Evolutionary Innovations in the Fossil Record: the intersection of ecology, development, and macroevolution', *Journal of Experimental Zoology (Mol Dev Evol)*, vol 304, no 6, 2005, pp 504–19.

45 Hewzulla, D, MC Boulter, MJ Benton and JM Halley, 'Evolutionary Patterns from Mass Originations and Mass Extinctions', *Philosophical Transactions of the Royal Society of London B*, vol 354, 1997, pp 463–9.

46 Gavrilets, Sergey and Aaron Vose, 'Dynamic Patterns of Adaptive Radiation', *Proceedings of the National Academy of Sciences*, vol 102, no 50, 2005, pp 18040–5; and Sole, RV, SC Manrubia, M Benton and P Bak, 'Self-Similarity of Extinction Statistics in the Fossil Record', *Nature*, vol 388, 1997, pp 764–7.

47 Upchurch Jr, GR, BL Otto-Bliesner and C Scotese, 'Vegetation and Atmosphere Interactions and their Role in Global Warming During the Latest Cretaceous', *Philosophical Transactions of the Royal Society of London B*, vol 353, 1998, pp 97–112.

48 Parmesan C and G Yohe, 'A Globally Coherent Fingerprint of Climate Change Impacts Across Natural Systems', *Nature*, vol 421, 2003, pp 37–42.

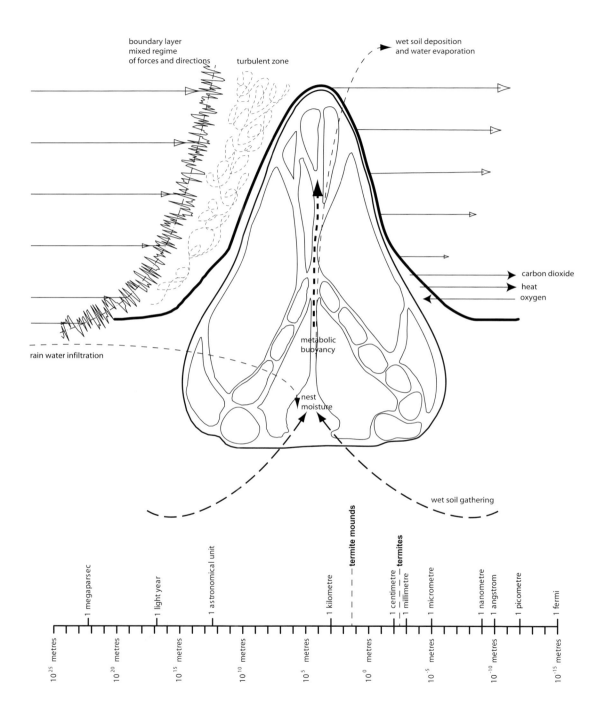

boundary layer
mixed regime
of forces and directions

turbulent zone

wet soil deposition
and water evaporation

carbon dioxide

heat

oxygen

metabolic
buoyancy

rain water infiltration

nest
moisture

wet soil gathering

1 megaparsec

1 light year

1 astronomical unit

1 kilometre

termite mounds

1 centimetre
1 millimetre
termites

1 micrometre

1 nanometre
1 angstrom

1 picometre

1 fermi

10^{25} metres

10^{20} metres

10^{15} metres

10^{10} metres

10^{5} metres

10^{0} metres

10^{-5} metres

10^{-10} metres

10^{-15} metres

The Forms of Metabolism

5

The varying metabolisms of all living forms are related to their morphology and scale, to behaviour and to their environment. Energy, information and material flows through individual forms are vectored through their populations, habitats and the ecological systems that they construct and live within. Where living forms organise themselves into collectively extended metabolisms, intelligence, social and spatial organisation, and material artefacts emerge. Collectively extended metabolisms are conserved and developed by positive feedbacks that modify the regime of natural selection.

All living forms must acquire energy and materials from their environment, and transform matter within their bodies to construct their tissues, to grow, to reproduce and to survive. D'Arcy Thompson argued that the morphology of living forms has a 'dynamical aspect, under which we deal with the interpretation, in terms of force, of the operations of Energy'.[1] Living forms are able to construct and dynamically maintain themselves by the exchange of energy and material through their surfaces, and in doing so excrete changed materials and energy back into the environment. Metabolism is the processing of energy, the 'fire of life',[2] and occurs at all levels from the molecular to the intricate dynamics of ecological systems. At the molecular level almost all living forms use the same chemistry, with varying modes and rates of process in manufacturing the three classes of molecule that are used in the construction of plant and animal cells and tissues: amino acids, carbohydrates and fats. There are also common metabolic characteristics for whole forms, in the relations between the geometry and overall size of the body plan, the internal operating temperature and the mode of existence in the environment. Morphology and metabolism are intricately linked through the processing of energy and materials.

5.1 Termite Behaviour and Orders of Magnitude
Colonies can produce three-dimensional material forms that are typically five or more orders of magnitude larger than the individual; for example, the termite *Macrotermes bellicosus*, each individual only a few millimetres long, produces a fully developed nest that is up to 10 metres high and 30 metres in radius. The nest constructions of wasps, bees, ants and termites exhibit a wide range of forms, but all of them provide a thermally and chemically regulated environment, so extending the suitable climatic range for the species and modifying the energy requirements and metabolic rates of its individuals.

Metabolism determines the relations of individuals and populations of forms with their local environment. Higher levels of biological organisation emerge from metabolic processes, in the relations between species, and in the density and patterns of distribution of species across the surface of the earth. All metabolic processes stem from the sunlight that falls on the surface of the earth. A very small percentage, perhaps less than 2 per cent, of that light energy enters ecological systems through the photosynthesis of plants. Light energy is transformed into chemical energy, bound in organic molecules, and used to construct the tissues of plants. The flow of energy through all living forms is often thought of as a food chain, and although this description is topologically inaccurate (web is a more accurate description than a chain), it is a useful description of the general direction of energy flow. Plants produce biological materials that can be reprocessed to release energy, and all other forms of life consume them in sequence; herbivores feed on the plants, converting them into heat energy, and in turn carnivores feed on the herbivores or other carnivores, and humans consume all other forms of life. Dead organic matter is broken down by microbes and fungi into prebiotic molecules. At each level, energy is used up so that only a small percentage of the energy available at one level is transferred to the next level. Matter is recycled, but energy is dissipated, used up and lost to the system. All metabolic processes cease without a constant source of energy, although most living forms are capable of storing some energy in chemicals to survive temporary fluctuations in energy supply.

The emergence and evolutionary development of systems for the transformation of light energy to chemical energy, in the cells of living forms, occurred in three major phases.[3] The most ancient metabolic system, when only simple bacteria existed, fed on carbon dioxide and hydrogen, and excreted methane. This first type of photosynthesis occurred in a world without oxygen, and so there were no 'aerobic' or oxygen breathing living forms. The subsequent emergence of cyanobacterial metabolisms differentiated living forms into aerobic and anaerobic realms, and generated the oxygen in the atmosphere. The emergence of the more complex cells, an intracellular symbiosis of energy-producing subsystems into the larger system of the eukaryotic cell, enabled the subsequent evolutionary development of multicellular organisms of increasing morphological complexity. There are other common features of organic energy systems. All organisms must not only produce energy, they must also transport it. The morphology of branching networks is found in all organisms of all species.

There is a relationship between energy, lifespan and body mass; small organisms are typically more metabolically active than larger organisms, and the larger the organism, the slower the metabolism. A fast life is a short life, and variations of this saying are common across the world. Perhaps one of the most memorable versions occurs in the film *Blade Runner*, 'The light that burns twice as bright burns half as long'.[4]

The understanding of the relationship between the pace of a life and its duration is thought to have originated at around the same time as Darwin and FitzRoy were setting out on their voyage.[5] It was formalised in 1928 as 'the rate of living',[6] and research in the following decades established that the energy used by a gram of tissue in a small organism is higher than in larger organisms. The pace of energy use in smaller living forms is measurably faster, and their lifespans are short, whereas bigger organisms live longer than small organisms.

Metabolic relationships to mass and lifespan are complex, but a gram of living tissue consumes approximately the same amount of energy during its whole lifespan, no matter which living form or species of which it is a part. Within any specific taxa, such as mammals or plants, the metabolic rate of activity will vary from species to species, but it is now widely agreed that the rate of energy consumption per unit of body mass declines as the body size increases. A gram of tissue in a mouse uses up 25 times more energy in any unit of time than a gram of tissue in an elephant, so that the mouse must eat much more frequently, and much larger quantities in relation to its body mass than the elephant. This means that a mouse must eat about half its body weight every day; an elephant needs a little more than 2 per cent. However, when unrelated taxa are compared that differ greatly in size, such as a comparison between bacteria and mammals, the metabolic activity per unit of body mass is approximately the same. What varies is the lifespan, by many orders of magnitude. A bacterium may live for a few hours, a mouse two to three years, and elephant up to 60 years. It is thought that the 'amount of living' is a constant, an invariant parameter that is a product of the metabolic rate of a gram of tissue multiplied by the maximum lifespan.[7]

PHOTOSYNTHETIC METABOLISM AND PLANT MORPHOLOGIES

Plants are 'autotrophs' or self-feeders, constructing their own materials, molecule by molecule from sunlight, water and carbon dioxide, and a few trace minerals in tiny proportions from the soil. The process is a sequence of chemical reactions known as photosynthesis, which drives the metabolism of marine unicellular organisms including cyanobacteria and algae, and all the larger plants of the surface of the earth. Oxygen is the by-product.[8] Carbon dioxide enters the plant and oxygen is excreted along with water vapour, through the stomata, the 'pores' in leaves and stems.[9]

Plants that are adapted to hotter regimes, including many of the summer 'annual' plants, have evolved a faster acting modified photosynthetic chemistry.[10] The stomata stay open for shorter periods during the day to absorb carbon dioxide, and so less water is lost by transpiration. A third modification of photosynthetic metabolism[11] is found in Crassulaceae and other cacti, succulents and bromeliads. The stomata open at night, minimising evaporation, and close during the day. In these plants metabolic activity may be internalised altogether in extremely arid conditions, and stomata are closed night and day. This enables the plant to survive dry spells, and when water is available again, there is a rapid uptake of water and recovery occurs. The body of the plant includes specialised water storage tissues, and some root systems are similarly adapted.

LEAF ARRAYS

The characteristic silhouette of trees, the outer boundary of the volume of leaves, is constrained by the shape and size of the individual leaf geometry specific to the species, and the extent to which leaves shade each other from the light.[12] In environments with high levels of light, several layers of leafs may be arrayed before the lowest leaf is so shaded that it cannot capture sufficient light for photosynthesis. It has been argued that 'pioneer' trees, the early species in developing forests, tended to have leaf arrays organised in deep multilayered crowns. In consequence, later 'climax' species adapting to the lower light environment between established species, reduce their self shading by developing flatter and shallow crowns, with a single layer of leaves on the boundary of the leaf volume.[13] However, many trees appear to have stacked monolayers, one above the other, and other varied morphologies do not strictly conform to either organisation.

The arrangement of leaves on a twig or stem, phyllotaxis or leaf ordering, is significantly related to the avoidance of self shading. Leaves spring from a twig or stem at more or less the same angle, but in sequence are rotated so that they are offset from each other. Elm trees, for example, have successive leaves on opposite sides of the twig, which is also expressed as an angle of offset, in this

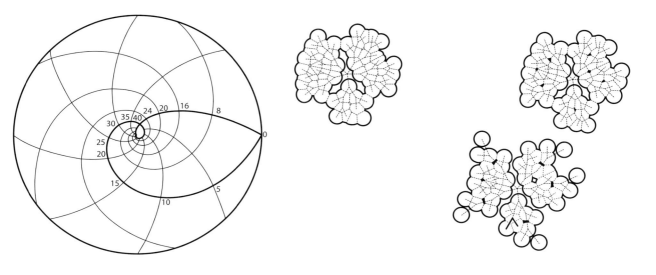

5.2 Phyllotaxis
The arrangement of leaves on a twig or stem, phyllotaxis or leaf ordering, is significantly related to the avoidance of self shading. Leaves spring from a twig or stem at more or less the same angle, but in sequence are rotated so that they are offset from each other.

case 180°. On beech and hazel trees the leaves are rotated 1/3 of the circumference of the twig or 120°, on oak trees the rotation is 2/5 or 144°, on poplar and pear trees it is 3/8 or 135°, and on willow and almond trees it is 5/13 or 130.46°. The fractional numbers are recognisable as quotients of alternative Fibonacci numbers[14] and are commonly found across many scales and in many different modular components, including petals and cones. There are three distinct phyllotactic patterns, spiral[15] and distichous (alternate) being the most common, with a third more complex whorled pattern emerging in some species. Changes in leaf shape and orientation and in stem length can compensate for the negative effects of leaf overlap produced by phyllotactic patterns. The effectiveness of phyllotaxy in limiting self shading is not absolute, and is modified by the shape and orientation of the leaves, and distance along the stem between leafs.[16]

All transpiration takes place through the stomata, and they typically slow down diffusion of water vapour into the atmosphere; the resistance to the flow of liquids is typically hundreds of times greater in leaves than it is in the roots, stem and branches.[17] The pattern of veins for the movement of fluids within the leaf varies across the species, but the rate of flow of water through the tree is slowed and controlled by the leaf array. Both gases and water vapour are controlled by the stomata, so the rate of transpiration is closely coupled to the rate of exchange of gases. Both gas and fluid flow are highly dynamic, varying between night and day, between young leaves and old leaves, and generally in response to changes in temperature and in the water supply from the roots. It follows that the photosynthetic metabolism of a tree is a product of the total surface area and mass of leaves in the array, and the lifespan of the leaves, and that these have an intricate mathematical relationship with the fluid distribution network of the whole tree and its overall morphology.[18]

BRANCHING NETWORKS

Branching patterns have been intensively studied in many disciplinary fields. Two of the most cited works in geomorphology are studies of the geometrical properties of hydraulic branching networks of streams and river systems.[19] In the anatomical organisation of trees the transportation network for fluids and the structural support for the leaf array have evolved as a fully integrated morphology.[20] Branch angles and the ratios of length in sequential 'mother to daughter' branches determine the effective leaf area,[21] and constrain the overall morphology of a tree. They are also intrinsic characteristics of a species, so that different angles and ratios appear in different species. The number and the position of a branch in the hierarchy of branches from outermost twig to the trunk, and the length of each branch, is said to have a logarithmic relation.[22]

There are two elaborate branching networks of vessels that extend throughout the plant, from the roots to the stomata of the smallest leaf. One system, the 'xylem', consists of many bundles of narrow tubes. Water that is absorbed from the soil into the roots is drawn up through the plant to the leaves, where it evaporates through the stomata. The evaporation creates a negative water pressure in the column of water in the xylem tubes. The other system, the 'phloem', moves the carbohydrates that are assembled in the leaves to other metabolically active parts of the plant. Water is needed to maintain the pressure inside the living cells, and most of the metabolic processes of the cells require water molecules. However, almost all of the water that enters the plant system is 'transpired', or evaporated from the leaves, and this movement of cool water

THE ARCHITECTURE OF EMERGENCE

up from the soil regulates the internal temperature of the plant. The humidity and temperature of the air around the plant will affect the rate of transpiration. Low temperatures or high humidity slow transpiration and high temperatures or low humidity accelerate transpiration. Very little of the energy that falls on a plant is used for the metabolic assembly of complex molecules, some light energy is reflected, but most, up to 75 per cent, is dissipated as latent heat in the water vapour that evaporates from the stomata.

As the leaves, twigs and branches bend and deflect under load, both compressive and tensile stresses are induced in the trunk. The pattern of growth during the year is differentiated, with new cells developing in the spring in the outer layers. The cells are large because there is plenty of water available, but as the summer progresses and the soil becomes drier, moisture decreases and new cells that develop are smaller. Cells cease to grow in the winter, they dry out and this tends to make the cells shrink. As they are strongly bonded to the inner part of the trunk they cannot shorten and so they are in tension. The trunk is then 'prestressed', with the outer layers of the trunk in tension, and the centre of the trunk in compression. In consequence the trunk is able to bend considerably without breaking. The differentiated pattern of growth is similar in branches and twigs, with similar results.

GRASSES

Grasses are thought to be more recent than trees in the history of evolution, radiating out from their origins in tropical forests when the global climate changed to more arid conditions. Subsequent rapid speciation produced multiple diverse forms.[23] New species of grasses emerged with an adapted faster photosynthetic metabolic chemistry[24] that is commonly found today in hotter climatic regions. This faster photosynthesis emerged several times in different but related lineages, and genetic studies have shown that it did not evolve the same way from each origination.[25] Grasses have the highest rate of photosynthesis and minimal rate of water transpiration, but are limited in their range by low temperatures that shorten the growing season in cold climatic regimes. Morphologies of grasses are very varied, but all grass species have two unique structures that do not appear in other plants, the slender 'spikelet' flower organisation, and a distinctive fruit structure, the grain or caryopsis. Among the 10,000 estimated species of grass are wheat, rice and maize, the major food sources for humans and animals bred for meat. Other forms include pineapples and some flowering plants.

There is a relationship between the total mass[26] of a plant form and its lifespan.[27] Big plants live longer than small ones, and this appears to be true for all plants, from phytoplankton that live for one day to giant sequoia that may live for up to 3,000 years.[28] Size is a critical factor in the rate of metabolism, and the geometry of the vascular network scales with the size, volume and mass of the plant form.[29] There are invariant ratios across the diversity of plant morphologies, relationships between the surface area of leaves, the total volume the plant occupies, the geometry of its branching networks, and the metabolic rate and lifespan. Variations of these characteristics are all dependent on the size, or rather the total mass, of the plant form. For example, the number and mass of leaves in a plant, the rate of fluid flow in the vascular network, and the total carbon assimilation or gross photosynthesis scale proportionately to each other. They all scale at the quarter power of the mass.

The primary relation of morphology and metabolism in plants is in the spatial organisation of large surface areas to capture light and for the exchange of gases, the structural system for the deployment of those surfaces, and an internal transportation system for moving water and metabolic products. The anatomical organisation of the trunk and branches is generally observed to maximise the photosynthetic potential of the three-dimensional array of leaves. The metabolic imperative of maximum surfaces for photosynthesis is constrained by the necessity for a stable structural configuration that will be strong enough to resist buckling under their own weight, and to resist additional imposed loads such as snow, or wind pressure from all directions. The structural properties of the trunk and branching network emerge from the differentiated pattern of growth, and the morphology in general emerges from the interaction of the volumetric array of leaves and the patterns of branching networks that support them.

THERMAL METABOLISMS AND ANIMAL MORPHOLOGIES
The metabolisms of animals process the chemical energy stored in plants, or the flesh of other animals. They are thermal or heat-producing metabolisms, and are characterised by the relation of their internal body temperature to the temperature of their immediate environment. It was once common to refer to 'warm blooded' or 'cold blooded' animals, but this is inaccurate. For example, the body temperature of 'cold blooded' reptiles can be extremely high when they are in sunlight for any length of time. Animal metabolisms may either maintain a constant internal temperature regardless of the ambient

temperatures, or they may allow their internal temperature to vary according to the rise and fall of the temperature of their environment. Most animal metabolisms are predominantly one or the other regime, but combine some behavioural aspects of both.

'Endotherms' generate heat internally to maintain their body temperature. Maintaining a constant body temperature is a demanding energy regime for a living form. The rate of metabolic activity is high and the majority of food must be used as fuel for body temperature, with little left over to be converted into body tissue or mass. Food consumption is up to 10 times more than a comparable size animal with a variable temperature metabolism, and elaborate morphological and system adaptations are necessary. This in turn presents difficulties when the external temperature rises and falls through seasonal variation. Constant temperature metabolisms have the advantage of remaining active in very cold climates, by increasing the rate of metabolism, but of course they do need to do so in order to acquire food to maintain their energy regime. The development of enhanced insulation in layers of fat, fur and feathers increases the retention of heat, but there are far fewer adaptations that enhance the shedding of heat. Few animals with constant body temperature metabolisms can survive in very hot environments.

'Ectotherms' absorb heat from their environment to raise their body temperatures. Variable temperature regimes, such as the metabolisms of most amphibians and reptiles, are less energy demanding. Metabolic activity is more chemically complex, but the rate of activity is slower, and heat production is so low that the external environment effectively regulates the body temperature a little below the environmental temperature. High body temperatures are achieved by basking in the sun, for example, lizards or snakes resting on warm rocks in the hot sun. Much more of their food intake can be converted in to body mass. They are less active as the temperature drops, but do not need to be so active to acquire food. In fact they can survive long periods without food, and some can reduce their metabolic rate when food is scarce. They cannot survive in very cold environments. The energy requirements of amphibian and reptilian metabolisms are lower than those of birds and mammals by a whole order of magnitude.

As the 'endothermic' avian metabolism and morphologies evolved from 'ectothermic' reptiles, and mammalian evolutionary development was quite separate, it follows that the physical constraints of surfaces and network distribution systems are critical factors in evolution. Natural selection has acted to evolve high energy thermal metabolisms, producing a significant reorganisation of the surfaces and systems involved in the exchange of oxygen and carbon dioxide, and in the transportation of metabolic products. The morphology of lungs was modified in mammals, and extensively so in birds, to produce larger surface areas for the exchange of gases. The circulatory system was enhanced by the development of more complex hearts and increased fluid pressures, as was the oxygen-carrying capacity of the blood being circulated. The evolution of increased mitochondrial surfaces within the cells amplified the energy-processing capacity of cellular tissues.

The difference in energy production capacity between the two thermal regimes is apparent in the organisation of body organs and tissues, and in the interior organisation of their cells. The endothermic metabolisms of avian and mammalian forms have larger internal organs than amphibian and reptilian forms, the organs have a far greater density of mitochondria, and the mitochondria themselves have a greater surface area.[30] The high metabolic rate of 'endotherms' is temperature sensitive, so that when ambient temperatures increase, the metabolic rate also increases. Body temperature is stabilised by increasing the speed of metabolic processes, requiring more energy flow through the system. By contrast, the ectothermic metabolisms of reptiles and insects reduce their metabolic rate as ambient temperatures increase, as they allow their internal body temperatures to fluctuate, and so the energy flow through the system is reduced. Ectothermic metabolisms are less energetically 'expensive' by an order of magnitude.

THE EVOLUTION OF BODY SIZE, SURFACES AND METABOLIC RATE

Metabolic processes have a relation to body mass – fluid energy transportation in particular is an essential determinant of body plan and overall morphology, and the size of elements in the transportation network, such as aortas, lung branches and tree trunks scale at the quarter power of body mass. The relationship of any morphological or metabolic characteristic to mass is known as allometry, a term that is thought to have been originated by Julian Huxley. Huxley published two seminal papers in 1924 on the relative differential growth[31] of the body parts of crabs, which in some species have very large abdomens, or in the case of fiddler crabs, one disproportionately large claw. He proposed the first mathematical formula (recognisably a power law) that related the size or mass of the whole body to the differential growth body ratio.

Size is critical[32] in many metabolic parameters, but most directly in the way it changes the ratio of surface area to the volume enclosed by that surface. Edward Cope argued in 1886 that fossil evidence suggested that vertebrates have increased in size over geological time.[33] The general evolutionary tendency towards larger sizes is also associated with the observations that body size in many species tends to be larger in lower temperatures and in higher latitudes; and that species that live in warm temperatures and close to the equator tend to be smaller.[34] Increased size does seem to offer a metabolic advantage in colder climatic regions.

It is logical to assume that heat loss is directly proportional to the external surface area, so the larger the surface area the greater the loss of heat. It follows that the overall external geometry of a living form is 'energetically' significant – conserving heat in cold climates is best done by large rounded forms, as proportionally they have greater enclosed volume for their surface area. In hot climates narrow slender forms shed heat more easily, as proportionally they have more surface area for their enclosed volume. The smaller the form is, the greater the surface area is in relation to the enclosed volume. But it is not only the external surface area that is significant. The body plan of living forms and the organisation of their internal surfaces for metabolic transactions also change as size increases. Thermal metabolisms evolved their long intestinal tube with its large number of convolutions to increase the surface area, and use muscles to accelerate the passage of food. The evolution of greater surface areas for respiration is a similar strategy, with the branching networks of lungs enabling very large surface areas for the exchange of gases.

Insect morphologies are limited in size by both structural and metabolic constraints. The interior volume of tissues and organs is contained by a rigid 'cuticle', a stiff external skeleton that has very little flexibility, and so as the body grows in size during their life cycle they must shed or moult the cuticle and replace it with a new and larger one. This determines a structural limitation on size, as the ratio of surface area to volume decreases as overall size increases, and the mass of the internal tissues would surpass the supporting capacity of the exoskeleton. Most insects have 'ectothermic' metabolisms and are 'aerobic' or oxygen consuming systems, with metabolic processes that are similar to all other animals. However, the respiratory system is quite different, in that oxygen is delivered directly to every cell in the tissues, rather than being carried indirectly by the haemoglobin molecules in blood. The cuticle has a number of openings or spiracles that lead to trachea, and

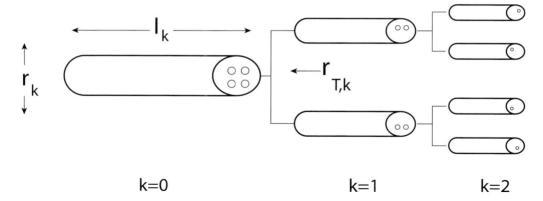

$$l_k \qquad r_{T,k} \qquad r_k$$

k=0   k=1   k=2

5.3 Metabolic Scaling
The quantitative model of GB West, JH Brown and BJ Enquist rests on the development of an abstract geometrical model of the maximally efficient branching network for the distribution of metabolic products and fluids. There are three constants in the model. First, the network branches in a hierarchical series to supply all parts of the living form, so that the branches are self-similar, reducing in cross section and length by a constant ratio; second, the end points of the smallest branches are always the same size no matter what the size or species of the living form is; third, the branching network minimises the time and energy used to distribute the fluids and metabolic products, and the metabolic rate of the whole living form scales at the 3/4 power of the body mass. Each branching generation can be described by its length (l_k), its branch radius (r_k), and its internal tube radius ($r_{T,k}$).

these branch directly from, or close to, the spiracle. Air diffuses directly through the trachea into the tissues. This organisation has an effective limit, as any significant increase in size will increase the distance between the spiracle and the tissues, and reduce the capacity for diffusion of gases. A very large insect would simply suffocate from lack of oxygen. Fossil evidence does show that very large insects did exist during the 'carboniferous' period, and it is thought that the oxygen content of the atmosphere was much higher than it is today. The largest insect fossil is of the dragonfly *Meganeura monyi*, which was recovered from a coalfield in France late in the 19th century,[35] and has a wingspan of 75 centimetres. It is thought that the higher oxygen content and temperature of the atmosphere overcame the limitations of diffusion over long distances in the larger bodies of these ancient insects. A further limitation on size is the insect intestine, which does not have the complex involutions and foldings of the mammalian intestine, and so has a proportionally much smaller surface area to process food. The small volume and proportionally large surface area of insects means that they have rapid heat loss. Body temperatures of flies are close to ambient temperature even during flight, when muscle activity is generating the maximum internal heat.

THE ARCHITECTURE OF EMERGENCE

METABOLIC SCALING

The first theories of metabolic scaling appeared late in the 19th century, and were based on the way that the surface area of any three-dimensional object scales in relation to the volume enclosed by the surface. The surface area of any solid form is geometrically proportional to the 0.67 (2/3) power of its volume, so it was argued that the resting metabolic rate must also be proportional to the 0.67 power of the volume or mass of any living form. It is logical to assume that the surface area of a living form is more critical than its mass for metabolic rate, as all energy and materials transactions occur via surfaces. However, the first systematic measurements of size and metabolisms in animals, made by Max Kleiber in 1932, revealed that the expected relationship between metabolic rate and mass was incorrect, and that across a range of animals it is much closer to 0.75 (3/4) rather than the anticipated 0.67 that the simple geometrical scaling of size predicts. Kleiber had analysed the metabolic rate in relation to the body mass of mammals and birds. He found that the resting or base metabolic rate changes as the body mass increases, and the famous graph of his analysis plots metabolic rate as proportional to the 3/4 power of body mass. The relationship of metabolism to body mass has been intensively researched over the 80 years that have passed since then, and it is now widely accepted that the 3/4 power scaling of metabolic rate is consistent across 27 orders of magnitude, from the smallest of microbes to the very largest blue whale, and in the differing metabolisms of ectotherms and endotherms,[36] and in the photosynthetic metabolisms of plants.[37]

Although there have been a very large number of empirical or observational studies of the ubiquity of power scaling in allometric relationships, it has long been a mystery as to why so many biological phenomena, such as lifespan, heart beats and respiratory rates should be related to body mass by 3/4, 1/4 or minus 1/4 powers. The quantitative model of GB West, JH Brown and BJ Enquist rests on the development of an abstract mathematical model of the maximally efficient branching network for the distribution of metabolic products and fluids. It provides a theoretical logic for the scaling of metabolic rate, and many other morphological parameters, in relation to the mass of a living form. There are three constants in the model. One, the network branches in a hierarchical series to supply all parts of the living form, so that the branches are self-similar, reducing in cross section and length by a constant ratio; two, the end points of the smallest branches are always the same size no matter what the size or species of the living form is; three, the branching network minimises the time and energy used to distribute the fluids and metabolic products, and the metabolic rate of the whole living form scales at the 3/4 power of the body mass. Since the first publication in 1997, the model developed by West, Brown and Enquist has been successfully tested with the available observational data for all living forms. The metabolic scaling characteristics emerge from the parameters of branching networks in the vascular system of trees and in both the cardiovascular and respiratory system of mammals. The model applies to the whole system of an organism, and it is argued that it incorporates both structural and hydrodynamic constraints, and is capable of accurately predicting many other allometric variables that scale in relation to mass, such as the parameters of fluid flow and the related dimensions of the vessels, the maximum height of trees, and ecological patterns of distribution[38] of plant populations and communities.

COLLECTIVE AND SOCIALISED METABOLISMS

There are species that have evolved metabolisms that are reliant on the presence of other species, so that their energy and material transactions can only be conducted in close association with a partner species. The most common examples of mutually beneficial associations are flowering plants and the many species of insects, bats and birds that pollinate them. The evolution of specialised morphological features for collecting nectar and pollen, such as the tubular proboscis in flies,[39] moths and butterflies, enables them to collect a rich energy source and at the same time the transfer of genetic information by pollen grains from the male anther to the female stigma enables fertilisation. Coevolution, speciation and adaptive radiation has produced great diversity in the morphology of flowering plants and in the species that act to pollinate them.[40] Although some mutual associations are generalised, most are highly specific, such as the fig and the wasp *Hymenoptera Chalcidoidea*, where each is absolutely dependent upon the other for survival.[41]

Not all associations are beneficial to both organisms, however, and some are entirely one-sided, with only one of the species gaining an advantage from the association. All orchids and many bromeliads attach themselves to the trunks or branches of trees, but do not take anything other than support from their hosts, and do not harm them in any way.[42] They are known as epiphytes, and these delicate plants would simply not be able to achieve such a height from the ground by themselves. They benefit from the attachment to their stronger and larger hosts by the superior exposure to sunlight; water and nutrients are taken from the air and rain. There are also many close associations that are parasitic, benefiting one species but harmful in varying degrees to the host species.

THE ARCHITECTURE OF EMERGENCE

Parasites such as bacteria, viruses, fungi and nematode worms are very common in plants and animals, living either on or in the body of the host species. Animals also host larger parasites such as tapeworms in their intestines and soft organs, and mites, fleas, and lice on the surface of their bodies. Parasites feed on the tissue of their host, and many are able to successfully transfer between species. In everyday language symbiosis[43] is commonly described as the 'mutually beneficial association of two different organisms'. It is traditional to categorise symbiosis as either mutualist, commensalist or parasitical. However, recent research has tended to concentrate on the emergence of novel metabolic processes or capabilities from the interaction of species,[44] and the conservation over time of the new metabolism by coevolution. Coevolution of two species requires the exchange of genetic information, which may be very ancient and conserved by natural selection as in the case of the mitochondria and chloroplasts, or more recent as in the case of some insects that feed on the phloem sap of plants.

Phloem sap has high concentrations of sucrose produced by photosynthesis, and is used for the transportation of nutrients around the branching network of the plant. Animals, however, cannot process the nutrient rich phloem sap, as they lack the appropriate amino acids. A small number of insect species, including whiteflies, mealy bugs and aphids, possess the necessary symbiotic micro-organisms in their gut to use phloem sap as their sole food source. These are the 'Hemiptera' insects, and they digest the phloem and excrete the residue as 'honeydew'. The 'honeydew' is chemically suitable for processing by a wide range of metabolisms, and is consumed by numerous other insect species, including wasps and bees, and by some bats and birds.[45] Species of beetles, wasps and ants have evolved that feed directly from the anus of the hemipteran insects, and these insects also 'tend' the aphids, protecting them as well as harvesting the 'honeydew'. Remarkably, some species of plants have evolved hollow structures for nesting ants, including those that 'tend' aphids, and the ants protect the plant from herbivores, so that there are crucial advantages to all three metabolic systems.[46]

Three-way symbiotic metabolic systems are not common, but it is evident that social and spatial organisations emerge from the collective metabolic interactions of a number of insect species. Sociality is, in fact, rare in all animals. Almost all of the species of fish, reptiles, birds and mammals are solitary, or have temporary social relations for mating and rearing young that are based on small family groups. Where social organisation emerges it is strongly coupled to metabolic processes. The social organisation of insects is typically a colony, with limitations on the number of fertile individuals. While each individual has a functioning metabolism of its own, the colony as a whole organises the energy and material transactions of each individual into a persistent and coherent pattern that is conserved and developed over time. There is no central controlling intelligence but nonetheless individuals work in collective patterns, and the metabolic performance of the colony emerges from the non-linear interactions between individuals and between individuals and their environment.[47] The numerical size of a colony varies from a few hundred to many thousands for wasps and bees, and may be up to many millions for ants and termites. Colonies can produce three-dimensional material forms that are typically five or more orders of magnitude larger than the individual; for example, the termite *Macrotermes bellicosus*, each individual only a few millimetres long, produces a fully developed nest that is up to 10 metres high and 30 metres in radius. The nest constructions of wasps, bees, ants and termites exhibit a wide range of forms, but all of them provide a thermally regulated environment, so extending the suitable climatic range for the species and modifying the energy requirements and metabolic rates of its individuals. By eliminating variations in temperature and humidity, the embryonic development of larvae and pupae takes place in optimum conditions, so that a high percentage achieve full maturity. Similarly, the metabolisms of individuals operate in a thermally regulated environment, with only minimal adjustments to shed or conserve heat, and further do not need to increase energy or fluid intakes to compensate for adverse climatic conditions. Wasps regulate the internal temperature of their nests to 30°C, varying only by a degree or so, and bees achieve a fine control of their hives, maintaining a temperature around 35°C when external ambient temperature varies from below freezing to above 45°C.

All bees store honey, a complex sugar that is resistant to bacteria and fungi, and so they eliminate the potential threat of natural variations in the available supply of nectar. When nectar is in short supply, worker bees are able to sip honey. The material form of the hive is organised as a collective metabolism, operating in a state of dynamic equilibrium produced by the interaction of independent activities of individual bees, each with a different critical threshold of response to stimuli. When the temperature in the hive falls, the bees generate heat with their muscles to warm the hive; but each bee will have a different temperature threshold at which this response is initiated. Similarly, if the temperature rises, the bees fan their wings to increase airflow and reduce the temperature, and each individual bee will initiate fanning at a different temperature. The variation in individual thresholds may be several degrees, and the multiple thresholds act as negative feedback so that there is no over correction.[48] Communication of spatial information, by the famous 'waggle dance', operates by the same principles, with each individual forager contributing information of direction and distance to nectar sources with individuals responding to the information. There are thought to be as many as 17 different communication signals, and at least 34 different environmental cues that trigger responses.[49] Construction and repair of the hexagonal cells also operates in the same way, with some individuals depositing wax and others removing it, and this is also true of the construction of the outer, enclosing form. The diameter of the bee head, the orientation of the antennae and the operation of the mandibles determine the geometry of each cell. The coherent construction and the coherent metabolic behaviour of the hive emerges from the interaction of the differing response thresholds of multiple individuals.

The complexity of collective metabolic systems is higher when social insects incorporate the processing of their principal food source within the colony, combining the 'tending' of symbiotic food organisms with the metabolic regulation of a large material form. The *Macrotermes* termites cultivate a single species of fungus within the colony, providing a substrate for it to grow on, and protecting it from disease with a variety of auxiliary microbes.[50] The principal food source for the termites is leaves, but they cannot digest cellulose directly. Fungus can digest cellulose in a warm and moist atmosphere, so they are 'planted' on the chewed fragments of leaves that the termites have brought into the nest. The fungus is tended in the lower chambers of the nest, which are maintained at the optimum temperature and humidity for growth. The termites feed on the fungus, but also store reserves of grass for the fungus in dry higher level cells, so that the hive can survive fluctuations in primary source of energy supply, the leaves and small twigs that are collected from the 'range' or area surrounding the hive. Galleries of tunnels radiate out from the hive to cover the foraging 'range', just below the surface of the earth. There may be one or more million individuals in the colony, so that the ambient temperature is raised by the accumulation of the metabolic heat produced by the fungus. The heat, and the carbon dioxide produced by their respiration, would reach fatal levels if it was not conducted away from their living chambers and replaced by fresh air.

Water is also needed to maintain the humidity. Tunnels are excavated down to the water table; in dry or arid areas these may be as much as 50 metres below the nest, and spread out in a radial pattern down at the water table to increase the wet surface area of the tunnels.

Termites do vary the gross morphology of their mounds, constructing the material form in response to the environmental characteristics of the local habitat, which may be either open savannah or forest. In the higher temperatures of the savannah habitats the mounds are tall and have many projecting ridges that increase the surface area relative to volume, tending to increase heat dissipation. In the cooler forest habitats, there is less surface articulation and the overall morphology is rounder, reducing the surface area and tending to conserve heat. The interior is spatially and structurally complex, with the portion above ground acting as the respiratory and thermoregulating infrastructure of the hive. The termites live below ground in the extensive hive galleries and nurseries, the fungus gardens and the royal chamber. The excavation of the underground spaces provides soil, which is mixed with saliva, faeces and cellulose pulp for the construction material. The occupied spaces are separated from the surrounding soil by walls and air spaces, and the superstructure rests on a base plate supported by columns and arches.

Above the ground, the interior of the mound consists of narrow vertical channels that run from ground level to the top of the mound, some 25 millimetres below the surface. These are linked to each other by a network of lateral channels, which also connect the vertical surface channels to a large interior void and to the underground spaces. Hot moist air rises through the network of conduits, and as it cools it becomes denser, falling down the peripheral surface channels and diffusing out through small holes to the exterior. In some forms, the cap at the top of the mound also has vents, and the interaction of peripheral and chimney venting produces a more complex convection pattern. Cooler drier air is drawn in at the base. The pattern of ventilation is complex, and the upper regions are strongly influenced by the external temperature and variation in the direction and force of winds in the immediate surroundings. The termites continually make fine adjustments to the network of lateral and connective conduits to modify the flow regime. Changes to the gross morphology also adjust the flow, as increasing overall height exposes the top part of the mound to increased wind. In the lower region, tunnels lead directly from the ground surface to the major source of heat, the fungus chambers, and these may be opened, enlarged or narrowed or closed completely as conditions demand. The optimum temperature, humidity and the ratio of oxygen to carbon dioxide are maintained throughout the year, despite the natural variations in the external environment and the fluctuations in the metabolism of the termites.[51]

These fine adjustments are made by removal and deposition of soil, and over the course of a year the quantity of soil moved up by 10 or more metres can be as much as 1,500 kilograms, moved a few grains at a time in many millions of separate actions by completely blind individuals, each with a body length of a few millimetres. Not only is the nest form being constantly modified to regulate the collective metabolism, but one nest is never exactly the same as that of another colony. Similarly, if a nest is damaged the termites rebuild, but the new form will be different from the previous form. It is clear that the three-dimensional pattern of material is not built to a single fixed template. Each individual termite has a very small set of innate behaviours or 'motor programmes' that include the removal and transportation of soil, and the gluing of fecal/soil pellets to a developing column, arch, wall or floor. Individual actions are thought to be triggered by sensitivity to small changes in air flow, and to the consequent changes in the concentrations of pheromones or chemical traces of other individuals, and to variations in the concentration of carbon dioxide concentrations. The threshold to these stimuli, and the degree of response to them, will vary from individual to individual, so that the coherent behaviour of the colony emerges from the interaction of a limited set of simple individual actions with the current state of the fluctuating internal and external material and metabolic conditions. The larger and more complex the material organisation of the nest is, the more complex the patterns of stimuli will be, and in turn the more complex the collective behaviour of the termites will be in the construction and modulation of their nest, even though the action of any single individual remains simple. The collective metabolism is dynamically maintained, responding to the internal fluctuation of the aggregated metabolic processes of their population, and to fluctuations in the external environment including changes in temperature, moisture and food supply. The more complex nests extend the energy and material transactions of an individual organism to a material construction that has all the functions of complex metabolisms – respiration and the regulation of thermal dynamics, the acquisition, transformation and transportation of nutrients combined with storage.

EMERGENCE AND THE FORMS OF METABOLISM

Metabolisms are the systems by which forms are able to live, to construct themselves and grow, to dynamically maintain themselves over time, and to reproduce. Metabolic processes enable and regulate the capture of energy and materials from the exterior environment, transforming and transporting it through the interior of the living form, and excreting changed materials and energy back into the environment. Matter is recycled, but energy is dissipated. All metabolic processes cease without a constant source of energy, although most living forms are capable of storing some energy in chemicals to survive temporary fluctuations in supply. Animals feed on plants and each other, and as only a small percentage of all the energy bound up in the tissues can be metabolised, at each level, as life is consumed by successively more complex forms of life, energy is lost.

Metabolism has a direct effect on the anatomical organisation of all living forms, and on their mass and their lifespan. Small forms have 'fast' and short lives, as the rate at which their metabolisms work is higher than that of large forms, which have slower processes and longer lives. Whatever the size or shape of a living form, they all must capture and transform energy from their environment, and transport it in fluids to every cell. These processes require surfaces and fluid transportation networks, and there are geometrical parameters in the branching networks of living forms that are constant across all scales, from microbes to the largest trees and animals. The rate of energy that flows through a metabolism determines other variables that scale in relation to mass, such as the rate of fluid flow and the cross section of the aorta or phloem vessels, or the number of heartbeats in a lifespan.

The metabolic processes of living forms change their environment over a range of scales. What is commonly thought of today as the primary condition for life to exist, the oxygen in the atmosphere, was produced by the metabolism of another form of life, the single cell cyanobacteria. The emergence of the more complex symbiotic eukaryotic cell, in which the simpler chloroplasts and mitochondria cells were incorporated as entire metabolic units into the cells, enabled the subsequent evolution of living forms of greater complexity. It is not the case that evolution necessarily produces metabolic and morphological complexity, as many single cell and simple living forms still exist in the world today. However, forms that are not well adapted to their environment tend to die off when there are changes in the environment, such as when energy resources become scarcer through climate changes or increases in the populations of competing species. Those species that are metabolically stressed or 'unfit' are disadvantaged in relation to the other species that exist within the same territory or ecological system. They will respond initially by contraction of their accustomed territories, or range shifts and migrations. Under these conditions, if they are unable to migrate to more favourable territories, for example, restricted by geographical boundaries, they will become extinct. This changes the dynamic relations of the other species in the ecological system, modifying the diversity and distribution of the species, and this in turn may have further consequences, such as changes in predator-prey relationships. Where there is a positive outcome for the other 'fitter' species, it is as a result of the elimination of the unfit. As it is metabolism that regulates the life processes of all forms, and determines the relations between living forms, it follows that metabolism is the most significant phenotypical constraint in the evolution of living forms, in the speciation of diverse forms and in the patterns of diversity and distribution of species. Ecological organisation emerges from the interaction of the metabolic processes of all the forms of life that coexist within a territory or habitat.

All species have a range or spatial area from which they gather energy, and over which they have an effect. An individual tree, for example, is anatomically organised to support its three-dimensional array of leaves for its photosynthetic metabolism. It will modify the soil and the atmosphere of its local environment by its metabolic processes – the transpiration of water drawn up from the ground will modify the structure of the soil, and the water vapour and gases excreted by the leaves will modify the temperature, humidity and oxygen content of the atmosphere. This in turn will affect the metabolism of other trees near to it, as will the shade it casts. The spatial pattern of a mature forest, the density and distribution of varying sizes and species of plants, emerges from the interaction of all the plant metabolisms within it. Furthermore, the collective effect of the totality of metabolic actions produces the environment that other species inhabit, the bacteria and fungi, the insects, birds and animals that coexist with the forest and within it. The processes of multiple individual systems, each acting across a range of spatial and temporal scales, interact with the soil and topography, with sunlight and climate, water and atmosphere, to construct an ecological system. The flow of energy and material through an ecological system is thus regulated by the collective metabolism of all the living forms within it, and over time the regime of natural selection within the ecological system may be modified. At a finer scale, populations of individual living forms have an effect on their local environment, and in doing so they modify their own 'niche' within the larger ecological system. Their descendants inherit and extend that local environment. Over many generations this changes the local regime of 'fitness' and consequently the dynamics of natural selection.

Many living forms extend their metabolism by a material construction that reduces the load or stress on some aspects of their metabolic processes. Some mammals excavate burrows, sometimes with multiple entrances and interconnected chambers that are inhabited by several family groups and are spatially arranged as a loosely organised colony. The metabolic functions of burrows usually include smoothing out the fluctuating temperatures that would occur above ground, food storage, and strategic access to their range or territory. Many species of birds also construct their nests in colonies, with similar metabolic properties and a relatively unstructured or opportunistic spatial organisation of the colony as a whole.

Insect colonies have highly structured social organisations, with restricted reproductive roles for individuals, generations that overlap in time, collaborative care of the offspring, and in many cases morphological distinction or castes for specialised roles. Insect 'agriculture' is thought to have emerged at nine quite independent locations and times over the history of biological evolution, and the symbiotic relationship of the insect and the fungi are prolonged through time by multiple coevolutions between the insect species, the fungi crop and other microbes that are used to prevent invasive pathogens. The material forms of the constructions of social insects are spatially complex and exhibit collective metabolic processes that are dynamically regulated to a very fine degree over time. The complex material organisation emerges from the interaction of millions of simple actions of individuals, each with a very small set of innate behaviours or 'motor programmes' that are triggered by chemical, thermal or hygroscopic stimuli. Individuals have differing thresholds and degrees of response to these stimuli, and so collective intelligent behaviour emerges from millions of slightly different interactions with the fluctuating internal and external material and metabolic conditions. Large colonies may have millions of individuals, and the scale of the material construction in relation to the size of an individual can span several orders of magnitude.

The material construction that extends the metabolism of insect colonies has a fixed spatial relationship to the territory over which they range, with the nest or hive tending to be more or less centrally located. By contrast, the metabolism and social organisation of the great apes determines a very different spatial relationship of their material constructions to the territory over which they range. The orangutan, chimpanzee, bonobo and gorilla species, the closest phylogenetic relatives to humans, exist in social groups and communities that exhibit a wide range of behaviours, many of which are socially transmitted and characteristic to particular collectives. In chimpanzees the collective group is typically up to 100 individuals with a territory that is determined by the distribution of the fruit, leaves and herbs that they feed on. This may be as much as 35 square kilometres of forest, and a very much greater area in more open and mixed habitats. The whole community moves across their territory in loose association, split into smaller sub groups of four or six individuals, but moving closer together at night.

In all species of apes each individual, from the age of three or four, constructs a nest by weaving branches and leafy twigs into a platform to sleep in, usually in trees. Ground nests are more differentiated, and may be simple heaps of leaves and twigs, or leafy surfaces that are woven around bushes, or vertically organised structures that use three rooted bamboo stalks or saplings as a frame. Beds are frequently reused by all species,[52] usually when in close proximity to fruiting trees. Both rainfall and temperature also influence nest construction, with an increase in fully constructed ground and arboreal nests strongly correlated with decreasing temperature and increased rainfall. Each individual will build thousands of nests in a lifetime, in varying habitats with varying food supplies and environmental conditions, so it follows that the material construction and metabolic regulation is a response to changing environmental stimuli.

The social organisation of groups tends to produce genetic variation, for example, in chimpanzees the males remain with the group throughout their lives and so are closely related, but the females tend to leave the group when they reach sexual maturity, and join other groups. Chimpanzees make and use tools: widening nest openings and extracting honey or insects with twigs, breaking open nuts with rocks, and using leaves to sip water. It is observed that knowledge and expertise of nest construction, tool making and use is passed down through generations, immature individuals learning by imitating older more proficient adults. Variations do exist, however, between communities in different regions with different climates, and differing food quantity and quality. This suggests a material 'culture',[53] which involves the social transmission of knowledge that modifies the inherited and genetically conserved responses to environmental stimuli.

Intelligence, spatial organisation and material artefacts emerge from the collective extension of metabolism of the social insects. Insect collectives continually modify and regulate their exterior environment, and over time modify their ecological niche, thereby enhancing their 'fitness' in that environment. The close interrelation between the extended metabolism of the collective and their environment changes the regime of natural selection in their favour. In insect collectives there are no individuals with a capacity for processing information, and no system for the flow of information to a dominant decision-making individual or group. Responses to internal and external changes emerge from the actions of individuals, so that behavioural complexity emerges at the organisational scale of the collective. The emergence of distributed intelligence, of social and spatial organisation, of collective and materially extended metabolism, is reinforced and developed by positive feedbacks acting across a range of spatial and temporal scales.

It is clear that there are many similarities as well as differences between the dynamics of 'collectives' of the various taxa and species of apes and insects. What is common between them is the large number of individuals with a range of different response thresholds, emerging from very small variations in the process of embryological development. Both positive and negative feedback occur in their interactions with each other and with their environment; in general the gradation of responses across the population are either reinforced and accelerated by positive feedback, or inhibited by negative feedback. There is a high degree of redundancy in the relation of individuals to the collective, so that the numbers committed to specialised roles can be varied according to the circumstances – it is probable that this characteristic is also produced by the varied response thresholds of the multitude of individuals.

The relations of the spatial pattern of extended metabolic processes and material constructions are very different. The spatial pattern of the great apes arises from the ecological distribution and seasonality of food plants across the large defended territory of the group, and individuals moving in loose association.

Material constructions are temporary and individual, but closely grouped at night for defence. The spatial pattern of the social insects also arises from the ecological distribution of food plants, but the material construction tends to be centrally located in their territory, and is permanent. The evolution of human forms and culture involves both spatial patterns, and the emergence of a complex system for the transmission of knowledge over time.

1 Thompson, D'Arcy Wentworth, Prologue to *On Growth And Form* (first published 1917), Cambridge University Press (Cambridge), 1961, p 19.

2 Kleiber, M, 'Body Size and Metabolism', *Hilgardia*, vol 6, 1932, pp 315–51.

3 Martin, W and MJ Russell, 'On the Origins of Cells: a hypothesis for the evolutionary transitions from abiotic geochemistry to chemoautotrophic prokaryotes, and from prokaryotes to nucleated cells', *Philosophical Transactions of The Royal Society of London B*, vol 358, no 1429, 2003; and Cavalier-Smith, T, 'Cell Evolution and Earth History: stasis and revolution', *Philosophical Transactions of The Royal Society of London B*, vol 361, no 1470, 2006, pp 969–1006.

4 '… and you have burned so very, very brightly, Roy'. *Blade Runner*, 1982, directed by Ridley Scott, The Ladd Company, USA, [film].

5 Attributed to the lectures of Michael Faraday, not included in the later publication in *Scientific Papers. vol XXX, The Harvard Classics*, PF Collier & Son (New York), 1909–14.

6 Pearl, R, *The Rate of Living*, University of London Press (London), 1928.

7 Charnov, EL, 'A Note on Dimensionless Life-Histories for Birds Versus Mammals', *Evolutionary Ecology*, vol 9, 1995, pp 288–91.

8 $6CO_2 + 12 H_2O +$ light energy $= C_6H_{12}O_6 + 6O_2 + 6H_2O$.

9 Referred to as C3 photosynthesis, as the first metabolic product has three carbon atoms.

10 Referred to as C4 photosynthesis, as the first metabolic product has four carbon atoms.

11 Referred to as CAM photosynthesis, Crassulacean Acid Metabolism, after the plant in which it was first discovered.

12 Poorter, L and MJA Werger, 'Light Environment, Sapling Architecture, and Leaf Display in Six Rain Forest Species', *American Journal of Botany*, vol 86,1999, pp 1464–73.

13 Horn, HS, *The Adaptive Geometry of Trees*, Princeton University Press (Princeton), 1971.

14 0, 1, 1, 2, 3, 5, 8, 13, 21, 34, 55 and so on.

15 Spiral phyllotaxis usually has a constant divergence angle of 137.5°, resulting in a spiral that runs in a clockwise or counter-clockwise direction. Secondary spirals, the contact or intersection 'parastichies', run in both directions. The number of parastichies in each direction represents consecutive terms in the Fibonacci series.

16 Niklas, J, 'The Role of Phyllotactic Pattern as a "Developmental Constraint" on the Interception of Light by Leaf Surfaces', *Evolution*, vol 42, 1988, pp 1–16.

17 Sack, L and NM Holbrook, 'Leaf Hydraulics', *Annual Review of Plant Biology*, vol 57, 2006, pp 477–96.

18 Price, CA and BJ Enquist, 'Scaling Mass and Morphology in Leaves; an extension of the WBE Model', *Ecology*, vol 88, 2007, p 1132–41.

19 Horton, RE, 'Erosional Development of Streams and their Drainage Basins: hydrophysical approach to quantitative morphology', *Geological Society of America Bulletin*, vol 56, 1945, pp 275–370; Leopold, LB and TM Maddock Jr, 'The Hydraulic Geometry of Stream Channels and Some Physiographic Implications', *US Geological Survey Professional Paper*, 252,1953.

20 Niklas, KJ, 'Branching Patterns and Mechanical Design in Palaeozoic Plants: a theoretic assessment', *Annals of Botany*, vol 42, 1978, pp 33–9.

21 Honda, H and JB Fisher, 'Tree Branch Angle: maximizing effective leaf area', *Science*, vol 199, no 4331, 1978, pp 888–90.

22 Leopold, LB, 'Trees and Streams: the efficiency of branching patterns', *Journal of Theoretical*

Biology, vol 31, 1971, pp 339–54.

23 Bredenkamp, GJ, F Spada, and E Kazmierczak, 'On the Origin of Northern and Southern Hemisphere Grasslands', *Plant Ecology*, vol 163, December 2002, pp 209–29.

24 Kellogg, EA, 'Evolutionary History of the Grasses', *Plant Physiology*, vol 125, March 2001, pp 1198–205.

25 Sinha, NR and EA Kellogg, 'Parallelism and Diversity in Multiple Origins of C4 Photosynthesis in Grasses', *American Journal of Botany*, vol 83: November 1996, pp 1458–70.

26 The weight, or mass of an organism is a function of its size, and is directly proportional to the organism's volume. Living forms are composed mainly of water, and as 1 cubic centimetre of water has a mass of 1 gram, living tissues are a little more than 1 gram per cubic centimetre.

27 Marbà, N, CM Duarte and S Agustí, 'Allometric Scaling of Plant Life History', *Proceedings of the National Academy of Sciences*, vol 104, no 40, October 2007, pp 15777–80.

28 Loehle, C, 'Tree Life History Strategies', *Canadian Journal of Forest Research*, vol 18, 1988, pp 209–22.

29 Price, CA, BJ Enquist and VM Savage, 'A General Model for Allometric Covariation in Botanical Form and Function', *Proceedings of the National Academy of Sciences*, vol 104, no 32, August 2007, pp 13204–9.

30 Else, PL and AJ Hulbert, 'Comparison of the "Mammal Machine" and the "Reptile Machine": energy production', *American Journal of Physiology*, vol 240, 1981, pp 350–6; and Else, PL and AJ Hulbert, 'Evolution of Mammalian Endothermic Metabolism: "leaky" membranes as a source of heat', *American Journal of Physiology*, vol 253, 1981, pp 329–33; and Else, PL and AJ Hulbert, 'An Allometric Comparison of the Mitochondria of Mammalian and Reptilian Tissues: the implications for the evolution of endothermy', *Journal of Comparative Physiology B*, vol 156, November 1985, pp 3–11.

31 Huxley, JS, 'The Variation in the Width of the Abdomen in Immature Fiddler Crabs Considered in Relation to its Relative Growth-Rate', *American Naturalist*, vol 58, 1924, pp 468–75; and Huxley, JS, 'Constant Differential Growth-Ratios and their Significance', *Nature* , vol 114, 1924, pp 895–6.

32 Demetrius, L, 'Directionality Theory and the Evolution of Body Size', *Proceedings of the Royal Society of London B*, vol 267, December 2000, pp 2385–91.

33 Cope, ED, *Primary Factors of Organic Evolution*, Chicago University Press (Chicago), 1886.

34 Bergmann, C, *Göttinger Studien*, vol 3, 1847, pp 595–708.

35 Brongniart, C, 'Les Insectes fossiles des terrains primaires. Coup d'oeil rapide sur la faune entomologique des terrains paléozoïques', *Bulletin de la Société des Amis des Sciences Naturelles de Rouen*, 1885.

36 Peters, RH, *The Ecological Implications of Body Size*, Cambridge University Press (Cambridge) 1986.

37 Niklas, KJ, *Plant Allometry*, University of Chicago Press (Chicago), 1994.

38 Enquist, BJ, 'Allometric Scaling of Plant Energetics and Population Density', *Nature*, vol 395, September 1998, pp 163–5; and West GB, JH Brown and BJ Enquist, 'A General Model for the Origin of Allometric Scaling Laws in Biology', *Science*, vol 276, 1997, pp 122–6; and Turcotte, DL, JD Pelletier and WI Newman, 'Networks with Side Branching in Biology', *Journal of Theoretical Biology*, vol 193, August 1998, pp 577–92.

39 Szucsich, NU and HW Krenn, 'Flies and Concealed Nectar Sources: morphological innovations in the proboscis of Bombyliidae (Diptera)', *Acta Zoologica*, vol 83, 2002, pp 183–92.

40 Ehrlich, PR and PH Raven, 'Butterflies and Plants: a study in coevolution', *Evolution*, vol 18, 1964, pp 586–608.

41 Ramirez, BW, 'Host Specificity of Fig Wasps (Agaonidae)', *Evolution*, vol 24: 1970, pp 680–91.

42 This kind of one-sided association is referred to as 'Commensal', and along with 'Parasitical' associations, was traditionally categorised as a kind of symbiosis.

43 The term 'symbiosis' was first used by Bary, Anton de, *Die Erscheinung der Symbiose (The Phenomenon of Symbiosis)*, privately printed in Strasbourg, 1879.

44 Douglas, AE, *Symbiotic Interactions*, 1994 Oxford University Press (Oxford); and Douglas, AE and JA Raven, 'Genomes at the Interface between Bacteria and Organelles', *Philosophical Transactions of the Royal Society of London B*, vol 358, 2003, pp 5–17.

45 Douglas, AE, 'Phloem-Sap Feeding by Animals: problems and solutions', *Journal of Experimental Biology*, vol 57, no 4, 2006, pp 747–54.

46 Heil M and D McKey, 'Protective Ant-Plant Interactions as Model Systems in Ecological and Evolutionary Research', *Annual Reviews of Ecology, Evolution and Systematics*, vol 34, 2003, pp 425–53; and Heckroth HP, B Fiala, PJ Gullan, U Maschwitz and HI Azarae, 'The Soft Scale (Coccidae) Associates of Malaysian Ant-Plants', *Journal of Tropical Ecology*, vol 14, 1999, pp 427–43.

47 Theraulaz, G, J Gautrais, S Camazine and J-L Deneubourg, 'The Formation of Spatial Patterns in Social Insects: From Simple Behaviours to Complex Structures', *Philosophical Transactions of the Royal Society of London A*, vol 361, no 1807, 2003, pp 1263–82; and a summary of vol 361, no 1807, 'Self-Organization: The Quest for the Origin and Evolution of Structure', 2003, pp 1263–82.

48 Gould, JL and CG Gould, *Animal Architects: building and the evolution of intelligence*, Basic Books (New York), 2007, pp 122–31.

49 Seeley, TD, 'Thoughts on Information and Integration in Honey Bee Colonies', *Apidologie*, vol 29, 1998, pp 67–80.

50 Mueller, UG, NM Gerardo, DK Aanen, DL Six and TR Schultz, 'The Evolution of Agriculture in Insects', *Annual Review of Ecology, Evolution, and Systematics*, vol 36, 2005, pp 563–95.

51 Turner, JS, 'On the Mound of Macrotermes Michaelseni as an Organ of Respiratory Gas Exchange', *Physiological and Biochemical Zoology*, vol 74, no 6, 2001, pp 798–822; and Korb, J and KE Linsenmair, 'Ventilation of Termite Mounds: new results require a new model', *Behavioral Ecology*, vol 11, no 5, 2000, pp 486–94.

52 Iwata, Y and C Ando, 'Bed and Bed-Site Reuse by Western Lowland Gorillas (Gorilla g. gorilla) in Moukalaba-Doudou National Park, Gabon', *Primates*, vol 48, 2007, pp 77–80.

53 Whiten, A, J Goodall, WC McGrew, T Nishida, V Reynolds, Y Sugiyama, CEG Tutin, RW Wrangham and C Boesch, 'Cultures in Chimpanzees', *Nature*, vol 399, 1999, pp 682–5; and Whiten, A, V Horner and S Marshall-Pescini, 'Cultural Panthropology', *Evolutionary Anthropology*, vol 12, 2003, pp 92–105.

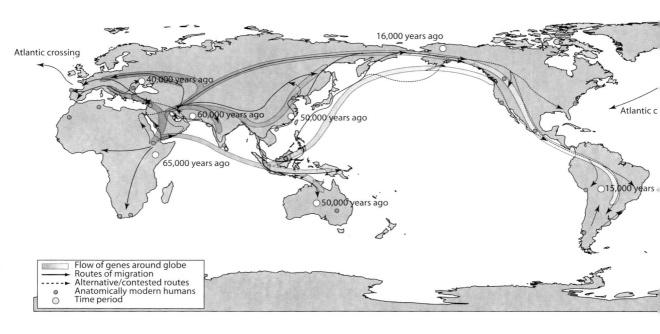

Atlantic crossing

16,000 years ago

40,000 years ago

60,000 years ago

50,000 years ago

65,000 years ago

50,000 years ago

Atlantic c

15,000 years

Flow of genes around globe
Routes of migration
Alternative/contested routes
Anatomically modern humans
Time period

6.1 Human Origins and Diaspora

Anatomically modern humans, *Homo sapiens sapiens*, emerged as a small
population of a few thousand in east Africa some 135,000 years ago. All
humans alive today are descendants of that founding population, and possibly
from one woman, the 'Mitochondrial Eve' within that population. The
successive waves of the diaspora 'out of Africa' began between 60,000 to
70,000 years ago, in to the Levant, and on in to Asia and Europe and
through Siberia to the Americas. As humans dispersed in to new climatic and
ecological zones, adaptive cultural variations emerged.

Humans – Anatomical and Cultural Forms

6

Anatomically modern human form coevolved with their material culture, so that human anatomical and cultural forms are inextricably entwined. Vectors of energy determined the diasporas 'out of Africa' and expansion of humans across the face of the earth, and variations arose in the mobility strategies, material constructions and the spatial patterning of their extended metabolism. The emergence of the founding system of civilisation integrated the development of language, long-term settlements, art and calendars into an informational system for the transmission of knowledge through space and over time. In all localities the founding system tended to evolve to the point of critical stability, and initiated significant changes in other living forms and ecological systems.

Like all other species, the evolution of humans has been constrained by their relations to other living forms, and to climatic regimes and the topography of the surface of the earth. These constraints, and the interactions between them, have produced the diversity and distribution of all the species across the surface of the earth. Living forms have in turn affected the processes of the atmosphere and oceans, the climate and the topography of the earth. Each system is dynamic, and each has shown dramatic fluctuations on timescales that vary from decades and centuries to millennia. The climate 'metasystem' generates very different regional and latitudinal regimes of temperature, precipitation and wind, with a range of variation and fluctuations in each regime. Continual climatic variability over a prolonged period produces a regime of natural selection in which species evolve that have the ability to survive in a range of environmental conditions.

Humans evolved from the morphologically varied 'Hominidae' family of the great apes, developing and expanding their populations through a series of changing topographies, fluctuating climates and varying ecological systems.[1] All species have some effect on their immediate environment, and in species that organise themselves as collectives, the construction of material forms provides a beneficial effect on the metabolism of the collective. Social organisations, intelligence and material constructions emerged in the behaviour of many species of living forms millions of years before the emergence of anatomically modern humans. The material constructions of social collectives have an effect on their local environment, each has a characteristic form, spatial pattern and range. These collective activities and their ability to persist down through the generations in their ecological system are known as 'niche construction'.[2] The evolutionary anthropologists KN Laland and FJ Odling-Smee argue that the modification of their local environment by a species positively changes the dynamics of natural selection, and so has an effect on the evolutionary development of that particular species. The beneficial modification of their environment increases their chances of survival, and in consequence enhances the chances of the genes that are responsible for that trait being inherited by the next generation. In effect, 'niche construction' acts as a positive feedback on natural selection. The impact that climate and food resources would otherwise have in limiting their populations is mitigated by the material constructions that spatially extend their collective metabolisms. Offspring are born into an environment that has been modified in their favour by the ancestral population, and the genes that are linked to these traits are passed on to their descendants. In doing so they create an 'ecological inheritance' for the next population.

Genetic inheritance is transmitted between individuals, from parents to their offspring, but the ecological inheritance of a modified environment is maintained from one generation to the next by the collective organisation and material constructions of the population as a whole. Evolutionary development of the collective proceeds because of the high level of fitness of the entire collective for its local environment, so that natural selection will act to conserve and disseminate the genes of the ecologically successful groups. The evolution of anatomically modern humans from the ancestral family of the great apes was coupled to the evolution of a material culture that increased their ability to extract energy from their environment, and so enhanced and extended their metabolism. In turn, they modified their environment and extended the range of territories and climates in which they could flourish. The emergence of the biological form of modern humans cannot be separated from the emergence of human culture; they have always been and continue to be interlocked in a coevolutionary process.

THE EMERGENCE OF HOMININ FORMS AND CULTURE

The original divergence and speciation of the hominin[3] from the ancestral apes occurred approximately seven million years ago in east Africa. New species of living forms, morphologically distinct from their ancestors, generally emerge from small populations that have been geographically separated from the normal territorial range of a numerous and widely distributed ancestor species. The geographical separation of the ancestral species on either side of the great Rift Valley in Africa occurred about 11 million years ago, when the land raised by tectonic forces subsided into an enormous valley some 6,000 kilometres long, in places hundreds of metres deep and up to 100 kilometres wide. The Rift runs from north to south, and to the west of the valley conditions remained humid and moist, with dense forests. The chimpanzee species evolved from the ancestral species in these conditions. To the east of the valley, the pattern of rainfall was changed by the new topography to a more seasonally varied pattern, with drier periods in-between. Over millions of years, the whole region gradually changed to a more seasonally arid condition. Grasses and plants able to flourish in these conditions proliferated and eventually the forests began to die back, opening up areas of grassland. The ancestral species were isolated in the now more varied climate of mixed forest and savannah, and in consequence experienced a quite different regime of natural selection to those on the other side of the Rift. The oldest hominin fossils are found in the grasslands of east Africa and are dated to between seven and eight million years ago.

The evolutionary diversification of the 'Hominidae' family continued, with morphological transformations occurring over millions of years and several variant species emerging. The upright body plan and bipedal walking are thought to have emerged about four million years ago, with substantial anatomical divergence from the ancestral great ape form. The species *Australopithecus afarensis*, now extinct, had a slender upright form, and is widely thought to be the ancestor of the genus *Homo*. Perhaps the most famous fossil of this species is a partial skeleton known as 'Lucy',[4] found in 1974 in Ethiopia by Donald Johanson. In the following year, the fossil fragments from 13 adult *A. afarensis* were found nearby.[5] The species, along with other closely related hominins, eventually became widely distributed across eastern and central regions of Africa, south of the Sahara, and down to the Transvaal in southern Africa.

Although no fossil evidence can exist[6] of hominin nesting and social behaviour, it is suggested that the early hominin constructed nests in trees.[7] It is reasonable to assume that the hominin had a similar 'material culture' and group organisation to that revealed by contemporary studies of the great apes, and that the 'niche' modifying traits of hominin were similarly genetically conserved. Coupled to the social transmission down through the generations of knowledge and expertise in nest construction and tool use, it is probable that the early hominin built nests of branches, stalks, leaves and lianas in trees, and on the ground, in a similar manner to their ancestral ape species. Anatomical analysis of the fossil skeletons supports this hypothesis, as the morphology of the knees and pelvis of *A. afarensis* are optimal for bipedal striding, and the morphology of the shoulders, arms and hands are optimal for the prehensile ability to grasp twigs and branches. This anatomy would have been ideally suited for the emergent environment of a patchwork mosaic of savannah and forest, with increased walking abilities extending the home ranges of bands of hominin, maintaining the group size despite the increasing distances between feeding sites in forest stands. Travel pathways between forest stands, linking frequently used feeding sites and habitually revisited nesting sites, produced a spatial patterning of the home range. The seasons produce differences in plant life, in the annual pattern of food resources such as fruit, seeds and nuts within the home range. It follows that the spatial patterning varied according to the time of year, and that the knowledge of the spatial and temporal pattern of the ecology of the extended territory was socially transmitted.

When the ice sheets of a new ice age began to advance from the poles, between 2.4 and 2.8 million years ago, sea levels fell as more and more water was bound up in the ice. The pattern of ocean and atmospheric circulations changed, and the subsequent global cooling produced changes in the African climatic regime. A speciation event occurred in many different mammalian groups, including grazing bovid and hominin.[8] Elisabeth S Vrba has called this a 'turnover pulse', arguing that the cooler and drier conditions produced changes to the distribution of plant life, and that the wet woodlands and forests were partially replaced by open grassland. Those species that were 'ecologically generalised' survived unchanged, but all the species that were 'ecologically specific' to wet forests either migrated or became extinct. However, when the climate undergoes multiple changes over a prolonged period, the continual variation in climate will also tend to conserve and develop species that are most able to persist in a range of environmental conditions. So the continual fluctuations in environmental conditions that prevailed in east Africa over such a prolonged period had a long-term effect on the regime of natural selection. The 'variability selection' hypothesis proposes that hominin evolved enhanced behavioural versatility as an adaptive response to these conditions.

As the whole region of east Africa became cooler and even drier, the seasonal differences in rainfall and temperature became more pronounced. The interaction of climatic variations over two differentiated timescales, the strong differences between seasons and the longer regional variations in the circulations of the atmosphere induced by global cooling, produced greater instabilities and fluctuations. Over several hundred thousand years these fluctuations would have caused frequent changes to the environment, to the streams and rivers, to plant life and to the surface of the land. Species with an ability to vary their behaviour in response to a range of conditions would have an advantage over those whose behaviour was fixed and specific to a particular habitat and weather pattern. In these circumstances, the 'fitness' of hominin species was not specific to the savannah habitat, but rather it was the capacity to vary their metabolic activities that counted. Over the longer timescale natural selection acted to increase the abilities of hominin[9] to vary the extent and spatial patterning of their home range, their nesting and their foraging behaviour.

The genus *Homo* emerged during this period, approximately 2.5 million years ago. It is now thought to have consisted of a small number of morphologically varied species, including the larger species now known as *Homo erectus*. The tall and slender narrow bodies of the *Homo* species were morphologically distinct from the shorter and broader *A. afarensis* hominin. The body plans of all *Homo* species are characterised by a slender and elongated overall morphology, and so were well adapted for thermoregulation in the hot climate.[10] Other morphological changes included changes to the skull, increasing the cranial capacity to twice that of the apes, and modifications to the jaw and teeth. There is fossil evidence to suggest that the increased cranial capacity was accompanied by a reorganisation of the brain, with the appearance of enlarged frontal lobes and areas associated with the control of speech.

The larger brain is strongly correlated with metabolic changes, particularly to the liver and the gastrointestinal tract. A large brain is metabolically 'expensive', having a much higher mass-specific metabolic rate than the rest of the primate body – a gram of brain tissue uses 22 times the amount of metabolic energy as a gram of muscle tissue. The 'expensive tissue hypothesis' of LC Aiello and P Wheeler suggests that the reduction in the size of the gastrointestinal tract of the slender body form coevolved with the enlarged brain. Increased cognitive abilities enhanced the social organisation of hunting and foraging in groups, and led to improved diets with a larger percentage of high calorie animal protein, and a

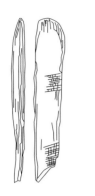

6.2 The Evolution of Tools
The making of stone tools is thought to have begun about 2.5 million years ago, with the emergence of the early species of the *Homo* genus. These skills, like those of chimpanzees and their use of rocks to break open nuts, are socially transmitted from parent to offspring down through the generations. The manufacturing technique is a single skilful blow of one rock against another.

proportional reduction in size of the digestive system.[11] The larger brain and increased cognitive abilities of *Homo erectus* are also correlated with the shaping and use of stone tools, with a more complex spatial and social mapping of extended home ranges, and with the first migrations and dispersals out of Africa.

The shaping of stone tools requires manual skill and an appreciation of the relation of shape and symmetry to the purpose of use. The making of stone tools, what anthropologists call lithic technology, is thought to have begun about 2.5 million years ago, with the emergence of the early species of the *Homo* genus. These are the simplest stone tools, shaped pebbles and stone flakes with one sharp face creating a cutting edge. It is a clear that these skills, like that of chimpanzees and their use of rocks to break open nuts, are socially transmitted from parent to offspring down through the generations. The manufacturing technique, a single blow of one rock against another, requires skill and the ability to recognise suitable crystalline rocks such as quartz or basalt. Analysis of finds in Ethiopia suggests that a single large stone had many flakes struck off it, and that a softer and more rounded stone was used to strike it. The sharp flakes extended the external metabolic activities of *Homo*, enabling them to cut open plants and animal carcasses and to gain more calories from them. Among the finds of the earliest stone tools are bone and horn tools that were evidently used to dig for tubers and insects. Over time, stone tools were transported away from the manufacturing site for tens of kilometres. Stone tools gradually became more standard in shape, and the small set of designs appear to have been remarkably stable for at least a million years over a very wide geographical area. That strongly suggests that the communication of manufacturing techniques was effective between bands of hominin, and raises the question as to how the dissemination of knowledge was accomplished.

The material evidence suggests that spoken language coevolved with the material culture and larger brains of *Homo*. The development of a spoken language cannot be incontrovertibly assigned to the early *Homo* species, but there is clear fossil evidence that the brain was not simply enlarged allometrically. The morphological modifications to the skull were differentiated and accompanied by internal reorganisation of the brain,[12] so that *Homo erectus* was at the very least functionally adapted for spoken language. It has been suggested that the learning and imitation of a set of vocalised sounds serves to identify and assert membership of a group in many species, particularly species that form social groups with a high degree of cooperation within the group. Elaborate sound sequences have other social functions too. For example, in aquatic mammals, such as whales and dolphins, the males produce complex 'songs' for courtship and for marking the boundaries of their territories.[13] Over time, natural selection acts to conserve and enhance the ability to produce and learn sets of sounds, and to elaborate the range down through the generations. 'Vocal learning' maintains social cohesion and organisation, and provides the instrument for the gradual development of an extensive set of arbitrary sounds from which spoken languages emerge.[14]

The transportation of tools away from the manufacturing sites suggests that the spatial organisation of the home range had begun to change. A differentiated pattern emerged, with a number of favoured locations dispersed around the territory being habitually revisited. The use of caves and rock shelters, often associated with tool manufacturing, is thought to have been seasonal, while other temporary sites were used for feeding and sleeping. The spatial organisation of individual nests into a coherent overall plan for defence, usually approximately circular, is common in apes, and is likely to have evolved further. There are no fossil finds of early *Homo* shelters, but the coevolution of human biological form and human culture necessarily includes the evolutionary development of shared rather than individual shelters. The evolution of enhanced cognitive capacity, tool making, communication, social cooperation and metabolic organisation were all interlinked. Sharp stone tools were available for the cutting of branches, and the practice of transporting tools and carcasses to other sites is likely to have eventually extended to the transportation of other materials. It follows that the cooperation and social organisation evolved for hunting, when extended to the shared construction of shelters, would inevitably lead to shared inhabitation.

The morphology may be inferred as an intermediate form between the approximately circular arrangement of individual nests of the great apes and the later archaeological finds of cave paintings depicting tent-like shelters and pit dwellings. The material construction of these shelters is likely to have consisted of the arrangement of cut branches in a roughly circular plan, leaning on each other to make an approximately conical form, and to have been covered with woven grasses and animal skins. *Homo erectus* used fire, although there is no precise dating of the controlled use of fire in constructed hearths. There are speculative theories concerning the cultural development of shelters and the use of fire, and the evolutionary loss of fur in the *Homo* species. The number of hair follicles in humans is similar to that of the great apes, but the hair is so fine that it does not function as fur. Other advantages of the cultural developments of shelters and fire, and the evolutionary loss of fur may have included the ability to easily shed parasites.[15] Infested shelters can be abandoned and new ones constructed, and infected skin is more easily cleaned than fur. The evolutionary development of sweat glands and associated dermal fat insulation in hairless skin changed the biological thermoregulatory regime.[16] Sweat enables the rapid shedding of excess heat through evaporative cooling, while fat insulation smoothes out rapid changes of temperature and provides some energy storage. These functional enhancements do have a cost in that naked skin is maladaptive for exposure and impacts, and in turn, increased environmental vulnerability is mitigated by clothing and shelter.

The anatomical form and the material culture coevolved. The emergence of increased brain size and enhanced cognition is strongly coupled to the evolutionary development of material technology and the subsequent extension of the range of conditions in which human metabolisms could function effectively. Positive feedback operated between brain size and the increasing complexity of culture, so that each has acted to accelerate the development of the other. Bigger brains enable a more complex culture, and a more complex culture enhances the ecological 'fitness' of the group and so positively modifies the regime of natural selection in favour of bigger brains.

THE DIASPORA OF HUMAN FORMS ACROSS THE EARTH

It is now generally, but not universally, agreed that there were several successive waves of migrations and dispersals of morphologically varied *Homo* out of Africa. Robert Foley and Marta M Lahr argue that fossil and stone tool finds suggest that differentiated populations moved at different times.[17] The primary route is thought to have been from Ethiopia up through the Nile valley in to Sinai and the Levant and then eastwards in to southern Asia, with a later movement from the Levant in to the southern regions of Europe. The waves of migration are of uncertain dates, but the morphological variation in fossil bones from different regions does suggest that the dispersals from Africa in to Asia and then in to Europe were episodic and extended over time for more than a million years.[18] During that time the descendant populations of earlier migration also evolved *in situ*. The most numerous and most widely distributed fossils are of *Homo erectus*. Throughout the last two million years or so there have been four major advances and retreats of the ice sheets, and several smaller glacial events, each producing large climatic changes. There was a pronounced periodicity to the advance and retreat of the ice, close to but not exactly matching the variations in the movements of the earth relative to the sun, known as the Milankovitch[19] cycles. In consequence, the climate continued to oscillate, and the regime of natural selection over the long term continued to act to conserve and enhance the evolution of the ecological niche modification tendencies of *Homo erectus*, extending their ecological range.

During this period[20] the global effects of the ice ages included very large changes of sea level of up to 100 metres, changing ocean currents, and regional cooling in weather patterns. All living forms retreated in front of the advancing ice or became regionally extinct, and expanded their populations and geographical distribution during the warmer interglacial periods. In consequence, the pattern of the migrations and expansion of the *Homo* species in Asia, and later in Europe, was mainly along east to west latitudinal axis. Expanding into areas of similar climate that had no substantial mountain barriers, *Homo erectus* spread right across southern Asia as far east as the Indonesian island Java. Westward migration into southern Europe occurred much later.

Homo erectus was widely dispersed across Africa, Asia and southern Europe 750,000 years ago. Finds of multifaceted hand axes and smaller blades over an extensive area of land indicate the coevolutionary development of the living forms of *Homo erectus* and their culture continued throughout that time, both in Africa and in Asia. Tools that are more complex first emerged in Africa around the same time. The development of tools with two symmetrically worked faces, known as 'bifacial' tools, is usually associated with the large teardrop-shaped hand axes. However, there were also many other smaller blades of similar shape, suitably sized as knives or points for lances and for throwing spears. The symmetrical morphology of these blades across a range of dispersed sites suggests a widespread appreciation of geometrical shape within *Homo erectus* populations, and a commensurate development of communication and social organisation. Bifacial tool forms were widespread across Europe 500,000 years ago, but have never been found in eastern Asia. The enhanced cognitive capacities of *Homo erectus* enabled better communication, more complex social organisation and the production of more complex material artefacts. For example, the Terra Amata site on the Mediterranean coast in what is now southern France has been dated to 380,000 years ago. The pattern of post holes indicates that multiple temporary timber structures, oval in plan and up to 15 metres long by 6 metres wide, were used seasonally over a period of years.[21] The size of the huts and the hearth found in the centre of each one suggests shared or socialised construction and inhabitation.

The development of the biological form and of culture was a coevolutionary process, each acting as a positive feedback on the other. The accumulation of small modifications to their ecological niche also had a positive effect on the survival rate, and resulted in a slow but persistent expansion of the general population. As the evolutionary process continued, so the energetic needs for higher quality diets gradually increased. In consequence, bands and groups would have tended to enlarge the spatial extension of their home ranges, expanding their metabolic activities over greater areas at the same time as the general population was growing. The variability of regional climates and subsequent episodic changes to local and regional ecological systems, would also have contributed to the pressures on local territories and the increasing populations.

The waves of dispersal were driven by the interaction of three major dynamics: the increase in population density; the increase in energy requirements to be processed through the collective metabolic activities of each group or band; and the climatic variations that constrained the availability of food resources within the ecological systems of local populations. The continual diaspora across Asia and into Europe was also accelerated by two positive feedbacks. First, animals had evolved in Asia and Europe without the presence of *Homo*, and so would have been much easier prey than the fauna of Africa that had coevolved with *Homo*. Second, the diseases that constrained the *Homo* populations in Africa were absent in the territories into which *Homo* was migrating. The principal negative constraints that inhibited the flows of *Homo* across the continents were topographical features; such as land over 12,000 metres in altitude.

Homo erectus is now widely accepted as the ancestral species from which anatomically modern humans[22] are descended. For much of the 20th century, however, it was thought that 'Neanderthals' were the intermediary form between *Homo erectus* and modern humans. Fossil evidence and the analysis of molecular DNA indicate that the lineage from *Homo erectus* diverged approximately 400,000 years ago into two descendant species, *Homo neanderthalensis* and the early form of *Homo sapiens*. There is little to separate the material culture of the Neanderthals and the first anatomically modern humans, and in the Levant they were virtually indistinguishable in terms of artefacts.[23] The cranial capacity of both forms shows a significant increase from *Homo erectus*, to about three times that of the great apes.[24] It has been suggested that this increase in brain size, and the consequent substantial increase in energy requirements, indicates a further episode of the coevolution of form and culture. The appearance of hearths and animal bones among fossil finds suggests that the control of fire and the development of cooking were strongly coupled to the expansion of brain size. Cooking breaks down the proteins and fibres in meat and plants, and so externalises part of the digestive process. The result is that fewer calories are required for internal digestion, so more energy is available from food. Cooking was evidentially a highly localised and social activity, and this suggests the further development of a fixed home base, and the further evolution of material culture. The increased brain size, and consequent increase in cognitive potential, was sufficient to have enabled a much finer neurological control over all physical activities, including speech, tool making and the use of tools for material constructions. This suggests additional development in the transmission of material knowledge and social organisation. The coevolution of biological form and culture accelerated in the populations dispersed across Africa, Asia and Europe.

The analysis of the DNA of contemporary populations, used in conjunction with fossils and climatic patterns of the past, is now used to plot the flows of ancient humans across the face of the earth. The mitochondria in human DNA passes down the generations from mother to offspring, and analysis suggests that the maternal lineages converge in a single female, a 'Mitochondrial Eve' who lived in a small population of a few thousand anatomically modern humans in east Africa some 135,000 years ago.[25] Fossil and genetic evidence, when taken together, suggests that this was the founding population of modern humans and that they rapidly expanded their populations until they extended across the entire African continent. The analysis also suggests that the chronology and geographical pattern of the diaspora of anatomically modern humans 'out of Africa' began as recently as 60,000 to 70,000 years ago with small populations of migrants moving in to the Levant, and from there in to Asia and Europe.[26] The subsequent expansions and further migrations extended the populations over all the surface of the earth except Antarctica,[27] so that all humans alive today are descendants of that founding population. It is likely that other human populations were living in Africa, Asia and Europe at the same time, but the flow of modern 'out of Africa' humans displaced locally established human species everywhere.[28]

Neanderthals had spread right across Europe by the time anatomically modern humans first emerged in Africa. They coexisted in the same geographical regions only between the migration out of Africa of the ancestral modern human populations 70,000 years ago, and the extinction of the archaic Neanderthal human form about 30,000 years ago. It is probable that the populations rarely encountered each other, and that when they were in close proximity they coexisted only when the population density of the modern humans was initially very low. Neanderthals evolved from *Homo erectus* to become morphologically distinct from modern humans, their skeletal morphology indicates great muscular strength and full mobility from a very young age. They had short stocky bodies and powerful thick limbs, so were well adapted for thermoregulation in the cool climates of Europe and western Asia. The energy requirements of this body form are higher than those of the more slender modern humans and they required a great deal more food to maintain their metabolisms.

At that time the environment of this region ranged from cold steppes and tundra to dense forests of cold-adapted trees, with brief summers and very severe winters. Fossil remains provide evidence that the spatial patterning of Neanderthal home ranges was similar to that of *Homo erectus*, strongly differentiated by season with winter refuges in caves and a number of temporary camps of shelters occupied in a shifting pattern during all other seasons. Large animal bones are commonly found in Neanderthal sites, typically mammoth and woolly rhinoceros, reindeer and arctic fox. Hunting of such large game requires collaboration and communication, and the burial of the dead in pits within rock shelters does suggest that Neanderthal culture was strongly socialised. Their stone tools were similar to those of other archaic human forms, and included hand axes, spear blades and simple borers, but did not evolve further.[29]

As the expanding populations of modern humans moved into new territories, the Neanderthals were gradually displaced southwards towards Iberia. There is no evidence to suggest that they were cognitively inferior to anatomically modern humans, and they were certainly well adapted by morphology and culture to cool climate territories and ecological systems. The displacement of Neanderthals in western Europe by modern humans, whose slender morphology was more suited to tropical climates, suggests that the Neanderthals may ultimately have been disadvantaged by the very specificity of their morphology and cultural adaptation to cool climates. The social and material culture of modern humans was sufficiently general to enable them to survive greater climatic fluctuations in a much wider range of environments. Climatic oscillations were extreme during the time that Neanderthals and modern humans coexisted. By 60,000 years ago the ice sheets had retreated somewhat, although the global climate was still generally rather cooler than it is today. During the long interglacial phase that followed, there were numerous rapid oscillations between very cold dry periods and warm moist periods. The development of the cultural system accelerated, enhancing human adaptation to the environmental variability, and so modern human populations continued to expand. Neanderthal culture, like their biological form, had become rather more specific to cool habitats, so their populations were more constrained and did not expand. It may be that humans simply outbred the sparser populations of the widely dispersed Neanderthals.

By 50,000 years ago modern humans had reached as far east as the islands of South-East Asia, New Guinea, Australia and the Ryukyu Islands south of Japan. However, the very high northern latitudes of Asia were not reached until many thousands of years later. There were plant and animal species distributed across the Arctic and the high northern steppe habitats. Fossil evidence shows that the steppe biome supported a range of vegetation and fauna that varied in scale from ground squirrels to mammoths.[30] Human biological forms had none of the metabolic advantages of the mammals of these latitudes, and so occupation did not occur until the material culture had evolved sufficiently for them to regulate their collective metabolism in this climate.

As the great ice sheets began to advance again towards the middle latitudes, the climate metasystem cooled. As more and more water became locked up in the ice, sea levels fell, less rain fell and the deserts were greatly expanded. The progressive change extended over thousands of years, the ice reaching its maximum extent[31] about 20,000 years ago. The cool and arid climate had profound effects on all life. The northern forests died back, ice at least one kilometre deep covered much of northern Europe and most of Canada, and cool steppe, alpine grasslands or alpine desert conditions extended from central Europe eastwards and northwards in to Siberia. Human populations in central and northern Europe contracted, flowing to the west in to southern France and Spain, or to the east along the valleys of the major rivers in the great plains of eastern Europe. Both regions became densely populated, and the numerous archaeological finds suggest that where caves and rock shelters existed, they were occupied in winter seasons only, with temporary encampments used in the other seasons.

As the ice began to retreat again after the 'glacial maximum', humans expanded from the lower latitudes up into the high northern latitudes. Siberia has always been very cold, and even during the glacial retreat it was an extremely harsh environment, remaining unoccupied by humans until about 20,000 years ago. Sea level was then at least 100 metres lower than it is today, and Asia and the Americas were connected by a wide 'land bridge' known as Beringia. Small groups of modern humans migrated in several waves, from northern Siberia along the newly exposed continental shelf of Beringia. Analysis of mitochrondrial DNA shows that some of this population settled there and became the ancestors of the Eskimo-Aleut people, and that the later descendants of the early populations were the Amerinds, who eventually went on to occupy the whole of North and then South America.[32] The expansion of humans down through the Americas expanded from what was an initially quite small founding population in Alaska,[33] although the sequence and route is unknown. It has long been thought that the principal route was through an ice-free north-to-south corridor that had opened around 11,000 years ago in the great ice sheet that covered what is now Canada. However, archaeological and linguistic evidence, together with dated human skeletons, strongly suggests that human expansion into the Americas may have begun somewhat earlier, about 15,000 years ago along the western coasts of the Americas,[34] and that later movements of people followed the inland route.

THE ACCELERATION OF CULTURAL FORMS

The acceleration of culture associated with the emergence of anatomically modern humans includes bone awls and needles, from which can be inferred a development in the use of animal hides for tailored clothing. Sea shells pierced for use as personal ornaments and decorated pieces of red ochre have also been found in pit burials. The widespread use of beads and pendants made from shell, bone, animal teeth or stone across Asia, Europe and in Africa and the Levant is evidence that the communication between local groups was effectively a network capable of transmitting cultural information across very large distances.[35] In parallel studies in linguistics and genetics, population geneticist LL Cavalli-Sforza has revealed strong correlations between the geographical pattern of variations in languages and the human genome, and the effects of multiple dispersals. He estimates that spoken language is likely to have evolved close to present day complexity at least 100,000 years ago,[36] and that linguistic evolution had produced substantial variations into the major language families around 40,000 years ago.

The finding of sea shells hundreds of kilometres from coastlines indicates extensive contacts and trading networks between dispersed groups in well populated regions. Personal ornaments are visual displays that convey information to outsiders, indicating the membership of a specific group, and more personal information such as married status or adulthood. There are clear regional differences observed in bead types, and the differing combinations shared with one or more neighbouring groups confirms other evidence of the interaction between groups within larger populations. Similarly, painted images and figurative objects emerge sporadically in Africa, the Levant, Europe and Asia. Although there is good evidence for the episodic appearance of these cultural artefacts and practices before the emergence of modern humans, the sites are dispersed in time and geography, and it is clear that they did not become widespread until about 50,000 years ago.

The carving of figurative sculptures and the painting of rock images are part of the widespread practice of recording information and transmitting data over time. Notched or engraved bone artefacts have been found in Africa, Asia and in Europe, indicating that counting or tallying was part of this practice. The oldest mathematical artefact is thought to be the 'Lemombo' bone, a section of baboon fibula found in Swaziland and dated to 35,000 years ago. It has 29 clearly defined notches, approximating the lunar cycle, and strongly resembles the calendar sticks that are currently used by the Namibia Bushmen.[37] The carved figures, rock engravings, paintings and notched bones are the material archives of the cultural knowledge and values of anatomically modern humans. They enabled the transmission of structured information over time, extending and augmenting the transmission of knowledge through spoken language. Images of animal forms and hunting techniques have been found in multiple sites right across western Europe, and they display more than the commonly observed beauty and graphical skills. Analysis of images in hundreds of sites reveals that only five species are depicted, and these are the largest animals: mammoths, horses, reindeer, ibex and red deer. Analysis of the relative frequency of images and bone remains in each locality reveals a strong but disproportionate correlation. The bones of red deer and reindeer are the most commonly found, but these animals are less frequently depicted than the rarer and larger species. Larger animals have a higher metabolic and material value, yielding more meat and hides. When examined as a set, the disproportion in the frequency of depictions of each species and the frequency of kills suggests a systematic proportional representation. The frequency of animal images indicates the prevalence of the different species in a locality in relation to their relative energy value.[38]

The spread of human culture is likely to have occurred in two different modes, each operating at different temporal scales. Over long timescales culture was spread by 'Demic' or demographic diffusion, carried with the flow of modern humans out of Africa and across the Levant into Europe and Asia. When existing populations expanded their numbers beyond the metabolic capacity of their own territory, the movement of people into new territories was initiated. The flow of people was slow, operating at the timescales of generations, and each generation is likely to have moved only a few kilometres. Although some groups may indeed have made extremely long journeys, the more significant phenomenon of the waves of migrations and dispersals across the face of the earth is likely to have consisted of the accumulation of numerous short local journeys on land and by sea. Each expansion increased the ecological pressures on the populated areas that migrating populations moved into. In consequence, a further migration would soon be induced. As people moved, they carried with them their material culture. Over shorter timescales, culture 'diffused' by contact and exchange between neighbouring populations, and so was very rapid by comparison. Whenever there was geographical continuity between populations that extended across a region, the rapid diffusion of artefacts, materials and practices was effective over very long distances. If the dating of the 'diaspora' from the founding population is accurate at 60,000–70,000 years ago, then the expansion into South-East Asia proceeded at an average rate of approximately 320 metres per year or about 8 kilometres per generation.[39] This suggests that the majority of groups were always within a few days' travelling distance of each other, enabling the diffusion and exchange of cultural artefacts and practices between neighbours.

THE FORMS OF TEMPORARY AND PERMANENT SHELTERS

The first durable constructions, known as 'pit houses' or 'pit structures' have been found across all of Europe and Asia in mid to high latitudes.[40] They are coupled to a seasonally differentiated pattern of activities as they were occupied only during the winter cool or cold season. Pit houses enabled modern humans to regulate their collective metabolism in a great range of climates and so expand into the very cold territories of the high northern latitudes. The archaeological evidence of early pit structures is clearest in the plains of eastern Europe, where there are no caves. Many structures, of varying size and complexity, have been found on the elevated terraces along the banks of the river Don; and in the same region the remains of what are thought to be temporary or seasonal shelters, constructed from timber or bone frames with animal hide coverings, have also been found. The climate of this region was much colder 35,000 years ago than it is today, quite similar to modern day cold steppe environments found above 60° of latitude. At Kostenki, in what is now Ukraine, there are known to have been at least 50 settlements that had constructed permanent dwellings, and it is thought that this region was continuously occupied for thousands of years. The most common finds are the simplest constructions, circular dwellings of up to 6 metres diameter, with a central hearth. These were built over shallow pits excavated into the ground, with mammoth bone and timber frames driven into the earth and covered by animal skins and earth. In early forms the pits were not deep, and the roof probably extended substantially above the ground surface. The circular plan determined the conical form of the above-ground construction, as the simplest arrangement is inclined timber poles or mammoth bones crossing each other and bound together at the apex of the cone. In forms constructed with deeper excavations, the mammoth bones were cut horizontally, exposing the hollow marrow channel within the bone into which timber frames were inserted. Timber rots easily in damp ground, and using mammoth bones as 'sockets' indicates substantial building experience, and when taken together with exterior 'paving' of flat stones strongly suggests a clear ambition to build more permanent dwellings. The smaller 'pit houses' were sufficiently large to accommodate a single family, and being semi-subterranean had the advantage of the insulation offered by the earth, and some have been found with floors covered by sandstone slabs. There is also evidence to suggest that hearth fires were not only used for cooking but may have been used for heating the internal space. Excavating into the ground and the use of earth as a construction material provides good insulation and the hearths would have offered the potential for regulating the interior temperature. Pit dwellings had clear thermodynamic advantages, by smoothing out the external fluctuating temperatures they would have significantly reduced the load on the individual and group metabolic processes of modern humans in the winter months. Warm shelter and stored food reduced the need for extra calories, and consequently the frequency of hunting or foraging trips during winter. It is likely that they were strategically sited, with good access to resources distributed across the territory or home range of the group.

Larger buildings appear to be aggregations of several single dwellings into a linear series, typically 'three hearth' dwellings with an overall length of 12 metres. There were also even longer dwellings, up to 30 metres long and 8 metres wide,[41] with 8 or 10 hearths arranged on the long central axis and numerous small storage pits in the floor. These 'longhouses' were carefully positioned in relation to the topography, situated along the axis of inclination so that surface water from the snow melts would run along the exterior walls. These tended to be constructed as deeper excavations, and were most likely covered with flatter roofs. The enclosed spaces were sufficiently big to be occupied by a large number of people, and it is clear that a more complex social order had emerged with the development of the material form of the pit 'longhouses'. There were no internal walls to subdivide the interior, but the spacing of the hearths at 2 metre intervals does define a spatial order that would have facilitated occupation by several families at the same time. The overall number of dwellings suggests a stable population living within a defined territory, and socially organised for the necessary planning cooperation required for the gathering of materials, foraging and for construction. The large number of 'finds' within or close to the structures indicates that they were also the principal sites for the manufacture of tools, the cleaning of hides and bones, and for the finer manipulation of material for clothing and for bone artefacts. Carvings of animal forms are rare among the finds, but numerous small statues of the pregnant female form have been found at Kostenki, carved from bone or limestone. Some of the 'Venus' carvings also depict woven clothing, and are thought to confirm other evidence of the widespread use of textiles.[42]

The rarity of substantive archaeological evidence of pit structures in western Europe is widely thought to be because the principal winter residences were either rock shelters situated by river banks, or caves typically between 1 or 2 kilometres away from the rivers. The form of temporary structures occupied in warmer seasons is suggested by paintings and markings within caves and rock shelters throughout the region. Among the many paintings found are images depicting tent-like forms and structures[43] consisting of frames with some kind of covering. Archaeologists call these images 'tectiforms', meaning either roof or tent like. They are graphically rather different to the depictions of animals, being made with lines only, are often symmetrical and they indicate the geometry of construction rather than a pictorial image of the form. There are many variations, including some that appear to enclose large animals such as mammoths or bison, suggesting that these structures were strongly associated with hunting. It is likely that the frames were made from shaped and trimmed timber poles, and that the coverings were animal skins and perhaps grass thatch. The locations of temporary hunting camps are indicated by the large heaps of reindeer bones, many of which exhibit cuts and marks typical of butchering and filleting. These sites rarely have any remains of shelters or constructions, and this suggests that the meat and hides were parcelled and transported from temporary hunting camps to the settled sites with more permanent dwellings.

ECOLOGY AND THE SPATIAL PATTERNING OF TERRITORY

Pit structures have been found right across the world in cool and cold climates above the 32° latitude,[44] the only exceptions being in high mountainous regions of east Africa and South America. They are always associated with winter residence, and the use of temporary structures occupied in seasonal patterns of movement around a territory or home range. The dynamic pattern of movements emerged from the interaction of three sets of variables: the local ecology and climatic regime of the home range from which humans extracted food energy and materials; the population density; and the cultural techniques and technologies of the particular 'hunter-gatherer' group. It is estimated that the mean density of population in warm and fertile environments was less than three people per square kilometre, so that a small band of 50 individuals required a home range of up to 20 square kilometres.[45] In cool, dry and less fertile environments the density was much less, in the order of one individual for every 3 to 4 square kilometres, so that a group of the same size would have occupied a very large home range of up to 175 square kilometres.

LR Binford has argued that the pattern of movement emerged from the variable relationship between two distinct patterns of mobility, that he called 'residential' and 'logistical'.[46] Residential mobility is the movement of the whole group from one site to another, and logistical mobility is the movement of small groups from a residential site. The energy invested in the construction of pit structures such as those found at Kostenki indicates no residential mobility at all, winter occupation with substantial food storage, and high logistical movements with a number of temporary structures used in other seasons. Pit structures are never found in tropical regions, where the spatial patterning of home ranges was close to the high residential mobility of the ancestral great apes.

The temperature gradient from the equator to the poles is marked by a general decrease in the primary biomass, such as fruits, grains and roots. Along the same gradient, animals, including humans, require increasingly larger home ranges to feed themselves. In cold regions gathering will bring lower energy yields and the proportion of energy gained by hunting will increase. Hunting in colder climates required travelling longer distances or greater 'logistical' mobility, but the high energy content of large fauna offset the energy expended, and the bone, hide and tendons were an essential material resource. Daily foraging radii are estimated to have been between 6 to 10 kilometres[47] for larger bands, with occasional longer distances lasting several days for hunting of very large mammals.

The ecology was, in turn, modified by the activities of anatomically modern humans. The extinction of large mammals, the megafauna,[48] on all continents, including the very large woolly mammoths and mastodons, occurred across the world between 50,000 and 10,000 years ago, the time varying continent by continent in a pattern consistent with arrival and expansion of humans. Analysis of archaeological finds suggests that the megafauna were driven to extinction by human predation and the indirect ecological stress to their habitats induced by human occupation. Climate change may also have contributed an additional stress to the ecology in some regions, particularly the far northern latitudes of Eurasia. The hypothesis that humans were the sole cause is known as 'overkill', and there is some evidence to support this hypothesis in America and in Australia. In North America the extinction of almost every mammal larger than a human occurred during a period of mild warming, at the same time as humans expanded across the continent.[49] In Australia the extinctions were also concurrent with the arrival and expansion of humans, during a period of mild cooling. Large mammals are more susceptible to extinction than smaller mammals simply because of their body size. Animals are constrained in their population numbers by their metabolism and body mass, the time span of each generation and the reproduction cycle, and the size of the home range needed to support them. These are allometric relationships – the maximum population scales at a quarter power of the body mass, as does the generation length. Large mammals have slower metabolisms, relatively lower populations than small mammals and their reproduction cycle is much longer. Consistent and regular killing over many years can easily exceed the capacity of these populations to regenerate their numbers. The critical threshold of extinction of 1,000 kilogram mammals has been calculated to be less than 10 per cent each year, so that if hunters were successful in killing only 1 in every 10 megafauna each year, extinction inevitably follows. For 100 kilogram mammals, the critical threshold of extinction is over 25 per cent or one in every four animals each year, and for 10 kilogram mammals it is approximately 37.5 per cent or one in every three animals. The larger the body mass of mammals, the more susceptible they are to extinction.[50]

Herbivores, particularly those species with large body mass, have a significant impact on the physical structure of their range, modifying the dynamics and energy flow of the ecological system within which they live. The extinction of megafauna by 'overkill' acted as a positive feedback, accelerating changes in the patterns of vegetation in many regions. In Beringia, for example, the fertile grasslands and steppe changed to the much less productive moss and tundra.[51] In other regions where rainfall was decreasing, in parts of Africa and what is now California, the change from grasslands to arid scrublands was accelerated.

There is evidence, too, that it was not only forest ecologies that were modified by humans. Similar ecological modifications are thought to have occurred in 'intertidal' zones and their associated flora and fauna.[52] It is clear that the consumption of shellfish, and the use of spears and nets for fishing, had an impact on the regime of natural selection in coastal sites. The use of fire, for cooking, driving game and land clearance, would have had both direct and indirect effects on the ecology, at the scale of local landscapes. Fires used in forest areas killed the tree seedlings, and over time promoted the slow spread of grasslands, replacing the mature forest.[53] The impacts of the gathering of wild grains, nuts, fruit and tubers for food may be thought to have been temporary on local spatial scales, but these practices modified the regime of natural selection to the benefit of those plants and trees favoured by humans. Over thousands of years preferential selection had an impact on the genetic diversity of the ecology.[54] There is evidence that anatomically modern humans had an extensive knowledge of the ecology. At Ohalo in the Jordan Valley, recent excavations have shown that almonds, pistachios, olives and figs were included in the extensive range of foods gathered. The earliest human occupation at Ohalo is dated to 23,000 years ago,[55] and the finds of the remains of wild grains, mainly wheat and barley, indicates that small-grained grasses made up a substantial part of the diet of anatomically modern humans in the Levant. Starch recovered from stone artefacts suggests grinding to make the grains more digestible, and oven-like hearths suggest the baking of grain flour.[56] It is clear that, as the energetic 'returns' from hunting began to wane when the large mammal populations declined, there was a gradual shift in this region towards a diet with a high proportion of grains.

It follows that the gathering of these grains, and their subsequent dispersal and propagation, acted to modify natural selection in their favour. Over many thousands of years these plants came to be prominent in the ecology of the region, and very large 'stands' of wild grains and other human selected plants extended across the western end of the Mediterranean and south-west Eurasia. The genetic changes necessary for the subsequent domestication of wheat and barley were initiated at least 20,000 years ago. Similarly, the domestication of rice and millet in China, and of maize in Mesoamerica, also arises from genetic changes initiated by human behaviour.

EMERGENCE AND THE ANATOMICAL AND CULTURAL FORMS OF MODERN HUMANS

The extreme fluctuation of climate, and subsequent rapid variations in ecologies, established a regime of natural selection within which hominin evolved the capacity to vary their behaviour. 'Fitness' in this regime required a general flexibility of behaviour, an ability to adapt to a variety of climates and habitats. The slender and elongated body plan of all the *Homo* species was ideal for thermoregulation in the hot climate, and the evolutionary development of a larger brain was strongly coupled to the increasing complexity of culture, each acting as a positive feedback to accelerate the development of the other. The evolutionary development of culture included the geometrical shaping and use of stone tools, a more complex metabolic, spatial and social organisation operating over extended home ranges, the shared construction and inhabitation of temporary shelters, and the first migrations and dispersals out of Africa. The diaspora from Africa into Asia and then into Europe was episodic, consisting of several waves that extended over more than a million years. By 500,000 years ago, the *Homo* species were widely spread, and their culture had evolved to include more complex 'bifaced' stone tools with a symmetrical morphology and variations in size for application as hand axes, knives and spear points. The continual expansion and flow of *Homo* across Asia and into Europe was driven by increases in local population density, climatic variations that constrained the local availability of food resources, and the increased requirements for energy that the evolution of larger brains required. About 400,000 years ago two descendant species emerged, *Homo neanderthalensis* and the early form of *Homo sapiens*. Morphological changes included a further increase in brain size, enabling finer neurological control over all physical activities, including speech, tool making and the use of tools for material constructions. The coupled cultural evolution included the control of fire, the development of cooking and a further development in the transmission of material knowledge and social organisation.

Anatomically modern humans, *Homo sapiens sapiens* emerged as a small population of a few thousand in east Africa some 135,000 years ago. All humans alive today are descendants of that founding population, possibly from one woman within that population, the 'Mitochondrial Eve'. They rapidly spread across the entire African continent. The diaspora of anatomically modern humans 'out of Africa' began between 60,000 to 70,000 years ago, into the Levant, and on into Asia and Europe. As humans dispersed into new climatic and ecological zones, adaptive cultural variations were produced. Spoken language had evolved close to present day complexity by 100,000 years ago, and the multiple dispersals produced substantial regional diversifications into the major language families by 40,000 years ago. Other regional variations emerged in culture, in tailored clothing, in personal ornaments and in pit burials. Communication between local groups intensified to become a network capable of transmitting cultural information across very large distances. Spoken language was extended and augmented by carved figures, rock paintings and notched bones. These material archives of the cultural knowledge and values of anatomically modern humans enabled the transmission of structured information over time. The evolution of modern humans from the ancestral family of great apes was coupled to a material culture that enhanced their metabolism, increased their ability to extract energy from their environment, and extended the range of territories and climates in which they could flourish. Human culture spread and diversified by 'Demic' or demographic diffusion, the slow flow of people operating at the timescales of generations. Over much shorter timescales culture 'diffused' by contact and exchange between neighbouring populations.

The evolution of the spatial patterning of territory retained one aspect of the seasonally and ecologically determined pattern of movement of the ancestral apes, but evolved to include a strategically located winter residence along with the use of tents and temporary structures occupied in seasonal patterns of movement around the home range. Excavated dwellings, or 'pit houses', were arranged in clusters, and included 'longhouses' for the communal occupation by several families at the same time. The overall number of dwellings suggests a stable population living within a defined territory, and socially organised for the gathering of materials, foraging and for construction. The large number of 'finds' within or close to these structures indicates that they were also the principal sites for the manufacture of artefacts. Pit dwellings enabled modern humans to regulate their collective metabolism in a great range of climates, and to expand into the very cold territories of the high northern latitudes. Excavating dwellings in the ground significantly reduced the metabolic load in the winter months, as warm shelter and stored food reduced the need for extra calories. Adaptation to differing regional climates, topographies and ecologies emerged through variation in the timing and frequency of movements and residency, and morphological variations in the depth and size of the excavation and construction. In general terms, the ratio of 'residential' moves to 'logistical' moves varied according to latitude, as the temperature gradient from the equator to the poles is marked by a general decrease in the primary biomass, and increasingly larger home ranges for all species. For example, in cold regions 'gathering' yields lower returns, and the proportion of energy gained by hunting will increase. The extra energy expended in greater 'logistical' mobility, and in the deeper excavations, was offset by the high energy content and materials derived from killing of the large fauna. In very warm and fertile tropical environments all movements were 'residential', with no excavated dwellings. The variability of dwelling morphology and mobility strategies enabled anatomically modern humans to occupy and flourish in all the continents and islands of the earth.

The assembly of the cultural system, sometimes referred to as 'behavioural modernity' by archaeologists and anthropologists, was episodic and distributed in geography and over many hundred thousand years. Cultural evolution accelerated rapidly during the evolution of anatomically modern humans, and is clearly coupled to the diaspora and expansion of humans across the world.[57] It had reached a critical threshold of complexity more than 35,000 years ago, when long-term settlements, complex language, calendars and the material archiving of social and ecological information emerged. Across the world, the total population of modern humans increased, but the increase in numbers was episodic, with rapid local population growth punctuated by less frequent local declines and crashes.[58] Anatomically modern humans began to have an impact on local ecologies at about the same time, suggesting that the accelerated culture propelled the 'niche construction' of humans to a new phase. The extinction of the megafauna and the use of fire to drive game and clear land accelerated the change in patterns of vegetation in steppe grasslands, in cool forests and in warmer grassland ecologies. As the large mammal populations were progressively reduced by human predation, the energetic returns from hunting lessened. It became necessary to increase the proportion of 'gathering', so that a high proportion of grains was included in the diet. The gathering of grains, and their subsequent dispersal and propagation, initiated the genetic changes that over many thousands of years led to the domestication of wild cereals.

The founding system of civilisation exhibited some of the characteristics of self-organisation that are found in biological systems, in that it was comprised of a very large number of components and local assemblies without the information processing and regulatory instructions of centralised control. Communication was effective over large distances, and over time, and the extended metabolism acted as a positive feedback for the propagation of wild cereals in three continents. The relation of the spatial pattern of its externalised metabolic processes to its fixed and mobile material constructions was varied locally across quite different climatic and ecological regions. The system was distributed across the surface of the earth, and in all localities tended to evolve to the point of critical stability, maximising the energy extracted from the environment and the population numbers. It had a high number of local and fewer regional connections and interactions, but these were not effective between continents. As a global phenomenon it can be described topologically as an array of small world networks that did not interact with each other.

The founding system of civilisation persisted for tens of thousands of years in many parts of the world, with multiple local and regional advances and retreats, with long periods of growth and some rapid declines. For example, in the Americas it flourished until the expanding wave of Europeans, with a system of higher complexity, arrived less than 700 years ago. The interaction of changes in the climate and the consequent ecological changes, with the high and increasing density of population and with the general depletion of easily gained energy from fauna led to a progressive collapse of the founding system in five ecologically distinct and geographically separated regions. This initiated the evolution of new variations, and the development of more complex cultural and metabolic systems, with distinct social orders, material technologies and evolving spatial patterning of territories. Cities and nomadic systems emerged from the founding system of civilisation, so that for many thousands of years the three systems existed at the same time in different regions of the world.

1 McGlade, J, 'Archaeology and the Ecodynamics of Human-Modified Landscapes', *Antiquity*, vol 69, 1995, pp 113–32.

2 Laland, KN, FJ Odling-Smee and MW Feldman, 'The Evolutionary Consequences of Niche Construction: a theoretical investigation using two-locus theory', *Journal of Evolutionary Biology,* vol 9, 1996, pp 293–316; and Laland, KN, FJ Odling-Smee and MW Feldman, 'Niche Construction, Biological Evolution and Cultural Change', *Behavioral and Brain Sciences*, vol 23 no 1, Cambridge University Press (Cambridge), 1999.

3 The word 'hominin' is widely used as a general term for any of the variant species of primates with an upright posture and bipedal walking, dating from the first evolutionary divergence from the great apes to the emergence of the genus *Homo*. Anatomically modern humans, *Homo sapiens sapiens*, are the sole surviving species of *Homo*. Hominin is the modern variant of the word 'hominid'.

4 The 40 per cent complete skeleton hominin fossil AL 288-1, named Lucy after the Beatles song 'Lucy in the Sky with Diamonds'.

5 This group is known as 'the first family'.

6 Fossils are rocks, formed by the slow infiltration of dead organic material by minerals. This occurs when the original form has been protected in some way, for example by being rapidly buried in silt for an extended time. Usually only the hard parts, skeletal bones or shells are fossilised. There are only a very few exceptions where soft tissue has been preserved, such as mammoths in the northern tundras.

7 Sabater Pi, J, JJ Vea and J Serrallonga, 'Did the First Hominids Build Nests?', *Current Anthropology*, vol 38, no 5, December 1997, pp 914–16.

8 Vrba, ES, 'Environment and Evolution: alternative causes of the temporal distribution of evolutionary events', *South African Journal of Science*, vol 81, 1985, pp 229–36; and Vrba, ES, 'Late Pliocene Climatic Events and Hominid Evolution', in (ed) FE Grine, *Evolutionary History of the "Robust" Australopithecines*, Aldine de Gruyter (New York), 1988, pp 383–403.

9 Potts, R, 'Evolution and Climate Variability', *Science*, vol 273, 1996, pp 922–3; and Potts, R, 'Environmental Hypotheses of Hominin Evolution', *Yearbook of Physical Anthropology*, vol 41, 1998, pp 93–136; and Potts, R, 'Variability Selection in Hominid Evolution', *Evolutionary Anthropology,* vol 7, 1998, pp 81–96.

10 Ruff, CB, 'Climatic Adaptation and Hominid Evolution: the thermoregulatory imperative',

Evolutionary Anthropology, vol 2, 1993, pp 53–60.

11 Aiello, LC, 'Brains and Guts in Human Evolution: the expensive tissue hypothesis', *Brazilian Journal of Genetics*, vol 20, 1997, pp 141–8; and Aiello, LC and P Wheeler, 'The Expensive Tissue Hypothesis: the brain and the digestive system in human and primate evolution', *Current Anthropology*, vol 36, 1995, pp 199–221.

12 Tobias, PV and B Campbell, 'The Emergence of Man in Africa and Beyond [and Discussion]', *Philosophical Transactions of the Royal Society of London B*, vol 292, 1981, pp 43–56; and Kay, RF, M Cartmill and M Balow, 'The Hypoglossal Canal and the Origin of Human Vocal Behavior', *Proceedings of the National Academy of Sciences* , vol 95, 1988, pp 5417–19.

13 Tyack, PL, 'Dolphins Whistle a Signature Tune', *Science*, vol 289, 2000, pp 1310–11.

14 Fitch, WT, 'The Evolution of Speech: a comparative review', *Trends in Cognitive Science*, vol 4, 2000, pp 258–67.

15 Pagel, M and W Bodmer, 'A Naked Ape Would Have Fewer Parasites', *Proceedings of The Royal Society of London*, vol 270, Letters, August 2003, pp 117–19.

16 Kushlan, JA, 'The Evolution of Hairlessness in Man', *The American Naturalist*, vol 116, November 1980, pp 727–9.

17 Lahr, MM and Foley, R, 'Multiple Dispersals and Modern Human Origins', *Evolutionary Anthropology*, vol 3, 1994, pp 48–60.

18 Bar-Josef, O and A Belfer-Chen, 'From Africa to Eurasia – Early Dispersals', *Quaternary International*, vol 75, 2001, pp 19–28.

19 Milankovitch theorised that the variations of the earth's movements relative to the sun were the cause of the ice ages – see Chapter 2; and Milankovitch, M, *Théorie mathématique des phénomènes thermiques produits par la radiation solaire*, Gauthier-Villars (Paris), 1920; and *Mathematische Klimalehre und Astronomische Theorie der Klimaschwankungen, Handbuch der Klimalogie Band 1*. Teil A, Bornträger (Berlin), 1930; and *Kanon der Erdbestrahlung und seine Anwendung auf das Eiszeitenproblem*, published in English as *Canon of Insolation of the Earth and Its Application to the Problem of the Ice Ages* in 1969 by US Department of Commerce and the National Science Foundation.

20 From 1.8 million years before the present to 10,000 years before the present.

21 Lumley, H De, 'A Palaeolithic Camp Site at Nice', *Scientific American*, vol 220, 1969, pp 42–50.

22 The taxonomy of anatomically modern humans is still debated and may include archaic and modern variants. The earliest form is generally described as *Homo sapiens* and the modern form is generally known as *Homo sapiens sapiens*.

23 Zilhao, J, 'The Emergence of Ornaments and Art: an archaeological perspective on the origins of "behavioral modernity"', *Journal of Archaeological Research*, vol 15, 2007, pp 1–54.

24 Lieberman, DE, BM McBratney and G Krovitz, 'The Evolution and Development of Cranial Form in Homo Sapiens', *Proceedings of the National Academy of Sciences*, vol 99, February 2002, pp 1134–9.

25 Forster, P, 'Ice Ages and the Mitochondrial DNA Chronology of Human Dispersals: a review', *Philosophical Transactions of the Royal Society of London B*, vol 359, 2004, pp 255–64.

26 An earlier migration, evidenced by the fossil finds in the Levant, dated to 100,000 years ago, has not left any descendants in the DNA of contemporary Asians or Europeans – see Forster, P, above.

27 Stringer, C, 'Modern Human Origins – Distinguishing the Models', *African Archaeology Review*, vol 18, 2001, pp 67–75.

28 Liu, H, F Prugnolle, A Manica and F Balloux, 'A Geographically Explicit Genetic Model of Worldwide Human-Settlement History', *American Journal of Human Genetics*, vol 79, 2006, pp 230–7.

29 Pettitt, PB, 'Neanderthal Lifecycles: developmental and social phases in the lives of the last archaics', *World Archaeology*, vol 31, February 2000, pp 351–66.

30 Zazula, GD, DG Froese, SA Elias, S Kuzmina and RW Mathewes, 'Arctic Ground Squirrels of the Mammoth-Steppe: paleoecology of Late Pleistocene middens (24 000–29 450 14C yr BP), Yukon

Territory, Canada', *Quaternary Science Reviews*, vol 26, April 2007, pp 979–1003.

31 Known as the Last Glacial Maximum.

32 Forster, P, 'Ice Ages and the Mitochondrial DNA Chronology of Human Dispersals: a review', *Philosophical Transactions of the Royal Society of London B*, vol 359, 2004, pp 255–64.

33 Goebel, T, MR Waters and DH O'Rourke, 'The Late Pleistocene Dispersal of Modern Humans in the Americas', *Science*, vol 319, March 2008, pp 1497–502.

34 Dixon, EJ, 'Human Colonization of the Americas: timing, technology and process', *Quaternary Science Reviews*, vol 20, 2001, pp 277–99.

35 Kuhn, SL, MC Stiner, DS Reese and E Gulec, 'Ornaments of the Earliest Upper Paleolithic: new insights from the Levant', *Proceedings of the National Academy of Sciences*, vol 98, June 2001, pp 7641–6.

36 Cavalli-Sforza, LL, P Menozzi and A Piazza, 'Demic Expansions and Human Evolution', *Science,* vol 259, January 1993, pp 639–46; and Cavalli-Sforza, LL, *Genes, People and Languages*, North Point Press (New York), 2000.

37 Bogoshi, J, K Naidoo and J Webb, 'The Oldest Mathematical Artefact', *The Mathematical Gazette*, vol 71, December 1987, p 294.

38 Rice, PC, AL Paterson, 'Cave Art and Bones: exploring the interrelationships', *American Anthropologist,* vol 87, March 1985, pp 94–100; and Rice, PC and AL Paterson, 'Validating the Cave Art-Archaeofaunal Relationship in Cantabrian Spain', *American Anthropologist,* vol 88, September 1986, pp 658–67.

39 Approximately 8,000 kilometres in distance, over a duration of 30,000 years. A generation is taken to be 25 years in this context. Mandryk, CAS, H Josenhans, DW Fedje and RW Mathewes, 'Late Quaternary Paleoenvironments of Northwestern North America: implications for inland versus coastal migration routes', *Quaternary Science Reviews,* vol 20, 2001, pp 301–14.

40 Daifuku, H, 'The Pit House in the Old World and in Native North America', *American Antiquity,* vol 18, July 1952, pp 1–7.

41 Grigor'ev, GP, 'A New Reconstruction of the Above-Ground Dwelling of Kostenki', *Current Anthropology,* vol 8, 1967, pp 344–9.

42 Soffer, O, JM Adovasio and DC Hyland, 'The "Venus" Figurines: textiles, basketry, gender, and status in the Upper Paleolithic', *Current Anthropology*, vol 41, August 2000, pp 511–37.

43 Lacaille, AD, 'The Magdalenian Tectiform of La Mouthe and its Modern Counterpart', *Man,* vol 54, July 1954, pp 108–9.

44. Gilman, PA, 'Architecture as Artifact: pit structures and pueblos in the American Southwest', *American Antiquity,* vol 52, July 1987, pp 538–64.

45 Marlowe, FW, 'Hunter-Gatherers and Human Evolution', *Evolutionary Anthropology,* vol 2005, pp 54–67.

46 Binford, LR, 'Willow Smoke and Dogs' Tails: hunter-gatherer settlement systems and archaeological site formation', *American Antiquity,* vol 45, January 1980, pp 4–20.

47 Morgan, C, 'Reconstructing Prehistoric Hunter-Gatherer Foraging Radii: a case study from California's southern Sierra Nevada', *Journal of Archaeological Science*, vol 35, no 2, 2008, pp 247–58.

48 Animals weighing more than 44 kilograms are generally referred to as 'megafauna' – but the mammoths and mastodons weighed over 1,000 kilograms.

49 Haynes, G, 'The Catastrophic Extinction of North American Mammoths and Mastodonts' in 'Ancient Ecodisasters', *World Archaeology,* vol 33, 2002, pp 391–416.

50 Brook, BW and MJS Bowan, 'One Equation Fits Overkill: why allometry underpins both prehistoric and modern body size-biased extinctions', *Population Ecology,* vol 47, 2005, pp 137–41.

51 Zimov, SA, VI Chuprynin, AP Oreshko, FS Chapin III, JF Reynolds and MC Chapin, 'Steppe-Tundra Transition: a herbivore-driven biome shift at the end of the Pleistocene', *American Naturalist*, vol 145, no 5, 1995, pp 765–94.

52 Mannino, MA and KD Thomas, 'Depletion of a Resource? The impact of prehistoric human

foraging on intertidal mollusc communities and its significance for human settlement, mobility and dispersal', *World Archaeology*, vol 33, no 3, 2002, pp 452–74.

53 Hope, G, 'Early Fire and Forest Change in the Baliem Valley, Irian Jaya, Indonesia', *Journal of Biogeography,* vol 25, 1998, pp 453–61.

54 Ledig, FT, 'Human Impacts on Genetic Diversity in Forest Ecosystems', *Oikos*, vol 63,1992, pp 87–108.

55 Nadel D, 'A Long Continuity: the Ohalo II brush huts (19.5 ky) and the dwelling structures in the Natufian and PPNA sites in the Jordan Valley', *Archaeology, Anthropology and Ethnology in Euroasia,* vol 13, no 1, 2003, pp 34–48; and Nadel D, U Grinberg, E Boaretto, E Werker, 'Wooden Objects from Ohalo II (23,000 cal BP), Jordan Valley, Israel', *Journal of Human Evolution*, vol 50, no 6, 2006, pp 644–62.

56 Piperno, DR, E Weiss, I Holst and D Nadel, 'Processing of Wild Cereal Grains in the Upper Palaeolithic Revealed by Starch Grain Analysis', Letters, *Nature,* vol 430, August 2004; and Weiss, E, W Wetterstrom, D Nadel and O Bar-Yosef, 'The Broad Spectrum Revisited: evidence from plant remains', *Proceedings of the National Academy of Sciences*, vol 101, no 26, USA, June 2004, pp 9551–5.

57 Lahr, M and R Foley, 'Towards a Theory of Modern Human Origins: geography, demography, and diversity in recent human evolution', *Yearbook of Physical Anthropology,* vol 41, 1998, pp 137–76; and McBrearty, S and A Brooks, 'The Revolution that Wasn't: a new interpretation of the origin of modern human behavior', *Journal of Human Evolution,* vol 39, 2000, pp 453–563.

58 Boone, JL, 'Subsistence Strategies and Early Human Population History: an evolutionary ecological perspective', *World Archaeology,* vol 34, *Archaeology and Evolutionary Ecology*, June 2002, pp 6–25.

1--one cell

2--two cells

3--three cells

4--four cells

5--five cells

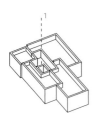 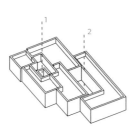 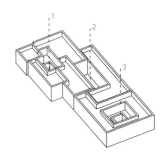

6--one courtyard house

7--two courtyard house

8--three courtyard house

 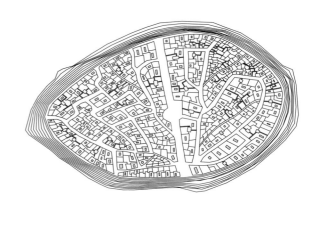

9--urban courtyards

10--City as a field of courtyards   (Irbil)

THE ARCHITECTURE OF EMERGENCE

City Forms

7

Cities simultaneously emerged from the collapse and reorganisation of the founding system of civilisation, in five geographically separated and ecologically stressed regions across the world. The evolutionary development of city forms and their extended metabolic systems was strongly coupled to multiple changes of the climate and ecological system within which they were situated, and to the rise in the flow of energy from intense cultivation, increased social complexity and to the evolution of information systems. The proliferation of cities, systems of cities and their extended metabolic systems across the world was characterised by episodic and irregular expansions and incorporations, collapse and subsequent reorganisation in more complex forms with greater flows of energy, information and material. The extensive modification of ecological systems at a variety of spatial and temporal scales is still evident in the arid and denuded landscapes that persist today.

Human forms and culture evolved over a period of extreme fluctuations in the climate, and consequent rapid variations in ecologies; a regime of natural selection that conserved and enhanced the ability to adapt their culture to a variety of climates and ecological conditions. The development of the elongated body plan and the large brain was strongly coupled to the increasing complexity of human culture, each acting as a positive feedback to accelerate the development of the other. Culture acts to transmit complex social and ecologically contextualised information down through the generations, and has tended to increase in complexity over time, a process that began over 130,000 years ago in east Africa with the emergence of anatomically modern humans, the diaspora 'out of Africa' and the spread of humans across the world.[1] By 35,000 years ago long-term settlements, complex spoken language, calendars and the material archiving of ecological information had emerged.[2]

7.1 Mesopotamia
The evolutionary development and elaboration of the courtyard, from the simple space between dwellings in the first settlements to its incorporation within spatially complex buildings of varying sizes and functions, occurred throughout the region. Courtyards also emerged within the dense pattern of dwellings, coevolving with social orders and values as urban spaces for collective functions. Walled cities emerged with populations of up to 10,000 people, within large arrays of extensively linked settlements of different sizes. Open space within the inner walled enclosure was organised as a series of courtyards, surrounded by tightly packed configurations of dwellings and narrow streets, often just wide enough for a pack animal, limiting the exposure of pedestrians to the sun, and restricting views.

Humans began to modify their local ecological systems about the same time, as the extinction of the megafauna and the use of fire to drive game and clear land produced changes in patterns of vegetation in steppe grasslands, in cool forests and in warmer grasslands. As the energetic returns from hunting were reduced, the increase in the gathering of grains initiated the genetic changes that over many thousands of years led to the domestication of wild cereals.

Excavated dwellings, or 'pit houses', provided humans with a fixed residential location for the winter months and enabled them to regulate their collective metabolism in a great range of climates, and to expand into the very cold territories of the high northern latitudes. In the other seasons, tents and temporary structures were occupied in ecologically determined patterns of movements around the home range. Pit dwellings were arranged in clusters and included 'longhouses' for communal occupation by several families at the same time. Adaptations to differing regional climates, topographies and ecologies emerged from variations in the patterns of movements around the territory, and in the depth and size of the excavation and construction.

The founding system of civilisation continued to develop local and regional variations over tens of thousands of years, with long periods of population growth and local episodes of rapid declines. In many locations it had developed to its maximum metabolic capacity, and had become highly vulnerable to climatic and ecological changes. The collapse of the founding system in five ecologically distinct and geographically separated regions led to the emergence of linked hierarchical patterns of settlements. As the flow of materials, energy and information intensified through the integrated arrays of settlements, populations expanded and social and cultural complexity increased. Cities emerged through a process of nucleation, condensing into nuclei within the extended 'metabolic' networks of the linked settlements.

Although the glaciers began to retreat at the end of the last 'glacial maximum' between 21,000 and 18,000 years ago, the dry cold climate persisted. Forest biomes were reduced in extent as the cold arid climate inhibited the growth of trees, and open steppe, tundra and savannah grasslands expanded. Forests and woodlands existed close to the equator, but the tropical rainforests in Africa and South America were reduced in area. In Europe, only a few isolated pockets had forest cover, while northern Europe and Canada were entirely covered by ice that was several kilometres thick. Most of northern Asia and Siberia were so dry that ice sheets could not form, although the ground was deeply frozen.[3] Sea level was about 100 metres lower than today, so that the shorelines were very different. Low land bridges were exposed between Siberia and Alaska, and between Europe and Britain. Many species, including humans, used these land bridges to expand into new territories.

The change from the glacial to the current 'interglacial' climatic period was marked by a number of episodes of rapid warming interrupted by short but intense cool arid periods. The most extreme climate variability occurred between 11,000 and 10,000 years ago[4] with large temperature fluctuations, but over those one thousand years, the overall trend was a rise in temperature across the globe. The cyclical changes in the orbit of the earth, the Milankovitch cycle, produced the maximum warming effect in the Northern Hemisphere 9,000 years ago.[5] As more summer sunlight fell on the Northern Hemisphere, the increase in energy received amplified the summer monsoon belt. However, the differential feedbacks from the ocean and atmospheric circulations, and from the ice fields and vegetation, produced regional variations in the absorption and distribution of heat over the following several thousand years. In this period,[6] substantially increased rainfall was accompanied by a more pronounced seasonality, with high summer temperatures. The temperatures are calculated to have been about 2°C higher than today, with larger increases in the high latitudes. Climatic changes in the mid latitudes were linked to changes in the 'inter-tropical convergence' zone, driven by the additional heat energy falling on the earth. This is the area from which warm, moist air rises up into the Hadley atmospheric cells, and it is evident that it had shifted substantially further to the north. Additional changes in the pattern of oceanic circulation are also implicated in changes to rainfall and monsoon cycles around the world, with complex outcomes. The strengthening of the African monsoon rain resulted in lakes and ponds in the Sahara, and further east, in a higher volume of water in the river Nile. Increases in rainfall also occurred across the Levant and south-west Asia.

The changes in the climate produced substantial ecological changes. Many species of animals and plants shifted their ranges, producing further ecological changes across the world. The rapid warming changed the ecology of the mid latitude tundra to deciduous woodlands, and the tundra populations of large herbivores such as reindeer and horse responded to the change by shifting their range further north. The red deer and boar that populated the expanding forests were more difficult to hunt than the large mammals of the tundra, but the forest biome was highly productive in fruits, nuts and tubers. The latitudinal band of arid deserts in the Northern Hemisphere began to experience substantially increased rainfall. The Sahara, for example, became savannah grassland with numerous lakes and a flourishing biome that supported large populations of fauna and of humans.[7] Savannah grasslands expanded in the mid to lower latitudes. In North America the expansion of the great prairie grasslands created a new ecological niche for the bison, and their populations increased significantly. The differences between the seasons became more marked, with very hot dry summers and warm wet winters. In south-west Asia and the Levant very large stands of wild cereals appeared, their dispersal and propagation accelerated by human 'selection' over more than tens of thousands of years. Sea levels rose, flooding coastlines and changing coastal ecologies and river systems were changed too as their base level was raised.

VARIATIONS OF THE FOUNDING SYSTEM

Climatic and ecological changes induced change and an increase in complexity of the founding cultural system. Additional stresses were created by the continuous increase in numbers and the consequential greater extraction of food and material energy from their surroundings. In all regions the extinctions of the 'megafauna' and other large mammals by human predation, coupled to the change from open tundra to forests with more widely distributed and less easily hunted fauna, resulted in a substantial decrease in energetic returns available from hunting. Animal skins, sinews and large bones became increasingly harder to come by, and their use in built structures and for tools lessened. However, 'gathering' in the highly productive forest and woodland biomes of southern Europe yielded substantially increased energetic returns, and in consequence the need for large territories was reduced. The total population rapidly increased. The material products of mammals began to be replaced with forest products; timber became more extensively used in the construction of shelters, along with woven grass mats and basketry.

The evolution of the longhouse, from excavated pit structure to freestanding timber buildings, was an adaptive variation arising from the climatic and ecological changes. There is no clear evidence of a single regional origin, or indeed when they may have originated, but they evolved in the climatic latitudinal band between the hot arid climates to the south and the very cold regions of the far north of Asia, where excavated pit structures persisted. By 7,000 years ago longhouses were common right across Europe and Asia, and there is evidence of very similar structures as far east as Melanesia.[8] The above-ground longhouses were narrower at one end than the other, and the roof was lower at the narrow end of the building. They were commonly 20 to 30 metres long and 5 to 8 metres wide, although some have been found as large as 40 metres in length. Settlements had six to 10 longhouses arranged in close proximity, suggesting that the population of settlements varied from 150 to more than 300 people. Earthworks for defensive perimeters were also quite common, some of them substantial.

The structure of longhouses consisted of substantial timber posts, set onto a sill or ground beam in excavated trench foundations. Walls and the pitched roofs were made from woven mats and plastered with earth. Analysis suggests that the roof members had a constant pitch, so that the wall height varied along the longitudinal axis. Axially pitched and tapering longhouses were usually aligned with the narrow end facing to the north-west, and it has been argued that the alignment of the narrow end was towards the prevailing winter winds and rain. The close concentration of timbers and stronger foundations frequently found at the narrow weatherly end, and the entrances found at the broader more sheltered end, are suggestive that alignment was thermodynamically beneficial.[9] In the more sparsely populated northern latitudes of Europe, the communities were usually smaller, and above-ground longhouses were simpler, usually constructed of undressed stones packed with earth, and with some internal timber supports. A variation in the pattern of mobility is associated with the development of the longhouses, which were often occupied for five to 10 years before the plant and animal resources of the local territory were exhausted. The longhouse and the territory were then abandoned, and the whole group moved to a new location.

In the savannah grasslands of the Sahara the founding system adapted to include much more extensive 'gathering' of wild cereals,[10] and archaeological evidence also suggests that humans had begun to enclose wild cattle in caves in the mountains during the winter seasons. The summer pattern of 'logistical' movements down to the lowlands for small game hunting and wild cereal gathering became modified to include the capture of wild cattle. The nomadic 'cattle-cultures' that eventually spread throughout Africa may have originated in the Sahara.[11] In the Levant and south-west Asia, the ecological outcome of increased rainfall and marked seasonality was an extensive open savannah with extensive stands of wild cereals, and large belts of oak and pistachio woodlands. This region had long been densely occupied for tens of thousands of years because it lay on the principal route of the diaspora 'out of Africa'.

The transition from 'low residential mobility' to fixed residential with high logistical mobility was established across the region by 12,000 years ago. At that time the dwellings were semi-subterranean, and were oval in plan, or rectangular with rounded corners. They were constructed over shallow excavations with foundations and low walls of undressed stone, while the upper structure and roofs were likely to have been made of light timbers and woven grass materials. Individual buildings varied between 3 and 6 metres in diameter and were usually sited in woodland areas, with some sites extending up to 1,000 square metres, although 500 square metre settlements were more common. Dwellings were arranged either linearly, creating streets and terraces, or in tight clusters, and there is archaeological evidence that in some settlements they were permanent fixed residences for large groups. The levelling of ground for construction, paving, and the use of plaster to line interior walls suggest significant investments of energy.[12]

It is thought that systematic cultivation of cereals, together with husbandry of semi-domesticated herds of sheep and goats, emerged in Levant and south-west Asia about 10,000 years ago, at the same time as the climate began to warm and become wetter. The archaeological evidence of intensive 'gathering' of cereals at Ohalo is dated to 23,000 years ago;[13] indicating a long and gradual evolution from the intensive 'gathering' of pre-domesticated wild cereals to the systematic planting and cultivation of their descendant species. The transition from storage holes in the floors of pit dwellings to specialised buildings and lined silos occurs over the same period.

The settlement at Beidha, to the north of Petra, was situated close the highlands of Jordan. The alluvial valleys there were grasslands 10,000 years ago, with woodland stands on the upper slopes. The sequence of construction and morphological changes reveals the evolution of settlements at that time. The early spatial organisation of the settlement consisted of small clusters of simple semi-subterranean buildings that had no internal differentiation, and a large open space or informal courtyard in the centre of the settlement. Differentiation in size emerged, as much larger and more spatially elaborate buildings were constructed opening onto the older courtyard, and individual freestanding buildings were built, one by one, over the ruins of simpler earlier dwellings. Other smaller courtyards were incorporated into the later buildings. The final enclosure of the central courtyard by a large building also defined a single point of entry. The increase in the diversity of building sizes, and the food storage chambers in the restricted central courtyard suggest an increase in social complexity.[14]

By 8,000 years ago there were village settlements right across this region, some with as many as 100 individual buildings, suggesting 500 or more inhabitants. A settlement of this size would require approximately 300 hectares of cultivated land to supply its population with grains through the year, with some surplus for storage.[15] The sites of larger settlements were in areas closer to wild cereal stands and rivers, and so more suited to cultivation than the woodland sites that were more favourable for hunting and foraging for nuts, fruits and tubers. The older and smaller sites were abandoned. Archaeological finds suggest that these large villages were almost wholly reliant on cultivated plants and domesticated animals. Groups with high residential movements also existed in the same region at the same time, and it is likely that trade in materials, goods and animals existed between them. Individual dwellings evolved to a more complex spatial organisation, with interior chambers connected to open courtyards that were either incorporated within a single dwelling or shared between several buildings.[16] Interior spaces and courtyards had plastered surfaces that were as dense as concrete, a process that requires controlled burning of the limestone at temperatures of 750 to 850°C. Walls were constructed of sun-dried brick on foundations of stone, and where they opened onto courtyards they had multiple openings. Storage for grains, either as discrete buildings or as silos built into the walls of interior chambers, were also lined with plaster. The development of the courtyard offered significant thermodynamic advantages in the hot climate for buildings in this region. The evolution of the courtyard, from a barely defined open space at the centre of clustered dwellings to an enclosed and regulated central space was coeval with linear streets and their subsequent evolution into linked networks that constrained and organised the movement of people.

COLLAPSE AND REORGANISATION

There has been a long held assumption that a benign 'interglacial' climatic regime was initiated 10,000 years ago and has persisted unchanged until today. That assumption was usually accompanied by the belief that it was the benign climate that enabled humans to 'invent' agriculture, cities and 'complex societies'. It is clear, however, that there have been many episodes of extreme variability in the climate, and that the effects have been far from benign. There is now a substantial accumulation of paleoclimatic evidence, from ice cores, tree rings, corals and sedimentary deposits in lakes and oceans, demonstrating that the Holocene has been far from a gentle and benign climatic regime. Many episodes of abrupt change to a cooler and drier climate have occurred in the last 11,000 years, most with a very rapid onset of less than a decade.

The consequence of severe drought and lower temperatures, varying in duration from three or four decades to several centuries, is widespread ecological change. It has been suggested that these episodes have a periodicity, occurring approximately every 1,500 years or so, and are coupled to the ocean thermohaline circulation, which has a similar timescale.[17]

It is also clear that cultivation was not an 'invention', but a system that emerged out of a process that was at least 15,000 years long, and was achieved by the gradual genetic modification of wild cereals by human rather than natural selection. Similarly, the domestication of cattle, sheep and goats was also achieved over many thousands of years through the capture and husbandry of wild herds, and by the cumulative effect of human selection. Furthermore, in the most populous regions, the mid latitudes of the Northern Hemisphere, the number of humans had increased to the maximum capacity of the founding cultural system, and in these regions it had evolved close to the critical threshold of stability. The social and material organisation of the dense population deployed across this region had persisted and developed over several thousand years, and large fixed settlements had emerged. The extended metabolic system had developed to include the organised cultivation and husbandry of plants and animals in combination with gathering and hunting, and included localised networks of trade in materials and storable food resources. The metabolic system was broadly based, but the sheer number of humans and the quantity of energy they extracted and consumed had risen to the point where the system had become highly vulnerable to ecological changes of the region. It is now widely accepted that severe climatic and ecological changes had a significant role in the emergence of cities.[18]

Abrupt climatic changes occurred in three major episodes, disrupting the warm and wet climate of the early Holocene.[19] Some 8,200 years ago the pattern of rainfall changed and a severe century-long drought occurred right across North Africa, the Levant and south-west Asia. Non-linear perturbations and variations in the global monsoon belt produced abrupt cooling in the Atlantic Ocean, and a general weakening of the Northern Hemisphere monsoons was accelerated by positive feedback from changes in the vegetation cover of the land surfaces of the region. Two further episodes occurred, at 5,200 and the most severe of all at 4,200 years ago, lasting for hundreds of years. The overall general trend of the climate switched from warm and wet to dry conditions with very hot summers throughout the lower latitudes of the Northern Hemisphere. In this region the

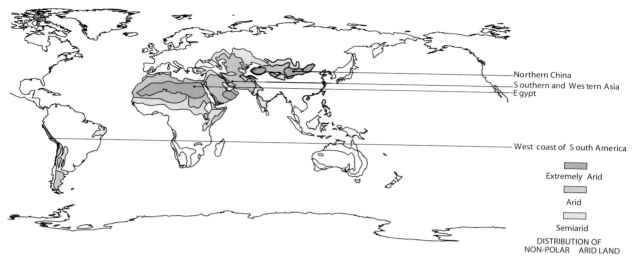

Northern China
Southern and Western Asia
Egypt

West coast of South America

Extremely Arid

Arid

Semiarid

DISTRIBUTION OF
NON-POLAR ARID LAND

7.2 Emergence of Cities
Between 6,000 and 5,000 years ago, the latitudinal band of deserts
around the world had broadened and developed the arid ecologies and
spatial extent they have today. Within the hot arid regions of the Levant,
south-west Asia, Egypt and the Indus Valley of southern Asia; and the cold
arid regions of northern China, and the north-west coast of South America,
river valleys provided the only ecologically favourable locations for all living
species, including humans. Cities emerged in these locations.

three abrupt episodes produced particularly hot dry conditions, and eventually
most of the region became completely arid, as it is today.[20] It is thought that
human clearance of the forests and woodlands also contributed to the positive
feedback caused by changes in the vegetation cover. The change in the structure
of houses, from wooden posts to masonry piers suggests a shortage of timber.
The fuel needed for the plaster making process, for cultivation and for
construction, required very substantial quantities of timber. Once a stand of trees
had been felled, the grazing herds of sheep and goats inhibited the regeneration
of the forests.

Across the region the arid conditions and consequential ecological changes
induced the failure and collapse of the founding system. In general usage, the
word 'collapse' implies a sudden and complete failure, and when used in the
context of buildings and infrastructure it is often associated with catastrophic
loss of life. However, the meaning is somewhat different when used in the
context of systems, where it is associated with a dynamical change in order or

organisation, and in complexity. The outcomes of system collapse can be the complete dispersal of the components or a complete loss of order; a regrouping of the components into smaller simpler dispersed assemblies or reorganisation to a lower level of complexity; and the reordering of the components into a more integrated assembly or reorganisation to a higher level of complexity. An increase in the flow of energy is coupled to increases in complexity.

In this particular context the archaeological evidence indicates that all three outcomes occurred. In areas that had severe ecological stresses many settlements, particularly large ones, were simply abandoned and their populations dispersed.[21] In other marginal territories, with dispersed small fertile patches, nomadic pastoralism developed and evolved. In the Sahara, for example, cattle husbandry ceased altogether, but the nomadic herding of sheep and goats developed to an annual pattern of movements between well-watered pastures, a pattern that persists today. Nomadic systems arose as a variant of the founding system, and evolved and proliferated across the arid regions of the world.[22] In other areas the dispersed settlements consolidated into fewer but larger concentrations on the fertile river floodplains. Cities emerged from a process of nucleation, in which the collapse and reorganisation of the founding system evolved to a higher level of complexity in ecologically favourable locations.

EMERGENCE OF THE CITY

Between 6,000 and 5,000 years ago, the latitudinal band of deserts around the world had broadened and developed the arid ecologies and spatial extent that they have today. Within the hot arid regions of the Levant and south-west Asia, Egypt and the Indus Valley of southern Asia; and in the cold arid regions of northern China, and the north-west coast of South America,[23] river valleys provided the only ecologically favourable locations for all living species, including humans. As recurrent episodes of severe climatic and ecological stresses continued,[24] cities emerged in all five regions within a few hundred years of each other. The relatively simultaneous emergence of city systems in five widely dispersed regions across the world, and the long distances between them, suggest that it is very unlikely that cities emerged first in one region and spread by cultural diffusion to the others. Cities emerged from the extended metabolic systems of dispersed settlements, condensing into nuclei within integrated arrays of settlements, with an amplified flow of materials, energy and information, and an increase in social and cultural complexity.

THE ARCHITECTURE OF EMERGENCE

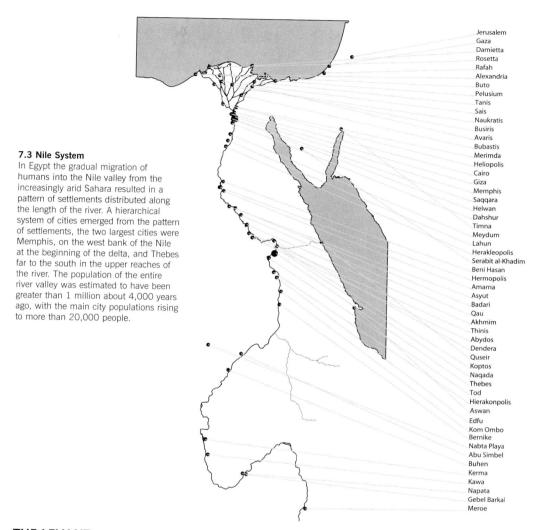

7.3 Nile System
In Egypt the gradual migration of humans into the Nile valley from the increasingly arid Sahara resulted in a pattern of settlements distributed along the length of the river. A hierarchical system of cities emerged from the pattern of settlements, the two largest cities were Memphis, on the west bank of the Nile at the beginning of the delta, and Thebes far to the south in the upper reaches of the river. The population of the entire river valley was estimated to have been greater than 1 million about 4,000 years ago, with the main city populations rising to more than 20,000 people.

Jerusalem
Gaza
Damietta
Rosetta
Rafah
Alexandria
Buto
Pelusium
Tanis
Sais
Naukratis
Busiris
Avaris
Bubastis
Merimda
Heliopolis
Cairo
Giza
Memphis
Saqqara
Helwan
Dahshur
Timna
Meydum
Lahun
Herakleopolis
Serabit al-Khadim
Beni Hasan
Hermopolis
Amarna
Asyut
Badari
Qau
Akhmim
Thinis
Abydos
Dendera
Quseir
Koptos
Naqada
Thebes
Tod
Hierakonpolis
Aswan
Edfu
Kom Ombo
Bernike
Nabta Playa
Abu Simbel
Buhen
Kerma
Kawa
Napata
Gebel Barkal
Meroe

THE LEVANT

Across the Levant and south-west Asia large concentrations of settlements grew and developed in the broad floodplains and estuaries as the ecological conditions continued to change.[25] The gradual habitat tracking of species and the migration of humans from the increasingly arid territories towards river valleys and their floodplains had begun more than 8,000 years ago. Existing settlements in the river valleys expanded as migrants from abandoned territories continued to arrive, and new settlements arose. Within a few hundred years the valleys and floodplains had closely packed settlements, with the rivers providing strong connections between them.

Jericho, on the West Bank of the river Jordan, is thought to be the oldest continuously inhabited settlement in the world. It sits today on a mound, known as a tell, which has been built up over millennia, as each new building is constructed on the ruins of an older one. Tells are common throughout the Levant and south-west Asia, some rising more than 20 metres above the plains upon which they stand. Buildings made from sun-baked mud bricks could only endure for up to 70 or 80 years before weathering led to loss of strength and the building collapsed. The rubble was levelled for the new building, so that Jericho was continuously being rebuilt, 'cell' by 'cell', in a dynamical process that persisted over millennia.[26] The very earliest construction dates from 11,000 years ago, and by 8,000 years ago Jericho was a large walled town with a population of up to 3,000 people, with water storage cisterns and storage buildings of different sizes for grain and materials. The streets were narrow and dwellings were tightly clustered, with many of the larger dwellings consisting of several rooms arranged around a courtyard. A series of smaller tells surround it, indicating that Jericho was the centre of an array of settlements.

The broad flat plains between the river valleys of the Tigris and Euphrates, historically referred to as Mesopotamia,[27] had many similar settlements of varying sizes. By 7,000 years ago a pattern of distribution with two levels of hierarchy had emerged. There were a few large settlements, up to 10 hectares in size, and many smaller settlements of 1 hectare. Functional differentiation is suggested not only by differences in size, but also by the bigger and spatially more elaborate buildings in the larger settlements. Larger centralised buildings were used for grain storage, redistribution and other social activities such as gatherings and ceremonies. The pattern of distribution also suggests that the inhabitants of the smaller satellite settlements were most directly involved with cultivation and husbandry, and that the inhabitants of the larger settlements were most directly involved with storage, the regulation of the flow of food, fuel and materials, and with social order. Irrigation canals and ditches were localised, integrating the extensive but irregular pattern of fields, groves and gardens across the land between the large and small settlements. Paths also persisted over time, beginning as tracks habitually used by people and pack animals, and subsequently paved as the flow increased. As settlements expanded over the land surrounding them, the existing patterns of canals, boundaries and paths often determined the configuration of streets and building plots.[28] The process of connection and nucleation, of concentration and expansion, continued and accelerated in this region throughout the following millennia.

The cities across the Levant and South-East Asia were quite homogeneous in their forms over a large geographical area, but the population density expanded most rapidly in the more ecologically favourable areas of southern Mesopotamia. The combination of variations in flow volume, changes in the pattern of river courses and prolonged droughts caused many areas to be abandoned, and the movement of people into southern Mesopotamia further increased the population density. Cities emerged as closely packed configurations of buildings, with populations of over 10,000 people, within large arrays of extensively linked settlements of various sizes. There were three or four different sizes of settlement linked into each city metabolism, with areas of cultivated land between them. The metabolic pattern of cities and their settlements had evolved to a hierarchical system, with very large numbers of the smallest settlements, a few larger settlements and one city. Each system was autonomous, with informal links to other systems close by.

The form of cities across the region was exemplified by the city of Ur, which was at that time close to the sea. The walled city sat on a tell on the west bank of the Euphrates, and enclosed an area of approximately 90 hectares. It is estimated that 5,000 years ago the population within the city was 35,000, with another 200,000 people living in the extended network of settlements linked to Ur. The largest open space was within an inner walled enclosure that was organised as a series of courtyards and contained the ziggurat. The majority of the city consisted of a tight-packed configuration of dwellings and narrow streets, often just wide enough for a pack animal, which limited the exposure of pedestrians to the sun, and restricted views. Two- and three-storey buildings developed, incorporating courtyards within their form, with windows opening onto the enclosed courtyard. Exterior walls tended to be blank and unrelieved by openings or surface articulations, usually with only one entrance. The protected domestic space was further isolated by having access only from small 'culs de sac', that were in turn connected to narrow streets that led to the main streets. Small courtyards in a variety of shapes were also integrated into the larger urban pattern, creating a gradation of spaces between public spaces, used for collective social functions such as markets, and the most private space behind the interior courtyard of the house. The social values associated with this urban configuration, with its layers of spatial separation and social protection within the family dwelling, coevolved with the urban form.

As cities expanded, systems of linked cities emerged. Informal trading links between neighbouring cities developed into more frequent flows of materials and energy, usually with one larger city linked to one or more smaller ones. The intense competition between established cities for fertile irrigated land led to conflicts, during which many cities and settlements built defensive walls. There were many different alliances formed over the following millennia, with dynastic successions and periods of systematic warfare resulting in different configurations of linked cities and settlements. The dynamic of the system of cities was characterised by successive iterations of gradual intensification of the links between cities, their integration into larger and more complex organisations, by abrupt collapses and a return to a less complex system of autonomous and smaller organisations. Akkad had been the first city in the Levant and south-west Asia to extend its system to a regional scale, covering a large area of what is now Iraq, Syria and southern Turkey. The cities and settlements in the north of the region relied on rain for their cultivation, but the southern cities had extensive networks of canals that supplied irrigation for the fields. When the climate changed abruptly to a more arid condition, rain-fed cultivation began to fail. Most of the people migrated south, abandoning the northern plains. The severe regional drought of 4,600 years ago lasted for more than 300 years and the migration of people was so massive that the population of the south was doubled. The increase in the flow of energy and materials accelerated the evolutionary development of systems of notation and mathematical calculation. Simple impressions were pressed into wet clay balls or tablets, and were used to record transactions, measurements of field area and quantities of grain.[29] Cuneiform script, derived from the wedge-shaped marks made by the cut end of reeds, extended the system and persisted for two millennia.

EGYPT

In Egypt the gradual migration of humans into the Nile valley from the increasingly arid Sahara resulted in a pattern of settlements distributed along the length of the river. The eastern Sahara was fully desiccated by 5,000 years ago, and as more people arrived the population density increased, new settlements arose and existing settlements expanded. The pattern of settlements developed in relation to the fluctuations in the fluvial processes of the Nile and the geomorphic dynamics of the floodplain.[30] The width of the floodplain ranges between 2 kilometres at Aswan and approximately 18 kilometres at Minia, and it carries a very high volume of silt. Deposition and erosion of silt can change the channel within a year. Settlements formed on the edge of the floodplain, but as the water levels dropped in the increasingly arid climate, new settlements formed on the floodplain closer to the river. The dwellings were constructed of mud brick, and periodic flooding accelerated the decay, so that the cycle of decay and rebuilding was much faster than in the Levant and south-west Asia. Retreating floodwaters deposited silt over extensive areas, and when the river was flowing at full volume the alluvial soils could be rapidly eroded.

The system of irrigation along the Nile was simple, locally organised and effective for cultivation of large areas. When the flood levels rose, the water was trapped in ponds created by rapidly constructed earth walls. Cultivation was strongly coupled to fluctuations in the flood volume. There were considerable variations between one year and the next, and extreme fluctuations in the abrupt episodes of climate change that altered the rainfall patterns in Ethiopia and equatorial Africa where the Nile rises. Persistently low river levels and major droughts occurred during the severe climatic regional episodes 8,000 years, 5,000 years and 4,200 years ago, with many fluctuations in-between.

A hierarchical system of cities emerged from the pattern of settlements along the river floodplain. The two largest cities were Memphis, located on the west bank of the Nile at the beginning of the delta, and Thebes far to the south in the upper reaches of the river. The population of the entire river valley was estimated to have been greater than 1 million at that time,[31] with the main city populations rising to more than 20,000 people. There were a series of small cities along the river between them, and numerous even smaller settlements that were linear in organisation, perhaps to maximise the river frontage. Many of the early settlements are now buried under the alluvial deposits, but it is evident that large and small settlements arose and were abandoned as the channels and banks of the river changed.[32]

There is archaeological evidence that 5,000 years ago the use of working river craft was extensive. Boats were commonly 12 to 18 metres in length, although a 43-metre-long boat was found at Giza. The 900 kilometre journey by boat from Thebes (now Luxor) to Memphis (now Cairo) is estimated to have taken only two weeks during the flood season,[33] and it is clear that the unified culture of Egypt was produced by the flow of people and materials on the river. It may also be that the fluctuations in flow, and the famines that occurred in dry periods, acted as a positive feedback to the cultural integration of the settlements dispersed along the river valley. As the integration of the culture increased along the river, the small cities and settlements became more differentiated in specialised manufacture of artefacts, but remained metabolically self-sufficient. For example, the pottery and stone artefacts from one of the early cities, Hierakonpolis, were widely distributed over upper Egypt. Hierakonpolis extended for four kilometres along the river and across the floodplain into a large 'wadi'[34] to the edge of the desert, it had its own extensive areas of cereal cultivation and animal husbandry. Smaller linked settlements extended its domain north and south along the river.

Occupation of the river delta began to increase in the dry conditions, as more dry land became available in the once swampy marshlands typical of delta regions. Memphis expanded rapidly, and the existing informal maritime links with the Mediterranean islands and the Levant were intensified. The collective metabolic system that developed along the Nile was hierarchical and differentiated, integrated by a coherent and literate culture. As the flow of energy and materials through the system increased, so too the social institutions expanded and developed. These were concentrated in Memphis, the string of cities along the Nile to Thebes contributed to the larger system, but regulated their own areas. Consequently, changes in the dynastic succession of kings, the large religious institutions and the administrative bureaucracies did not affect their own metabolic system greatly, and it is clear that the remarkable longevity of the extended system of cities and settlements can be attributed to this pattern of organisation.

The construction of new cities on the floodplain was a systematic process that occurred many times, and was exemplified by el-Amarna on the east bank of the Nile about 275 kilometres north of Thebes. The general organisation of the city was 'designed' or ordered by a governmental decree, but the detailed articulation of blocks and individual buildings was determined by the families and their contractors who built them. The city was linear in plan, with three main streets parallel to the river, of which one was wide enough to be a processional route. The general arrangement consisted of residential zones at either end, to north and south, with a large administrative zone in the middle. A very large temple compound was marked out to the north beyond the residential area. City blocks were defined by locally determined streets interconnected to the main streets at a variety of angles, so that there was no standard size of block, or plots within blocks. The richest families built large houses fronting right onto the main

THE ARCHITECTURE OF EMERGENCE

streets, with smaller buildings facing onto the side streets. All domestic and administrative buildings were approximately rectangular, but the variation in size and the irregular spacing and orientation of the minor streets resulted in a differentiated urban form.[35] The contractors' encampments were quite different, with uniform small rectangular buildings set out on an orthogonal grid of regularly spaced streets.

The systems of transmitting and archiving of information evolved rapidly as the flow of food energy and material culture intensified. Hieroglyphic inscriptions, on clay tablets and slabs of slate, had emerged by 5,000 years ago, along with a calligraphic script written with ink brush on papyrus. The written script, known as 'hieratic'[36] was not a descendant of hieroglyphics, but a parallel system that allowed rapid notation by priests. It evolved into a more complex notational system known as 'demotic' script or 'writing for documents', and is associated with the development of a specialised and extensive bureaucratic system of governance.

THE INDUS

Cities emerged in the Indus Valley from the process of nucleation coupled to climatic and ecological changes during the early and mid Holocene.[37] The river systems covered a far larger geographical area and had a larger population than either Egypt or Mesopotamia, but the migration of human populations from dispersed and long-established settlements to the river valleys was similar. It has not been extensively excavated, but now more than 1,000 settlements have been found along with several large cities such as Mohenjo-Daro, Harappa, Chanhu-Daro, Kalibangan and Lothal that were comparable in size to Memphis. For example, 86 settlements have been found close to Mohenjo-Daro, although the links between them are not known. Cities were distributed along the Indus and the coastline, although there is a quite different coastline today and the river course has changed.[38] As in Egypt, the flow of people and materials along the river united the culture along its length.

The forms of the cities and of artefacts were quite consistent over an area in the order of 800,000 square kilometres, with rectangular brick buildings of varying sizes, paved streets, water conduits and drainage systems. There is also substantial evidence of trade operating at an interregional scale, with many finds of artefacts from Mesopotamia and other cultures.[39] Most, but not all new cities, were built on previously unoccupied land, and the urban pattern suggests that the main streets were systematically organised with the irregular blocks occupied in a similar manner to those in el-Amarna and other cities of the Nile. Mohenjo-Daro, for example, had wide main streets that were approximately orthogonal to each other, but the connecting streets were not at strict right angles to main streets, and the lesser streets not strictly at right angles to them. The patterns within the blocks of the city are varied and irregular assemblies of rectangular buildings, ranging in size from large private houses that enclose several courtyards to aggregations of single-room dwellings. The larger houses had their own wells, and privies connected to extensive brick-lined drainage systems.[40]

The city was functionally differentiated, with separate large manufacturing areas, residential areas, and a walled enclosure that contained granaries and warehouses. The presence of these buildings in the enclosed 'citadel' indicates the regulation of distribution and that the enclosed area was administrative rather than religious. The paved public streets and the water conduits and sewage system also indicate an organised regulatory system. There was a system of weights and measures, and a widespread use of a system of inscriptions on artefacts that was unique to that region. Recent analysis has shown that it did not encode speech and was not a written form of language. The set of symbols is limited and the inscriptions on artefacts have very short sequences. There were no standing armies and no monumental architecture, but it is speculated that use of this symbol set may also have contributed to the cultural integration of material production across the region.[41]

NORTHERN CHINA

Cities emerged on the plains of the southern part of the Loess Plateau in northern China, through nucleation strongly coupled to the episodes of abrupt climatic and ecological changes. At the end of the last glacial period the ecology of this region was a cool arid steppe, and it was transformed by the rapid warming in the early Holocene to a wetter shrub and grassland steppe. The changes to the Northern Hemisphere monsoon belt around 8,000 years ago transformed the hydrological system across China, causing prolonged episodes of drought in the northern plains and changes to the course of the Yellow River that led to frequent flooding in the southern regions.[42] Settlements emerged across the Loess Plateau, developing from the longhouse variant of the founding cultural system. The material construction of the longhouses was differentiated in relation to the regional ecology, constructed of earth, mud brick and timber in the drier north, and standing on wooden stilts or columns in the warmer and wetter south. The cultivation of cereals, mainly millet, was widespread. As the population expanded, systematic plant cultivation intensified, and the increased yield supported a further increase in numbers. The critical threshold of stability of the system was exceeded in the abrupt episode of climatic change at the end of the early Holocene, and across the northern steppe the soil degraded until the land was arid.[43] The founding system collapsed, with two outcomes: 'habitat tracking' or home range shifting of living species, including people, into the river valleys, and the emergence of the nomadic tribes of the northern steppes.

In the valley of the Yiluo, part of the Huang He or Yellow River system, large settlements developed links between them, and two and three level hierarchal systems emerged. The topographical constraints are severe, as the valleys of the Loess plain are typically deeply incised by the rivers, and tend to be either very steep or cliff like. During the prolonged periods of drought, the vegetation binding the loess together died back, and during the brief seasonal storms, severe erosion occurred. When aridity further increased, the movement of people into the river valleys accelerated. Settlements located outside the Yiluo river valley collapsed during abrupt falls in temperature and accelerated aridity 6,000 years ago.[44]

The forms of the settlements combined the longhouse and the courtyard. A thick earth wall was constructed to enclose a large open courtyard or *ting*. The principal opening was in the south wall, and a freestanding longhouse was built on an elevated platform close to the inside of the northern wall. The east and west sides of the courtyard were each occupied by a simpler undivided longhouse built up against the outer wall.

Over time, walled courtyards were aggregated into a number of different interlocking combinations of greater morphological complexity. Cities emerged, enclosed by substantial walls arranged in a rectangular plan. The walls of the city of Erlitou enclosed over 300 hectares. Within them were a series of interlocking walled courtyards arranged in a hierarchy of varying sizes and configurations, around a centrally placed large courtyard of over 10,000 square metres. The city was functionally differentiated, with separate areas for manufacturing workshops, foundries, kilns and residential areas. The freestanding longhouse developed into a large hall situated across the intersections of the walled courtyards, and smaller variant forms were arrayed along the walls. Erlitou is thought to be the capital city of the Xia, the first large culturally unified system of cities and settlements that extended over a large area of the Yiluo river valley about 4,000 years ago. Zhengzhou was some 80 kilometres from Erlitou, and somewhat larger. The walls were 10 metres high and 5 metres deep, with a total length of 7 kilometres. The climatic and ecological fluctuations had a severe effect, with evidence suggesting that the system of cities collapsed, reverting to a simpler organisation along the valley of numerous but smaller walled settlements and reduced population.[45]

The earliest symbols found in the first cities of northern China are the pictographic symbols incised on pottery. Over time, the evolution of the complex Chinese script developed from this small set of pictographs, through combinations of symbols that became increasingly regularised as square characters, to new compound symbols that combined sound and meaning. As in Egypt, the coevolution of script and social complexity is associated with the development of a specialised and extensive bureaucratic system of governance.

THE ANDES

Less is known of the emergence of cities in this region than any other, and most of the archaeological research is very recent in comparison to Egypt, the Levant, South-East Asia and northern China. Peru lies on the western coast of South America, and the topography, hydrology and ecology are distinct from the other river valley systems within which cities emerged.[46] The western coast of the continents of the Americas, like the other continents, is morphologically distinct from the eastern coast. The western coast is the leading edge of the tectonic plate as it moves slowly westward, colliding with and subducting the tectonic plate of the Pacific floor and so creating an 8,000 metre deep ocean trench that runs all along the coast of Peru and Chile, and the characteristic mountain chain that runs the entire length of the continent. The coastal strip between the mountains and the sea is very narrow in Peru, and today is a cold and exceptionally arid desert.

Desertification arose from changes in the pattern of the ocean currents rather than the Northern Hemisphere monsoon belt. An increase in the upwelling of deep ocean water lowered the sea temperatures along much of the west coast of South America. The sea temperatures in this area were known to have once been 3°C to 4°C warmer than today, and in consequence the ecology would have been quite tropical. It is thought that about 5,000 years ago the volume of upwelling of cold water increased significantly. The colder water reduced the temperature of the atmosphere above it, causing an alteration in the rainfall pattern. The change from the warm wet tropical climate to a cool arid climate had a profound effect on marine and land ecologies,[47] including the development of the strip of desert lying between the sea and the high mountains inland.

The tropical variant form of the founding system in South America had a pattern of high logistical movements from fixed settlements, usually formed around large cleared circular spaces in the dense forests. In this variant, the dwellings were large timber constructions with thatched roofs arranged around the periphery of the central space. Like the longhouses of the Northern Hemisphere they were communally occupied, but the large circular space was quite distinctive. When the ecology of the immediate area was exhausted the whole group would move and construct a new clearing and dwellings in a previously untouched area. Small temporary hunting camps, including coastal sites, were part of the metabolic pattern. As the climate changed, species and people shifted their range, migrating into the ecological 'refugia' of the river valleys.

The Andes mountains have many valleys, from which 25 small rivers run down across the desert to the sea, and their small fertile floodplains are isolated from each other by the desiccated land. A functionally differentiated system arose between coastal and mountain settlements, and cities emerged with systematic cultivation and canal irrigation in the mountain valleys.[48] Between the mountain city and the coastal settlement there were a series of smaller settlements linked into the metabolic system. The river valleys occur at approximately 30 kilometre intervals, and vertically link the two quite different ecological areas. It has been argued that the social evolution of 'semi-autonomous city states' was determined by the topographical isolation and ecological independence of these river valleys.[49] It is likely that the diminished ecological resources in both the mountains and the coastal strip, caused by the abrupt climate change, accelerated the development of the system of settlements in these isolated valleys.

The river Supe, for example, has 18 known settlements along its 90 kilometre long valley, with the city of Caral located in the mountains, and the coastal settlement of Aspero some 23 kilometres lower down in the low foothills, close to where the river delta begins. Caral covered over 65 hectares, with six distinct large residential areas, each with a large mound or platform.[50] The residential areas are differentiated spatially and materially; the largest consisted of a complex of large rooms built in dressed stone with plastered walls, and others had smaller rooms built in timber and earth. Irrigated plant cultivation is known to have included beans and squash, and cotton used for the manufacture of fishing nets has been found in the coastal settlement. Caral, and most other cities, had two or more very large circular plazas. The evolution of plazas from the cleared central space of the founding system is evident. The smaller coastal settlement at Aspero was located in a natural basin that encloses the flat valley floor in the low foothills close to the sea. Narrow terraces cut into the sides of the basin are thought to be the sites of dwellings, with numerous dwellings on the valley floor extended over 14 hectares. There are also low masonry-faced stepped platforms, of uncertain purpose, that have been interpreted as monumental in character.[51] The basin topography was well suited to floodwater irrigation for plant cultivation, and the proximity to the sea provided marine food sources.

No evidence of notational systems has yet been excavated at Caral, with the exception of a 'quipu' or array of knotted strings. The complexity of information that can be encoded in knots was once thought to be lower than in numerical systems, but recent analysis includes both the different colours of the individual wool and cotton strands and the knots. It is now recognised that the system is a three-dimensional hierarchical array.[52] In a society with complex textiles the system would have been widely accessible.

DESCENDANT SYSTEMS

Nomadic systems evolved from a variant form of the founding system, moving herds of domesticated sheep and goats for grazing between isolated fertile pastures in differentiated seasonal patterns. Across the Levant and south-west Asia, the systems of cities and settlements were spatially constrained to valleys and irrigated floodplains between the rivers Tigris and Euphrates, leaving large areas within which only smaller and widely separated settlements existed. The metabolic system of these settlements covered extended territories, with a pattern of seasonal mobility that combined residential and logistical mobility. During the winter season the whole population remained in the settlement, and cereal cultivation was reliant on the winter rains. In the spring and summer a proportion of the population moved with the herds to temporary camps.[53] The pattern of high mobility during spring and summer with a winter return to a fixed settlement was consistent as the nomadic system developed and proliferated across the world. Nomadic systems expanded across the marginal territories from the southern tip of Africa to the steppe grasslands of Eurasia to Siberia and to many parts of Northern America. Their interaction with the systems of cities and settlements had two principal vectors, trade and war.

Material necessities were traded for their own subsistence, and supplied the systems of cities with meat and hides. They also transported, manufactured and cultivated high value items across extended territories and regions, and so acted to diffuse cultural values between cities in a range of scales from local to regional. Organised defence of the herd from natural predators was an essential part of the system since animals were first captured and herded. In some regions, most notably in north-east Asia, nomadic tribes evolved formidable strategies and technologies of systematic warfare.[54] In both the animal and human populations of the nomadic system, genetic modifications occurred. Until 8,000 years ago the human metabolism was unable to digest milk; the genetic mutation that enabled them to do so is thought to have occurred independently in Africa and in Europe. That genetic modification is now widespread but not universal in human populations today.[55]

Cities evolved from trading settlements along the extensive patterns of nomadic systems that linked Egypt to the Levant and south-west Asia, and on to the Indus Valley. In middle Asia very recent excavations in the valley of the Helmand River have revealed a city at Shahr-i Sokhta that extended over 150 hectares, with more than 350 other settlements in Jiroft, the central region of what is now Iran.[56] Little is known of the form and systems of these cities, but the overall pattern of ruins suggests that they are likely to have been variant forms of the cities of the Levant and south-west Asia. In the Arabian peninsula the most extreme desert conditions existed, as they do today, and the population was very small and widely dispersed. Settlements and cities emerged on the trading routes that extended between Mesopotamia and the dispersed pattern of the fertile oasis close to the southern coasts. City forms in the peninsula are also clearly descended from the cities of the Levant and south-west Asia, with tightly packed patterns of dwellings and narrow streets, with courtyards integrated into both dwellings and into the larger urban pattern. The social values associated with this urban configuration, with its layers of spatial separation and social protection within the family dwelling, coevolved with the urban form. The spatial organisation of mosques, caravanserai and markets emerged with the evolutionary development and elaboration of courtyard systems.

A significant variation of the nomadic system emerged between 6,000 and 5,000 years ago. It is now widely accepted that rafts and simple water-craft were used in the human colonisation of the islands of South-East Asia, New Guinea and Australia more than 50,000 years ago. River craft were extensively used in the river system of the Nile, and perhaps to a slightly lesser extent in the Euphrates/Tigris, the Indus and the Yiluo and Huang He of China. Sailing ships capable of extended coastal and sea voyages coevolved with the rise in trade between the systems of cities around the Mediterranean, the Indian Ocean and the South China Sea. The emergence of seafaring populations, coupled to the established nomadic systems in Eurasia and Africa, produced the vector of cultural diffusion to the islands of the Aegean and to mainland Greece. The movement of materials and people from the Nile valley and the coast of the Levant to Crete had existed for more than a thousand years before cities emerged on Crete about 4,000 years ago, and some 500 years later in Greece.

Greece has a range of mountains that run from north to south, bisecting the peninsula. Almost 80 per cent of the land mass is mountainous, with dry flat plains in the north-east and in the south-east. The climate has a marked seasonality, so that the rivers flow at high volume in the winter but dry up in the summer. The plains are isolated from each other by the mountains, and are just sufficiently fertile for plant cultivation of moderate intensity. The topographical and ecological constraints determined the distribution and concentration of settlements, and the emergence of loosely aggregated independent city systems. The cities of 'classical' Greece, between 3,000 and 2,400 years ago, had a compact form; few were completely enclosed by walls as the topography had historically provided some protection against wars with neighbours. The ecological constraints on the city and its extended system of differentiated settlements and fields were severe; as the population rose and the intensity of cultivation increased, the soils were degraded and yields began to decline. Most homes and artefacts were constructed from timber, and wood reduced to charcoal was the only fuel for homes and the kilns used in many manufacturing processes. The mountain forests were cut down, and grazing sheep and goats inhibited the regrowth of trees.[57] Soil erosion increased commensurately, and the silting of rivers acted to further increase the ecological stresses on the land, and on the extended metabolisms of the city systems.

The city systems of Greece had evolved so that they were operating near to their maximum capacity, and many were poised close to the edge of critical stability.

Kroton
Anaktorion
Skiros
Phokaia
Leukas
Sardis
Chalkis
Hipponion
Smyrna
Chios
Eretria
Naupaktos
Kaulonia
Lipara
Medma
Kolophon
Zankle
Lokroi
Patrai
Himera
Sikyon
Athen
Rhegion
Kephalonia
Megara
Samos
Mallos
Korinth
Naxos
Andros
Selinunt
Elis
Milet
Aspendos
Karia
Katane
Zakynthos
Tenos
Argos
Akragas
Side
Halikarnassos
Megalopolis
Leontinoi
Gela
Delos
Kos
Selinunt
Megara Hyblaia
Kelenderis
Phaselis
Kamarina
Sparta
Syrakus
Naxos
Knidos
Paros
Melos
Rhodos
Kameiros
Lindos
Kyreneia
Thera
Kythera
Salamis
Soloi
Karpathos
Kydonia
Paphos
Knossos
Apollonia
Kyrene
Barke
Taucheira
Euphesperides
Naukratis

7.4 Greek Colony Systems
The total population of Greece and its colonies is estimated to have grown by an order of magnitude over a period of 500 years, from one million to 10 million people. Many of the independent cities became the 'mother' city of an overseas colony, for example Corinth was the 'mother city' or metropolis of Syracuse.

Expansion was locally inhibited by the topography and ecology, but all along the coasts of the Mediterranean and the Black Sea there were many ecologically favourable sites, with small populations, unexploited forests and fertile plains for agriculture. New cities proliferated along the coasts, each planned and constructed by one of the many independent cities of Greece, enabling them to intensify the flow of livestock, timber and other materials from the new cities. The total population of Greece and its colonies is estimated to have grown by an order of magnitude over a period of 500 years, from one million to 10 million people. Today the word 'metropolis'[58] is most commonly used as the term for a very large set of cities that are so physically close to each other that the boundaries between them are barely perceptible. Metropolis had a different meaning in 'classical'

Greece, where many of the independent cities became the 'mother' city of an overseas colony, for example, Corinth was the 'mother city' or metropolis of Syracuse. More than 30 Greek cities are known to have expanded the range of their metabolic systems with overseas colonies. Miletus was the largest Greek city 2,500 years ago, and was probably the most prolific, having founded more than 60 overseas 'colonies' or subsidiary cities. Each of the subsidiary cities developed their local system of linked settlements, so that the metabolic system of Miletus extended over much of the Black Sea coastal territories.[59]

EMERGENCE AND THE FORMS OF CITIES

Cities emerged from a process of nucleation in five topographically and ecologically defined regions within a latitudinal band characterised by either hot or cold arid climates. In each region recurrent episodes of climatic change induced further ecological stresses on the widely distributed pattern of settlements that had already made pronounced changes to local and regional ecological systems. River valleys were the most favourable areas, and the flow of migrants from the ecologically stressed territories into the valleys increased the population in topographically and ecologically delimited territories. The concentration of people, and the consequential increase in the volume of exchanges between settlements of food, fuel and materials, established the integration of the individual metabolic system of groups of settlements into larger systems. Severe climatic and ecological changes induced the process of nucleation and the subsequent emergence of cities.

City forms are material constructs that are composed of a spatial array of dwellings, a pattern of streets and public spaces together with differentiated buildings of varying sizes associated with the regulation of energy and material flow, and the extension of a metabolic network across the surrounding territory. City forms emerged within different topographies and ecological systems, evolving from regional variations of the founding system and the established patterns of settlements from which they condensed. The forms expanded and developed, strongly coupled to the dynamic changes of climate and ecology within which they were situated.

When further sequential episodes of prolonged drought occurred throughout the latitudinal band, the flow of energy through the system of cities was substantially reduced as crops failed, animal pastures withered away, and rivers dried up. Systems poised close to the critical threshold of stability are sensitive, and a small change may precipitate collapse. In Egypt, the Levant and south-west Asia, the Indus Valley, Crete and Greece, the systems of cities had all expanded their populations to the maximum capacity of their system, each close to the critical threshold of stability, and the links between them had intensified.

There were several century-long episodes of drought and high temperatures in the millennia between 6,000 and 2,500 years ago, and several sequences lasting three or more decades. In each case the consequence was drastically reduced flow in the river systems. In the territories that were not directly fed by rivers that were wholly reliant on seasonal rains, the failure of agriculture led to widespread famine and subsequent collapse. Some systems of cities persisted longer than others in the severe droughts, reverting to a simpler and more localised array supporting a lower population, but eventually many cities were simply abandoned, and their peoples migrated to more ecologically favourable locations.

In the Levant and south-west Asia, there were many iterations of gradual expansion and intensification of links over increasingly large areas, growing complexity and subsequent collapse and reorganisation. Two of the largest geographical expansions and later collapses were centred on the city of Ur, and on Babylon. In Middle Asia and the Indus Valley the collapse was followed by abandonment and migration of the population towards the east. Those people that did remain reverted to a simpler system of settlements with fewer links, smaller populations and reduced complexity. No further rise in complexity occurred in these areas for thousands of years. In northern China, climatic and ecological changes induced contraction and a subsequent reorganisation. Cities and settlements in the colder arid territories were abandoned to the emerging nomadic system of the Mongol tribes about 3,500 years ago.

The collapse of regional scale systems of cities led to the dispersal of populations and reversion to simpler systems of linked settlements. Over time, as the population density slowly increased in the southern part of the Loess Plateau, new cities emerged with dense localised distribution of smaller settlements, and a higher level of complexity. In both Peru and Greece the expansion of cities was severely constrained by the topography and ecology, with quite different outcomes. It is thought that cities and settlements in Peru were abandoned, with the peoples migrating to the north where the Inca later emerged. In Greece, the reorganisation of the systems of the metropolises or 'mother cities' was achieved by the proliferation of 'colony' cities along the

1-- longhouse

2-- double longhouse

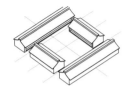

3-- new buildings facing existing yard

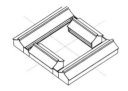

4-- enclosed yard

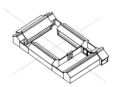

5-- single-enclosure courtyard

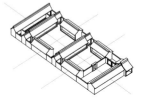

6-- double-enclosure courtyard

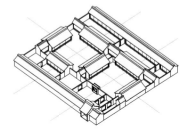

7-- double-route courtyard

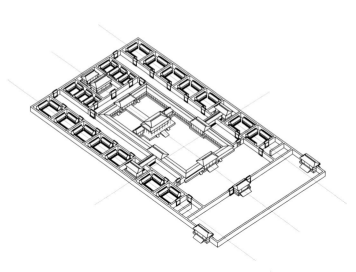

8-- triple-route courtyard

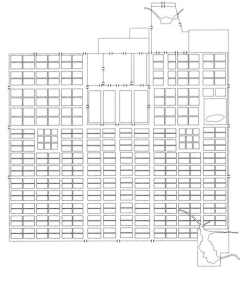

9-- City as a field of courtyards (ChangAn 1390-1101 years ago)

7.5 China

Cities emerged on the plains of the southern part of the Loess Plateau in northern China, through nucleation strongly coupled to the episodes of abrupt climatic and ecological changes. The material construction of the longhouses was differentiated in relation to the regional ecology, constructed of earth, mud brick and timber in the drier north, and standing on wooden stilts or columns in the warmer and wetter south. The evolutionary development and elaboration of urban configurations proceeded by iteration and recombination of the longhouse and the courtyard to produce complex spatial organisations and material forms at a variety of scales.

coastlines of the Mediterranean, the Black Sea, as far north inland as the Ukraine, and as far south as Alexandria in Egypt. Energy, in the form of food and materials, flowed from the overseas cities back to the metropolises. Information flowed in the reverse direction as knowledge and expertise in the organisation and construction of buildings and cities, and in the manipulation of timber, bricks and ceramics, stone and metals.

As cities emerged within a latitudinal band characterised by arid climates, and arose from variations of the common founding system, their evolutionary development tended to be convergent, exhibiting many similar patterns, arrays and forms. Convergent evolution has occurred widely in living forms, and many animals and plants that emerge from quite different evolutionary trajectories exhibit strong similarities in their body plans and the processes of their organs.[60] Likewise, there are common material, spatial and metabolic organisations in the forms of cities, most notably in the hot arid climatic regions of the Levant and south-west Asia, Egypt and the Indus Valley, and in their descendants in the Arabian peninsula and around the Mediterranean. The evolutionary development and elaboration of the courtyard, from the simple space between dwellings in the first settlements to its incorporation within spatially complex buildings of varying sizes and functions, occurred throughout the region. Courtyards also emerged within the dense pattern of dwellings, coevolving with social orders and values as urban spaces for collective functions. Within the cooler regions of Eurasia and the cold arid climate of northern China, the longhouse evolved and was developed, and in combination with the courtyard was elaborated to complex spatial organisations and material forms at a variety of scales.

Variation of the form of individual and groups of dwellings occurred locally, through the idiosyncrasies and necessities of the local topography and local knowledge of construction, or in response to irregularities in the flow of materials and available energy in 'manpower'. The emergence of larger building forms and the evolutionary development and elaboration of variant forms was strongly coupled to the rise in the flow of energy from intense cultivation, increased social complexity and the evolution of information systems. As the populations in extended city systems continued to expand, plant cultivation and animal husbandry were intensified and the flow of materials and energy increased. In turn, the built area of cities expanded over the established patterns of cultivated fields, pastures and irrigation canals.

Along the Nile valley new cities and associated agricultural field systems were laid out and rapidly constructed as variations in the river flow changed the river geometry and modified existing floodplains. The shallow gradient of the river enabled the evolutionary development of river craft and enabled the flow of materials, energy and people between cities and settlements. There were similar developments in the Euphrates/Tigris, the Indus and the Yiluo and Huang He rivers of China.

The subsequent development of maritime nomadic systems initiated the processes from which extended sets of colony cities arose. As the collective metabolic systems extended over increasingly larger geographical areas, the integration of colony cities into larger and more complex hierarchical systems acted as a positive feedback to the development of information systems including notation, calculation and writing. Information systems related to the differentiated and fluctuating flows of energy and materials evolved, the complexity of the system increased commensurately. Variations arose in the built form of individual buildings, in the scale, function and spatial organisation of groups of buildings, and in the overall patterns of cities.

The growth and development of cities and systems of cities across the world was characterised by episodic and irregular expansions and incorporations, and by local and regional scale patches of collapse, the abandonment of cities and dispersal of the people, and subsequent reorganisation. Systems of cities all tended to develop and expand so that they were operating close to the limit of their capacity to extract energy and materials from their environment, and to manage the complexity of flows through their system. Systems of cities developed multiple processes, each with flows of energy and materials through them, and with critical thresholds at differing scales of distance and time. They developed and grew until they were delicately poised close to their critical threshold of stability, and were then extremely sensitive to changes within their environment.

The outcomes of system collapse can be: the abandonment and migration of the people and a complete loss of order; a regrouping of the 'components' of the system into smaller dispersed assemblies with fewer links and reduced flows of energy, materials and information; or reorganisation to a lower level of complexity and the reordering of the 'components' into a more integrated assembly with increased flows; or reorganisation to a higher level of complexity.

THE ARCHITECTURE OF EMERGENCE

The ecological system of each of the five regions within which cities emerged and developed was modified by humans at a variety of spatial and temporal scales. The intensive cultivation of land supported large populations, but also resulted in the depletion of nutrients in the soil, and in some areas caused a marked salinisation of the soil. The use of timber for construction and for fuel, coupled to the clearance of land for agricultural use, resulted in deforestation at a regional scale, the spread of grassland savannahs and the extinction of animal and plant species. Successive cycles of drought, coupled to the elimination of tree root systems that bound the soil together, exposed the soil to further drying and erosion. The changes were cumulative and long lasting, and in many regions the modifications of ecological systems by humans are still evident in the arid and denuded landscapes that persist today.

1 Lahr, M and R Foley, 'Towards a Theory of Modern Human Origins: geography, demography, and diversity in recent human evolution', *Yearbook of Physical Anthropology,* vol 41, 1998, pp 137–76; and McBrearty, S and A Brooks, 'The Revolution that Wasn't: a new interpretation of the origin of modern human behavior', *Journal of Human Evolution,* vol 39, 2000, pp 453–563.

2 Noble, W and I Davidson, 'The Evolutionary Emergence of Modern Human Behaviour: Language and its Archaeology', *Man: Journal of the Royal Anthropological Institute*, vol 26, 1991, pp 223–53.

3 Roberts, *The Holocene, An Environmental History, An Environmental History* (second edition), Blackwell Publishing (Oxford), 1998, pp 7, 62–3.

4 This period is known to geologists as the Younger Dryas, from about 11,000 to 10,000 years before the present. It marks the boundary between the current epoch, the Holocene, and the previous epoch, the Pleistocene.

5 The axial tilt of the earth was then 24° and the nearest approach to the sun was during summer.

6 Generally known as the early to mid-Holocene.

7 Roberts, N, *The Holocene, An Environmental History*, pp 115–6.

8 Marshall, A, 'Environmental Adaptation and Structural Design in Axially-Pitched Longhouses from Neolithic Europe', *World Archaeology*, vol 13, 1981, pp 101–21.

9 Ibid.

10 Wendorf, F, R Schild, R Said, CV Haynes, A Gautier and M Kouseiwicz, 'The Prehistory of the Egyptian Sahara', *Science*, vol 193, 1976, pp 103–14.

11 Cremaschi, M and S Di Lernia, 'Holocene Climatic Changes and Cultural Dynamics in the Libyan Sahara', *African Archaeological Review*, vol 4, 1999.

12 Bar-Yosef, O, 'The Natufian Culture in the Levant, Threshold to the Origins of Agriculture', *Evolutionary Anthropology*, vol 6, 1998, pp 159–77.

13 Nadel D, 'A Long Continuity: the Ohalo II brush huts (19.5 ky) and the dwelling structures in the Natufian and PPNA sites in the Jordan Valley', *Archaeology, Anthropology and Ethnology in Euroasia*, vol 13, no 1, 2003, pp 34–48; and Nadel D, U Grinberg, E Boaretto and E Werker, 'Wooden Objects from Ohalo II (23,000 cal BP), Jordan Valley, Israel', *Journal of Human Evolution*, vol 50, no 6, 2006, pp 644–62.

14 Byrd, BF, 'Public and Private, Domestic and Corporate: the emergence of the Southwest Asian village', *American Antiquity* 59, 1994, pp 639–66.

15 Based on a yield of 50 kilograms per hectare (100 x 100 metres), and approximately 65 per cent of the total calorific requirement of 250 people over the year.

16 Garfinkel, Y, 'Yiftahel: A Neolithic Village from the Seventh Millennium BC in Lower Galilee,

Israel', *Journal of Field Archaeology*, vol 14, 1987, pp 199–212.

17 deMenocal, PB, 'Cultural Responses to Climate Change during the Late Holocene', *Science*, vol 292, 2001, pp 667–73.

18 Smith, HJ, 'Did Climate Rock the Cradle?', *Science*, vol 312, no 5777, May 2006, pp 1109.

19 Gasse, F and E Van Campo, 'Abrupt Post-Glacial Climate Events in West Asia and North Africa Monsoon Domains', *Earth and Planetary Science Letters*, vol 126, 1994, pp 435–56.

20 Staubwasser, M and H Weiss, 'Holocene Climate and Cultural Evolution in Late Prehistoric-Early Historic West Asia', *Quaternary Research*, vol 66, 2006, pp 372–87.

21 Banning, EB, 'The Neolithic Period: Triumphs of Architecture, Agriculture, and Art', *Near Eastern Archaeology*, vol 61, December 1998, pp 188–237; and Banning, EB, 'Housing Neolithic Farmers', *Near Eastern Archaeology*, vol 66, June 2003, pp 4–21.

22 Di Lernia, S and A Palombini, 'Desertification, Sustainability, and Archaeology: indications from the past for an African future', *Origini*, vol XXIV, 2002, pp 303–34.

23 Solis, RS, J Haas and W Creamer, 'Dating Caral, a Preceramic Site in the Supe Valley on the Central Coast of Peru', *Science*, vol 292, 2001, pp 723–6.

24 Steig, EJ, 'Mid-Holocene Climate Change', Science, vol 286, 1999, pp 1485–7; and Brooks, N, 'Cultural Responses to Aridity in the Middle Holocene and Increased Social Complexity', *Quaternary International*, vol 151, 2006, pp 29–49.

25 McCorriston, J and F Hole, 'The Ecology of Seasonal Stress and the Origins of Agriculture in the Near East', *American Anthropologist*, vol 93, 1991, pp 46–69.

26 Morris, AEJ, *History of Urban Form: Before the Industrial Revolutions*, Prentice Hall (New Jersey), third edition, 1994, pp 6–7.

27 The term Mesopotamia is now widely used to refer to the larger region of the Levant and south-west Asia, but its literal meaning 'between the rivers' suggests a much smaller territory.

28 Bonine, ME, 'The Morphogenesis of Iranian Cities', *Annals of the Association of American Geographers*, vol 69, 1979, pp 208–24.

29 Schmandt-Besserat, D, 'Decipherment of the Earliest Tablets', Science, vol 211, 1981, pp 283–5; and Friberg, J, 'Counting and Accounting in the Proto-Literate Middle East: examples from two new volumes of proto-cuneiform texts', *Journal of Cuneiform Studies*, vol 51, 1999, pp 107–37.

30 Hassan, FA, 'The Dynamics of a Riverine Civilization: a geoarchaeological perspective on the Nile Valley, Egypt', *World Archaeology*, vol 29, June 1997, pp 51–74.

31 Ibid.

32 Trigger, BG, 'The Rise of Egyptian Civilization', in (eds) Trigger, BG, BJ Kemp and D O'Connor, AB Lloyd, *Ancient Egypt: a social history*, Cambridge University Press (Cambridge), 1983, pp 143; and Wenke, RJ, 'Egypt: Origins of Complex Societies', *Annual Review of Anthropology*, vol 18, 1989, pp 129–55.

33 Hassan, FA, 'The Dynamics of a Riverine Civilization: a geoarchaeological perspective on the Nile Valley, Egypt', *World Archaeology*, vol 29, June 1997, pp 51–74.

34 A wadi is a dry river valley, with steep sides and a flat floor, along which water flows only in the occasional wet periods.

35 Kemp, BJ, 'The City of El-Amarna as a Source for the Study of Urban Society in Ancient Egypt', *World Archaeology*, vol 9, *Architecture and Archaeology*, 1977, pp 123–39; and Kemp, BJ, 'The Window of Appearance at el-Amarna, and the Basic Structure of this City', *The Journal of Egyptian Archaeology*, vol 62, 1976, pp 81–99.

36 Derived from the Greek word *hiertikos*, pertaining to the priesthood.

37 Gupta, AK, DM Anderson, DN Pandey and AK Singhvi, 'Adaptation and Human Migration, and Evidence of Agriculture Coincident with Changes in the Indian Summer Monsoon during the Holocene', *Current Science*, vol 90, 2006, pp 1082–90.

38 Raikes, RL, 'The End of the Ancient Cities of the Indus', *American Anthropologist*, vol 66, 1964, pp 284–99.

39 Lawler, A, 'Unmasking the Indus: Boring No More, a Trade-Savvy Indus Emerges', *Science*, vol 320, 2008, p 1276.

40 Morris, AEJ, *History of Urban Form: Before the Industrial Revolutions*, Prentice Hall (New Jersey), third edition, 1994, pp 30–4.

41 Possehl, GL, 'Revolution in the Urban Revolution: the emergence of Indus urbanization', *Annual Review of Anthropology*, vol 19, 1990, pp 261–82.

42 Wenxiang, W and L Tungsheng, 'Possible Role of the "Holocene Event 3" on the Collapse of Neolithic Cultures around the Central Plain of China', *Quaternary International*, vol 117, 2004, pp 153–66.

43 Huang, CC, J Pang, Q Zhou and S Chen, 'Holocene Pedogenic Change and the Emergence and Decline of Rain-Fed Cereal Agriculture on the Chinese Loess Plateau', *Quaternary Science Reviews*, vol 23, 2004, pp 2525–35; and Lee, G, GW Crawford, L Liu and X Chen, 'Plants and People from the Early Neolithic to Shang Periods in North China', *Proceedings of the National Academy of Sciences*, vol 104, 2007, pp 1087–92.

44 Liu, L, X Chen, YK Lee, H Wright and A Rosen, 'Settlement Patterns and Development of Social Complexity in the Yiluo Region, North China', *Journal of Field Archaeology*, vol 29, 2002, pp 75–100.

45 Ibid.

46 Sanders, T, 'Cultural Ecology of Nuclear Mesoamerica', *American Anthropologist*, vol 64, 1962, pp 34–44.

47 Brooks, N, 'Cultural Responses to Aridity in the Middle Holocene and Increased Social Complexity', *Quaternary International*, vol 151, 2006, pp 29–49.

48 Dillehay, TD, HH Eling and J Rossen, 'Preceramic Irrigation Canals in the Peruvian Andes', *Proceedings of the National Academy of Sciences*, vol 102, 2005, pp 17241–4.

49 Stanish, C, 'The Origin of State Societies in South America', *Annual Review of Anthropology*, vol 30, 2001, pp 41–64.

50 Solis, RS, J Haas and W Creamer, 'Dating Caral, a Preceramic Site in the Supe Valley on the Central Coast of Peru', *Science*, vol 292, 2001, pp 723–6; and Sandweiss, DH, ME Moseley, J Haas and W Creamer, 'Amplifying Importance of New Research in Peru', *Science*, vol 294, 2001, pp 1651–3.

51 Mosely, ME and GR Willey, 'Aspero, Peru: A Reexamination of the Site and Its Implications', *American Antiquity*, vol 38, 1973, pp 452–68.

52 Mann, CC, 'Unraveling Khipu's Secrets', *Science*, vol 309, 2005, pp 1008–9; and Mann, CC, 1491: new revelations of The Americas before Columbus, Random House (New York), 2005, pp 345–9.

53 Levy, TE, 'The Emergence of Specialized Pastoralism in the Southern Levant', *World Archaeology*, vol 15, 'Transhumance and Pastoralism', 1983, pp 15–36.

54 Lomax, A and CM Arensberg, 'A Worldwide Evolutionary Classification of Cultures by Subsistence Systems', *Current Anthropology*, vol 18, 1977, pp 659–701.

55 Tishkoff, SA, et al, 'Convergent Adaptation of Human Lactase Persistence in Africa and Europe', *Nature Genetics*, vol 39, 2006, pp 31–40.

56 Lawler, A, 'Middle Asia Takes Center Stage', *Science*, vol 317, 2007, pp 486–590.

57 Hughes, JD and JV Thirgood, 'Deforestation, Erosion, and Forest Management in Ancient Greece and Rome', *Journal of Forest History*, vol 26, 1982, pp 60–75.

58 Derived from the Greek *meter* meaning mother and *pólis* meaning city.

59 Morris, AEJ, *History of Urban Form: Before the Industrial Revolutions*, Prentice Hall (New Jersey), third edition, 1994, pp 40–4; and Gwynn, A, 'The Character of Greek Colonisation', *The Journal of Hellenic Studies*, vol 38, 1918, pp 88–123.

60 Morphologists refer to the general anatomical architecture as the body plan, and similar or related body plans are generally classified together in groups or 'phyla'. This taxonomy does not normally take into account metabolic processes.

8.1 Beijing
The first city ever built by the steppe nomads, known as 'Dadu' or
great city, conformed closely to the Chinese *Kao Gong Ji* model cities
in plan and material construction, and is today part of Beijing.
Travellers from the small dense cities of Europe, including Marco Polo,
were astonished by the number of cities in China, the enormous areas
enclosed within their walls, and the dense populations two or three
times larger than that of any city in Europe.

The Forms of Information, Energy and Ecology

8

The integration of the collective metabolism of systems of cities into complex hierarchical systems acted as a positive feedback on the evolutionary development of information systems. Graphical and numerical notation, calculation and writing arose from the regulation of the fluctuating flows of energy and materials, and the complexity of the system increased commensurately. As more extensive and complex metabolic networks emerged, they have extracted energy and materials over regional and continental scale territories, with many periods of expansion to the critical limit of stability, and subsequent collapse and reorganisation. The evolutionary development of continental scale systems and the current worldwide system is strongly coupled to extensive modifications to the surface of the earth and to the ecological systems that live upon it. In consequence the interactions between the surface of the earth and the atmosphere at local, regional and global scales have been altered.

In humans, like all other living forms, information and the ability to extract energy from their environment are strongly coupled. The assembly of an integrated cultural system had reached a critical threshold of complexity more than 35,000 years ago. Complex spoken language, graphical arts in the form of cave paintings and engravings on shell and bone, and the beginnings of mathematics in simple lunar calendars were in use in most populated regions of the world. The information transmitted down through the generations was ecological and social knowledge, a set of instructions of how to live as member of the group or tribe, how and where to hunt and to gather, how to make weapons, tools, clothes and implements, and how and where to construct dwellings. Information enabled the metabolic, spatial and social organisation of the founding system to expand their numbers and flow across the surface of the earth. As humans dispersed into new climatic and ecological zones and adapted to them, new variations of the founding system arose. Seasonally and ecologically determined patterns of movement, inherited from the ancestral apes, also evolved to include long-term settlements of excavated 'pit dwellings' as winter residences, along with the use of tents and temporary structures in warmer seasons. Pit dwellings enabled modern humans to regulate their collective metabolism in a great range of climates, and to expand into the very cold territories of the high northern latitudes. Adaptation to differing regional climates, topographies and ecologies emerged through variation in the timing and frequency of movements and residency, and morphological variations in the depth and size of the excavation and construction.

The variability of dwelling morphology and mobility strategies enabled anatomically modern humans to occupy and flourish in all the continents and islands of the earth. Knowledge of how to make a dwelling was passed down from one generation to the next, and incorporated into the set of skills, social and ecological knowledge of each family and tribe. The use of graphical arts in cave paintings predates written language by 20,000 years, and it follows that the use of drawing in construction is most likely to have arisen at the same time with the marking out of the 'plan' of the dwelling on the ground with pegs and cords. There was little differentiation between individual dwellings in areas with similar climate and ecologies. It is likely that when variations did arise they were produced by differing circumstances of climate, topography and material resources during the building process.

Human populations grew to the maximum densities that could be supported in the ecology within which they were situated. The lowest population densities were in the hot and wet tropical forest ecologies, where the minimum density is estimated to have averaged only one or two people per 100 square kilometres, but in more temperate regions where gathering and fishing were the main activities, population densities were much higher – averaging up to 90 people or more per 100 square kilometres. The energy gained from gathering tubers, fruits and grains, or hunting and killing animals, averaged between 10 and 20 times the energy expended in those activities. Hunting small animals had such a minimal gain that in many situations it resulted in an energy loss, but hunting large herbivores including bison and mammoths produced as much as a 19-fold return. The extinction of the megafauna was part of, but not the only modification, of ecological systems that human activities induced. The cutting down of trees for the construction of dwellings and for fuel, the use of fire to drive game and to clear land, and the extinction of megafauna produced permanent changes in steppe grasslands, in cool forests and in the warmer grasslands. As the populations of humans continued to spread and grow, the increase in gathering of grains altered the regime of natural selection and initiated the genetic changes in wild cereals that enabled the development of more systematic plant cultivation.

The world population is thought to have been about five million people 10,000 years ago.[1] Across the surface of the earth the peoples had increased their numbers to the maximum capacity of their ability to extract energy and materials from their home range. Within the mid latitudes the climate became increasingly arid and plant life diminished, so that fewer animals could be supported and in turn the sources of food available for humans were greatly reduced. As the extended metabolism of the founding system failed across large open territories, settlements and territories were abandoned, and the founding system collapsed. In five geographically separated and ecologically distinct regions the peoples migrated to the more ecologically favourable valleys of the major river systems[2] in Egypt, the Levant and south-west Asia, India, China and Peru. The flow of migrants increased the size and number of settlements, and accelerated the development of increasingly complex networks of links between them. Cities emerged, between 5,000 and 6,000 years ago, through a process of nucleation, condensing into nuclei within the extended 'metabolic' networks of the linked settlements in the river valleys.

The spatial, material and metabolic characteristics of the early cities were intricately linked to the ecological and climatic system within which they emerged, and to the regional variant of the common founding system from which they descended. Where climate and ecology were similar, their evolutionary development tended to be convergent, with approximately similar spatial patterns and material organisations. What was common to them all was the increasing ability to extract energy from their locality, to manipulate and transform materials, and the accumulation and propagation of information. Information systems arose from the recording and transmission of differentiated and fluctuating flows of energy and materials, and evolved as the metabolic system of cities increased in complexity. Variations also arose in the form and scale of individual buildings, in the inventory of building functions, in the spatial organisation of groups of buildings, and in the arrays of cities and settlements. As more extended and more complex 'metabolic' systems developed, the intensified flow of energy and materials acted as a positive feedback to the further evolutionary development of energy and information systems.

Land-based nomadic systems, evolved from a variant form of the founding system, also exhibited common material characteristics and seasonal mobility patterns as they developed and expanded across ecologically marginal territories in Africa, Eurasia and Siberia, and Northern America. The principal vectors of interaction with the systems of cities were trade and war. They transported information and high value items across local and regional territories, and in doing so diffused cultural values. In many regions and particularly in north-east Asia, they also developed advanced strategies and technologies of systematic warfare.[3] A significant variant system arose from the intensive use of river craft that extended the metabolic activities of the systems of cities along the Nile, the Euphrates/Tigris, the Indus, and the Yiluo and Huang He rivers of China. Maritime nomadic systems coevolved with the development of sailing ships capable of longer coastal and sea voyages around the Mediterranean, the Indian Ocean and the South China Sea. As extended arrays of cities and their colonies were established, linked by maritime and land-based nomadic systems, the flow of energy and materials intensified at a regional scale. The quantity and complexity of information to regulate the flows through the expanding systems increased accordingly.

CITIES AND INFORMATION SYSTEMS

The evolutionary development of scaled plan drawings may be inferred from the stone statue of Gudea,[4] currently in the Louvre, which is known to be a little more than 4,000 years old. The seated figure has a tablet on his knees on which is inscribed the plan of a temple, along with a graduated scale rule. The plan is orthogonal, and defines a thick wall with buttresses, appropriate for the brick construction of that region and time. Gudea's robe has an intricate inscription that includes an account of the construction, and the distant source of materials such as cedars from Lebanon and stone from northern Syria. Two inscribed stone cylinders have also been found that document the construction.[5] Scaled plan and elevation drawings were also used in Egypt. One of the few surviving drawings on papyrus, known as the Turin papyrus, sets out the front and side elevations of a shrine at Ghorab. The elevations were drawn in black ink against a red grid, suggesting the method of transferring the drawing at full scale to the stone block. Few papyrus drawings survive, perhaps because only important drawings were made on the fragile and expensive papyrus and leather surfaces.[6] Most construction drawings were made on temporary plaster surfaces or on flat timber panels as working templates during construction. Site measurements were made with a cord knotted at 12 equally spaced intervals, a flexible 'ruler' also used by the city surveyors to mark field boundaries.

In Mesopotamia, Egypt and in China the first forms of systematic writing arose about 5,000 years ago, at the same time as the emergence of cities. In Mesopotamia small clay tablets had been in use for at least a thousand years to record quantities and transactions of grains, livestock and materials. The inscribed signs were stylised but recognisable pictorial representations such as of ears of wheat, or bundles of reeds. Abstract symbols were developed when reed styluses became widely used to press marks into the fresh clay. The resulting written language is known as cuneiform.[7] Egyptian hieroglyphs emerged around the same time, developed through a similar process of gradual abstraction from pictograms. Writing systems of this kind are referred to as logographic systems, and include Chinese and its descendants.

By 3,500 years ago in Mesopotamia, Egypt and China, mathematics had developed to include many geometrical constructions and arithmetical computations. In Mesopotamia detailed surveys of land, property boundaries and parts of cities were recorded on clay tablets as, for example, the map of the city of Nippur[8] that is annotated in cuneiform. Other fragments that survive from the Turin Papyrus show a large Egyptian map indicating the recording of topographical and geological characteristics. The papyrus is extensively annotated and it was probably made in preparation for an expedition to quarry for stone and gold.[9] The Mayan glyphs and other written languages from Mesoamerica emerged a little later, but quite independently. The collapse of the system in the Supe valley and Caral in Peru resulted in abandonment, and the migration of people to the north. The later development of the Inca notational system, manifested in textile strands, threads and knots, known as 'quipu', may have first emerged in Caral. It is not known at present if the 'quipu' system equates in complexity to fully developed writing systems. It has been argued that the development of 'quipu' is analogous to cuneiform, originating as a system of accounting records and evolving into a unique three-dimensional writing system.[10]

Phonetic writing, in which symbols represent the basic sounds or phonemes of spoken language, and syllabic writing in symbols which represent syllables, emerged from the evolutionary development of logographic writing. Today, all writing systems are combinations of logograms and phonetic symbols, augmented by 'silent' or unspoken signs known as 'determinatives' that are used to resolve ambiguities.[11]

In Mesopotamia, Egypt and China the use of writing was limited to professional bureaucrats and scribes. The Greek alphabet of 24 letters, developed from Phoenician consonants and extended by the innovation of signs for vowels, arose approximately 3,000 years ago and is still in use today. It has been used to write other languages, and many other alphabets are descendants, most notably Latin. A significantly larger proportion of the population used written language in the Greek system, although the majority of the population were not literate. Written specifications, or *syngraphai*, described the building, with sufficient information for the craftsmen to understand its form, dimensions and materials and method of construction. The general spatial arrangement of dwellings was long established, and widely known. As in Mesopotamia and Egypt, drawings used in Greek construction were made at full scale on the ground to set out the building to be constructed, or on temporary flat surfaces of plaster or timber as working templates. The master craftsman or architect set out the geometries on the site, and important details were first made in wood or clay at full size. These three-dimensional templates or prototypes were known as *paradeigm*, and precise measurements were taken from the *paradeigm* to the material construction. The Naval Arsenal at Piraeus, the port of Athens, was built 2,300 years ago as a store-house for the rigging and sails of 400 triremes. A stone tablet was incised with the complete specification for the building, including the foundations, site and dimensions, and the size of the stone blocks from which it was constructed.[12]

The archiving of information arises from data that is metabolically significant and ecologically contextualised. Information grows exponentially as populations increase, and greater quantities of energy and materials have to be extracted from the surrounding environment. The development of systems for the collection, storage and redistribution of energy and the manipulations of material was strongly coupled to the evolution of information systems, of administration, governance and the regulation of energy and material flows through the system of cities. Written language emerged from the evolutionary development of its antecedents: spoken language, drawings and material archives. Writing and specialised construction drawings coevolved with systems of cities, and enabled the accurate transmission of greater quantities of more detailed information over larger distances and longer durations. The establishment of distant colonies enabled cities to expand their populations beyond the energetic and material constraints of their local topography and ecology.

Metropolitan or 'mother' cities developed increasingly complex information systems, that in turn enabled the further development of systematic transformations of materials for the construction of artefacts, buildings and cities. Information flowed back to the colonies, accelerating their local expansion and increasing their complexity in turn. Increased complexity required higher levels of organisation, increased numbers of specialists to process, manipulate and to communicate greater volumes and more kinds of information, and they had to be supported on the surplus production of energy and materials in the system. Complexity consumed energy, and each increase in complexity required a further increase in the flow of energy. The process of finding, developing and collecting more energy and materials over greater distances and larger territories required an increase in information processing and consumed yet more energy. The emergence and subsequent evolutionary development of information systems and the systems of cities were strongly coupled, each acting as positive feedback on the expansion and growth in complexity of the other.

The systems of cities within the latitudinal band of the Levant and south-west Asia, the eastern Mediterranean and North Africa[13] all had had similar developmental sequences, with initial phases of rapid increases in population and city size, together with rapid accelerations of the flow of energy, materials and information through their systems. Although there was pronounced variability of climate 2,500 years ago, the overall trend had been a fall in temperatures across southern Eurasia, and the colder, wetter climatic regime extended as far as China. At the same time, the northward shift in the monsoon belts reduced rainfall in the subtropical latitudes and induced extended periods of drought. Sea level fell by 1 metre as more and more water was taken up into the expanding ice sheets.[14] Lower temperatures and changes in the global pattern of precipitation, varying in duration from decades to several centuries, produce substantial ecological changes. It is argued that these climatic variations are coupled to the deep ocean circulation, and so have a similar periodicity, occurring approximately every 1,500 years or so.[15] In the less ecologically favourable locations, expansion slowed and then ceased, and territorial contractions began, followed by declines in populations and migrations. In the most arid and ecologically stressed locations cities were abandoned. In Egypt, Mesopotamia, Crete, Greece and south-west Asia there was an irregular series of contractions and expansions, prolonged periods of famine and warfare that induced large migrations, but in China the systems of cities developed slowly but continuously, expanding the number of cities and doubling the population.

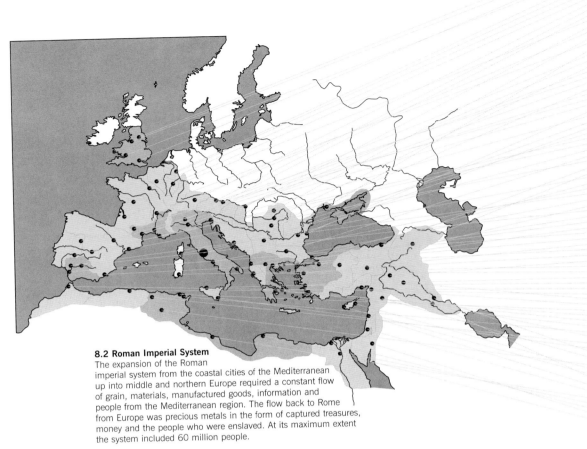

Isca Silurum
Colonia Ag
Durocortoru
Lutetia
Augusta T
Augusta V
Vindobona
Lauriacum
Limonum
Aquincum
Lugdunum
Napoca
Burdigala
Olbia
Mediolanu
Aquileia
Apullum
Arelate
Tolosa
Cremona
Sarmizege
Caesaraug
Salamantic
Narbo
Tomis
Massilia
Naissus
Durostoru
Salonae
Toletum
Emerita A
ROMA
Philippopo
Tarraco
Trapezus
Artaxata
Aleria
Byzantiur
Neapolis
Italica
Dyrrhach
Ancyra
Corduba
Thessalo
Pella
Nicaea
Gades
Tarentur
Pergamu
Carthage
Caesarea
Edessa
Caralis
Buthrotu
Panorm
Ephesus
Caesare
Tingi
Nisibis
Antioch
Utica
Corinth
Miletus
Athenae
Carthag
Tarsus
Cirta
Syracus
Ctesiph
Palmyr
Thevest
Salamis
Paphus
Babylo
Tyrus
Hierosc
Leptis M
Cyrene
Alexan
Petra
Mempl

8.2 Roman Imperial System
The expansion of the Roman
imperial system from the coastal cities of the Mediterranean
up into middle and northern Europe required a constant flow
of grain, materials, manufactured goods, information and
people from the Mediterranean region. The flow back to Rome
from Europe was precious metals in the form of captured treasures,
money and the people who were enslaved. At its maximum extent
the system included 60 million people.

THE IMPERIAL SYSTEMS OF ROME AND CHINA

The imperial[16] systems of Rome and Han China extended over continental scale
territories of approximately 6 million square kilometres each, and by 2,000 years
ago almost half of the world's population lived in either one or the other system.[17]
Their trajectories through time were similar; they arose, expanded and collapsed at
more or less the same time. Each system developed the largest cities of the world
in that period, with in excess of half a million urban residents. Both imperial
systems developed and extended over climatically and ecologically varied
territories; the Roman system expanded from the Mediterranean northwards up
into the cooler and wetter temperate latitudes of Europe, and the Han Chinese
system expanded to the south from the cooler Loess Plateau down into the
warmer and wetter climatic regime of southern China. They were linked by an
extensive network of overland routes, now known as the Silk Road, that began in
Chang'an in China and connected Asia and India to the Mediterranean regions.
People, together with materials, manufactured artefacts, information and diseases

flowed along its 8,000 kilometre length, and through the many trading cities that emerged and expanded along its routes. Both systems developed from antecedent systems within their region. The increase in complexity of imperial systems relative to their antecedent systems was characterised by an increase in differentiation, requiring an extended social order with more specialised occupations, and a more complex network to collect, process and disseminate more kinds and greater quantities of information. Both the Roman and the Han Chinese system developed many new techniques of material transformations, and built many more different forms of buildings than their antecedent systems.

THE ROMAN IMPERIAL SYSTEM

By 2,000 years ago the city of Rome had a population estimated at 500,000 people resident within the city[18] reaching a total of as many as 1 million over the extended urban area some 200 years later. For centuries before the imperial system was created, Rome had already expanded beyond the capacity of its hinterland to feed its citizens and to provide fuel for its industries. It had conquered and controlled the coastal cities of the Mediterranean, and grain flowed from Egypt and North Africa, Sicily, and Sardinia.[19]

The expansion of the imperial system up into middle and northern Europe required constant flows of grain, materials, manufactured goods and people from the Mediterranean region. The flow back to Rome from Europe initially was precious metals in the form of captured treasures, money and people who were enslaved. The continual rebuilding and enlargement of the harbour and granaries at Ostia and Portus during the imperial expansion suggests that grain and materials flowed from Egypt and other fertile territories to Rome, and were shipped from there to the mouth of the Rhône in southern France, and from there by river and overland to all the territories of the imperial system.[20]

The city of Rome had developed from a group of settlements arrayed around a small valley on the floodplain of the Tiber River. Each of the settlements expanded from their small hills down into the valley, eventually coalescing into a continuous urban form. The single-floor brick houses with internal atria and courtyards were variant forms, descended and modified from the courtyard antecedents in Greece, Crete, Mesopotamia and Egypt. In the early centuries this was the dominant form of dwelling in the city, as it was for its antecedents. As the city grew and developed over time, a new form of dwelling emerged, multi-floor buildings that occupied a whole city block. Known as *insulae*, the simplest form consisted of two parallel rows of repeated modules of single chambers, built from brick and extending from the street to the inner space between the rows. Other blocks consisted of parallel rows of two- or three-floor modules, and the most spatially complex had four rows arranged in a rectangle around a paved inner courtyard. Many were six or more floors high, although the legal limit was 21 metres. There were many variations in the spatial, material and structural organisation of the courtyard *insulae*.[21] The number of rooms in the blocks suggest that the occupation of these city block 'apartment' buildings was very high, and there are many records of fires and structural collapse, often attributed to poor building technique, the difficulty of pumping water higher than one or two floors, and the general lack of water in the city.

The Severan Marble Plan of Rome shows the ground plan of every building and block in the city, with a level of detail that included the smallest alleyways and staircases. The marble, also known as *Forma Urbis Romae*, was carved about 1,800 years ago and is known to have been approximately 18 metres by 13 metres when complete, with a scale of 1:240.[22] It is known that detailed surveys were made of all the buildings within Rome, and it is suggested that a more detailed annotated copy existed on sheets of papyrus. Roman maps were made to scale, and were used to record dimensions, ownership and building taxes. Analysis of the plan suggests that the courtyard *domus* with an internal atrium, once the general dwelling for all the population, persisted as the form of dwelling for the rich minority, and that the courtyard *insulae* apartment buildings became the most common form of dwelling for the mass population. The map also shows clearly that the urban blocks were very mixed, with no clear segregation of rich and poor into separate districts, nor of commercial buildings from residential.

There are a few surviving medieval copies of Roman surveyors' manuals. Although often poorly made, the copies that survive include surveying and measuring techniques, town plans, and theoretical sections on astronomy and applied geometry.[23] Surveyors also played a significant role in the establishment of new colonies; choosing the site, drawing the plans for the new city, setting out and allocating the plots of land, and making written records. The Roman army was the principal vector of urbanisation of all the territory under the imperial system. There was one language used in the army, Latin, and the flow of information from Rome to the furthest periphery, and from all regions back to Rome was through the army. The standard plan of the army camp was universally applied, although variations arose according to the local topography. A ditch and a wall enclosing a rectangular area of 20 hectares or so was constructed, either of earth with strong timber facing for temporary camps or of stone and brick for permanent fortresses. Two main streets were set at right angles to each other and around the intersection were set out the main administrative building, the hospital and the granaries. Each quadrant was subdivided by streets, with 15 barrack buildings in each quadrant, each legion having a nominal strength of 6,000 men divided into centuries. As people and goods, food and materials flowed into the camps and fortresses, buildings accumulated outside the walls, often extended for a kilometre or more and eventually developing into large towns. The Roman military origin of many large European cities can be seen in the street patterns that have persisted until today, as in Strasbourg, Cologne and Vienna.[24]

Maintaining the flow of grain, materials and information over the enormous distances to the northern and eastern frontiers was immensely expensive and very slow. When the expansion by conquest was over, the energetic costs of the imperial system rose and the returns began to decline. Once the system had expanded to its maximum extent, changes in climate and ecology accelerated the fall in energetic returns. Prolonged droughts in the eastern Mediterranean reduced the agricultural capacity of even the most fertile agricultural lands, which had already been exhausted by the intensity of cultivation and overgrazing. The cultivation of additional but less fertile territories was required to compensate, requiring more energy input for increasingly diminishing returns.[25] Throughout the imperial system local grain and livestock surpluses were used to supplement the flow from Rome, imposing an oppressive tax regime that required a larger and more expensive bureaucracy to administer. The complexity of the system was increased, by doubling the size of the army and the government, which was paid for by debasing the silver currency with 'base' or cheaper metals and massive inflation. When the climate became rapidly cooler in the high latitudes of northern Europe and Asia, the returns from livestock and grains diminished in ecologically marginal lands that had also been overgrazed and intensively cultivated. The demands for energy extraction placed on the provinces were so high that they could not be met. The oppressed provincial populations were alienated and reduced by migrations, while marginal lands were abandoned throughout the northern territories of the system and the people migrated to the south.[26] The army was increasingly unable to defend the enormous length of the frontiers against mass migrations and, in some areas, hostile invaders. The geographical extent of the imperial system began to shrink back until a little more than 1,500 years ago the city of Rome was conquered and sacked.

THE HAN IMPERIAL SYSTEM

By 2,000 years ago the population of Luoyang was similar to that of Rome, approximately 500,000 people,[27] and the total number of people within the entire Han imperial system was also similar to the Roman system at 60 million. The system extended from the tropical southern coast up to the Great Wall that had been built close to what is now the edge of the cold arid Gobi Desert. The Han system emerged from the collapse and reorganisation of the previous and short-lived Qin system, of which Chang'an, also known as Xi'an, had been the administrative capital; it later became the capital of the first or Eastern phase of the Han imperial system. The antecedent Qin system had unified the separate warring feudal states of China, although once that was accomplished it lasted only another decade.[28] The construction of the Qin mausoleum, the massive necropolis[29] of the first Emperor Qin Shi Huang, is now known for the 'terracotta army' of ceramic figures, of which more than 8,000 have been excavated to date. The construction of the Great Wall of China was completed during this phase of the imperial system, connecting and extending by thousands of kilometres the existing short sections that had been built by smaller independent states to defend against the incursions of the nomadic tribes of the steppes. Flood control and irrigation systems were already comprehensive, having emerged very early in China, and Qin extended the systems, with a new navigable canal connecting the Yangtze and Pearl Rivers, and new reservoirs and irrigation channels. Road construction and their dimensions were standardised, as were weights and measures, and the forms of written language with what is now known as the 'Qinzhuan' font. Military conscriptions involved a very high percentage of the population, and the tax demands, to be paid in labour on the construction of the Great Wall and in grain, were so high that they could not be met without mass starvation. It has been estimated that more than 60 per cent of the total output of all the population was required to keep the system functioning. The energetic demands of the Qin system could not be met and the system collapsed.

The Han imperial system inherited and developed the administrative system, and an imperial academy was established to train government officials, who had to undergo a formal examination. A two tier, central and local, administration was developed in order to minimise the expense of supporting a professional bureaucracy over the huge area of China. Metallurgy industries were nationalised, taxation was reduced and 'labour' conscription for government projects was limited to one month in each year. The population expanded very rapidly. As in the Roman system, a professional army of mass infantry was developed. Both the Han and Roman armies built roads and bridges as they moved during wars of conquest, infrastructures for the movement of people, food and materials. Armies also generate and manipulate vast quantities of information. Civil administration and the flow of information, energy and material were accelerated in both systems by the military. Mass migrations were also used to populate new colony cities in uncultivated lands and to integrate them into the imperial system.[30]

Information for the organisation and construction of cities was set out in the manual *Kao Gong Ji* which translates as *The Records of Examination of Craftsmen*. The manual may have originated in the Qin system, but it was revised and extended during the early Western Han system. It was widely used for the examination and assessment of craftsmen of all trades, guidance on the manufacture of artefacts such as weapons and musical instruments, and the building of dwellings. It has instructions on how to survey and level the ground, set out the square plan according to the cardinal points with a length of 1,200 metres per side, organise the internal subdivisions of the city, and orientate and position all of the principal internal buildings and structures.[31]

The walled cities of the Han imperial system were 'descendants' of the cities that emerged on the northern plains thousands of years earlier. The city of Chang'an, a few kilometres north-west of the modern city of Xi'an, was built on the site of ancient settlements, and has been continuously occupied and rebuilt many times over the 7,000 years since.[32] In the first centuries of the Han imperial system, sometimes referred to as the Eastern Han, it was the capital city. It was approximately square in plan, with massive rammed earth walls enclosing an internal area of 10 square kilometres that was divided into 160 interlocking walled courtyards of varying sizes, three larger walled courtyards of many tens of thousand square metres, and an orthogonal street pattern organised on north to south and east to west axes.[33] The spatially and functionally differentiated organisation, with separate areas for dwellings, granaries, arsenals, manufacturing workshops, foundries and kilns, is clearly descended from much earlier cities, such as Erlitou and Zhengzhou, although it was very much larger and had an extensive inventory of building functions. The northern and western outer walls had to be rebuilt according to the course of the river, and so were irregular in plan. When the capital was moved to Luoyang in the east, the population of Chang'an and its immediate surroundings declined substantially for several centuries. Luoyang, the capital of the later Eastern Han system, extended between the Mang Mountains and the Luo River, and was rectangular rather than square in plan with the long axis running north to south between the mountains and the river. The area enclosed by the rammed earth walls was 10 square kilometres, similar to Chang'an. There is scant archaeological evidence of Luoyang at this time, but it is thought that there was a significant amount of unoccupied land within the enclosure during the Han period.[34]

Most cities were set out and built on the northern side of fertile river-banks on land that was already cultivated, so that large cultivated areas were enclosed within their walls. Lakes were always constructed and this enabled walled cities to have an internal supply of food and water, a significant advantage especially in the semi-arid regions of northern China and in times of warfare when the city gates had to be closed for extended periods.[35] The internal organisation of the walled cities into a differentiated series of interlocking walled courtyards of varying sizes and an orthogonal street pattern was not necessarily fixed over time. The materials used for construction were rammed earth and timber, strong but relatively easy to construct or remove, and with a limited lifespan. In consequence, courtyards within the city frequently needed to be rebuilt, offering opportunities for reconfiguration. Chang'an and Luoyang were rebuilt many times over the following millennia, in response to changes in the course of the rivers, to demographic and political changes, and after destruction in warfare.

The total population of the Han imperial system had risen to 60 million and covered a vast territory. The quantity of information generated, manipulated and disseminated to regulate the system was immense. Although the geographical extent of the Han system was similar to that of the Roman system, four times as many professional administrators were employed. The rivers of China are orientated mainly on the east/west axis, making the flow of grains and livestock, raw materials and manufactured artefacts comparatively easy. However, movements on the north-south axis had to be by road, requiring more human and animal labour and so a higher energy cost. The energetic costs of the system continued to rise, and higher taxes were imposed. Excessive taxation and continuous warfare and incursions on the northern boundaries led to widespread social unrest. The rapidly cooling climate across the northern steppes began to diminish plant and livestock returns, inducing widespread famine and migrations to the south. Communication between the remote northern Xiongnu, Xianbei and Qiang provinces and the capital cities on the central Loess Plateau became irregular and eventually hostile. The Han imperial system collapsed, and fragmented into warring independent states.

COLLAPSE AND REORGANISATION

A thousand years ago the population of the entire world is thought to have been 310 million people, only marginally increased over the previous millennium.[36] The climate was then in the middle of the 300 year warming[37] that is sometimes referred to as the 'Medieval Optimum'. Very dry conditions prevailed across the mid latitudes of the Mediterranean region and southern Europe, south-west Asia and east Africa, and the south-west regions of North America, and strengthened the seasonal monsoons in eastern Asia.[38]

The middle centuries of the previous millennium had been much cooler and very dry across the high latitudes of the Northern Hemisphere. Polar and steppe grasslands are particularly sensitive to small changes in climate, and in dry cold conditions vegetation dies back and new growth is restrained. The nomadic system had evolved in these, and in other, ecologically marginal lands as a variant of the founding system, and their interaction with systems of cities had developed in two principal vectors, trade and war. In north-east Asia the nomadic peoples had developed formidable strategies and technologies of systematic warfare,[39] and as the resources in their homelands declined, waves of migration southwards persisted for hundreds of years. Large movements of armed nomadic peoples into the northern territories of the Roman and Han imperial systems, coupled to the diminishing ecological resources in those territories already under stress from the increasing energetic demands of the imperial systems, triggered a cascade of failures in both systems. The effect of local failures in the systems increased the stresses on the parts of the system to which they were connected, and where there were more connections the further the effects were transmitted. The more complex a system is, the more connections it has, so that what may appear to be a series of independent and unrelated localised failures act as negative feedbacks that amplify and accelerate the decline and collapse of the whole system.[40] Warfare, famine and plague caused severe population decline in both regions; both systems fragmented into separate autonomous and less complex systems, with reduced flows of energy, information and materials. The outcome of the collapse in China was quite different to that in Europe and the Mediterranean.[41]

In China, cooler conditions and changes to the pattern of rainfall had persisted for more than half of the previous millennium,[42] but although the flow of energy and information through the cities and settlements on the central plain of the Loess Plateau and in the south was diminished, it did not break down completely. The independent smaller states were gradually brought back into the system, the invasions of nomadic peoples were contained, the plague did not recur and the imperial system was reassembled and reorganised over a period of some 300 years. As the climate began to warm again towards the 'Medieval Optimum', the strengthening monsoon rains increased agricultural returns substantially, populations expanded, and the flow of energy through the system intensified. A new and much larger city of Chang'an was set out and built south-east of the former Han city. The walls enclosed an area of 84 square kilometres, within which more than a million people lived.

The use of timber for construction and for making the charcoal used as industrial and domestic fuel, and the clearance of land for agricultural use, coupled to climate change, resulted in deforestation and soil erosion at a regional scale, encouraging the spread of savannahs and the extinction of many animal and plant species. The Loess Plateau was once a flat terrain with extensive forests and grasslands, but by the end of the Han imperial system deforestation and changes to the hydrology had accelerated such extreme erosion of the soil that the topography was entirely changed. Thousands of years of human occupations, culminating in the increasing intensity and quantities of energy and water resources extracted during the densely populated Han and successor systems, produced the very steep low hills and valleys and the low water table that characterise the Plateau today.[43]

In Europe and the Mediterranean, the Roman imperial system had been reorganised into two autonomous parts, conventionally referred to as the Western Empire and the Eastern or Byzantine Empire, each with its own Emperor and administration. In the western Mediterranean lands and over all the former territory of the Roman system in Europe, the eventual outcome of the collapse was the emergence of small independent walled cities and fortified towns with sufficient local territory and local connections to be self-sufficient.[44] The medieval feudal pattern, and ultimately the pattern of today's small nation states of Europe, emerged from the collapse and fragmentation. The Eastern system persisted for a thousand years after the fall of Rome, gradually ceding territory and shrinking until only the capital city of Constantinople itself remained. It has been argued that this may be the only example in human history of a system of cities extended over a very large territory, that when faced with declining resources of energy and material chose to reduce the complexity of its organisation and the flow of information, and to revert to a simpler system.[45] The centralised administration was progressively reduced, local militias replaced the professional army, and cities were abandoned.

THE ARCHITECTURE OF EMERGENCE

A thousand years ago the Islamic imperial system had expanded from the original and principal city of Mecca in the Arabian peninsula, to Damascus in Syria and Baghdad in Persia, around the northern rim of the Mediterranean as far as Cordoba and Granada, to Fez in Morocco in North Africa, and up into Asia as far as Samarkand. Under the administration of the Abbasid Caliphate it extended over a greater geographical area than the Roman and Han imperial systems combined, to more than 13 million square kilometres, but with only half the density of population. Existing inhabited cities that had been extensively rebuilt by the Roman imperial system, such as Alexandria, Cordoba and Damascus, were again expanded and incrementally rebuilt. The recombination of successive and distinct spatial and social orders is still evident today. New cities such as Al-Qahirah and Madinat as-Salam, now known as Cairo and Baghdad, were set out and built as fortified walled cities, and imperial libraries were established in both cities to translate and preserve Persian and Greek texts. Baghdad grew rapidly, with a million inhabitants. Within it the library, the 'House of Wisdom', developed into what today might be described as a scholarly research institution, collecting, translating and systematising key ancient and current texts from all across Europe and Asia, and then generating new forms of knowledge. The first organised institution, the Al-Nizamiyya – what today might be called a university, offering free education for the populace – was also founded in Baghdad and the model was adopted by many other cities within the system.

The beneficial warming of the climate across the temperate latitudes of Europe and Asia was coupled to reduced rainfall and increased aridity over the eastern Sahara, the highlands of Ethiopia, around the eastern rim of the Mediterranean and the lands to its east. The consequent ecological stress reduced agricultural returns and diminished the flow of energy through the Islamic system. Although overland caravan and maritime routes extended as far as the more ecologically favoured territories of China, the very long distances prohibited the bulk flow of grains and livestock. Similar difficulties arose to those experienced by the earlier Roman and Han imperial systems: vastly expanded territory, diminishing resources and increasing complexity of the administration required to regulate the flow of information, energy and materials over very long distances. Theological disputes and war between rivals fragmented the system into increasingly independent regional territories, each bounded to their particular regional ecology.

The intensity of energy extraction around the whole Mediterranean region and south-west Asia also contributed to pronounced ecological changes that persist today. Forests provided timber for charcoal making, for the construction of buildings and ships and for the artefacts of war and fortifications. Deforestation had resulted in scarcity of timber all around the southern and eastern Mediterranean before the Roman and Islamic imperial systems,[46] but by 1,000 years ago the entire region was deforested, with depleted and eroded soils. The scarcity of forest resources resulted in intense competition and local warfare between cities and systems of cities, and in turn increased demand. Soil depletion and erosion diminished the energetic returns from agriculture, reducing the population that could be supported so that intensification of agricultural production was necessary. In turn, intensification further increased the depletion of nutrients and further accelerated erosion. Climate and water supply are modified by the metabolic activities of trees, and in the arid and semi-arid regions the cutting down of trees and clearance of forests eliminated the ameliorisation of episodes of drought, and the deserts advanced. In areas with moderate seasonal rainfall, such as the northern shores of the Mediterranean, the leathery shrub and small tree ecology, known as 'maquis', replaced the forests and persists today.

In North America, the changes to the global climate had an even more severe effect. A series of droughts, each at least one and some more than two decades long, occurred all across the southern plains and south-western region of North America. The climate of this region was hot, with a fluctuating pattern of low rainfall. The soil had few nutrients, so even with flood irrigation agriculture could not be intensified. Once the trees had been cut down for fuel and construction and the soil exhausted in a particular location, the people abandoned their settlements and moved to a new site. This system requires a large territory to support a small population that moves and resettles every two or three decades. Over time, the whole region was deforested, erosion accelerated and the soil exhausted. On the Great Plains, as in the Sahara, the dying back of vegetation produced a positive feedback that accelerated the process of desertification and increased the persistence of droughts over time. The long droughts and the consequent ecological changes substantially reduced the agricultural returns of the Anasazi, Mogollon, Hohokam and Patayan peoples, and led to the substantial decline of their populations. Over three centuries of drought there were successive waves of abandonment of the *Pueblo* settlements,[47] and the migration of the people to the more ecologically favourable valleys of the Colorado and Rio Grande rivers. The marginal soils and aridity persist across the entire region today.

The series of severe decadal droughts also had a pronounced effect in the Central American region of southern Mexico and the isthmus connecting the North and South continents of America. The Mayan system had expanded its population to about 5 million people across the region, close to the maximum that the system could support. Agriculture had been intensified by stepped terraces, raised fields and irrigation canals, but further intensification was constrained by the absence of domesticated animals for food and transport systems, and by the lower food energy in the main crop of maize compared with rice or wheat. Individual cities were thus limited to the resources available within a radius of two or three days' walk from the centre. As all materials had to be moved on human backs and all heavy work such as ploughing was done entirely by humans, there was a much higher ratio of human energy invested for lower energy returns than in Europe and Asia.[48] A greater percentage, up to 80 per cent, of the population was involved in agricultural work. The energy flow through the Mayan and other Mesoamerican systems, was in consequence very closely matched to the energetic demands of the cities and settlements. The limestone karst terrain with very few rivers and the long-term regional pattern of fluctuating rainfall made the supply of water a particular problem for cities. In consequence most were built on or close to naturally occurring sinkholes that were lined with plaster to make large cisterns that collected water from extended plastered catchment surfaces. However, the quantity of water stored was rarely sufficient to last more than a year or so, and as a result the series of decadal droughts had a severe effect on the agricultural and water resources of the cities. There were numerous small cities, closely packed together and often competing for favourable agricultural territories but with few links between them. Although written language, numerical and graphical information systems were advanced, and trade in small high value items had reached a regional scale, localised but prolonged warfare between cities was common.[49] Flows of information, energy and material between cities never did develop into a larger and more complex system to distribute resources across the region. Deforestation and soil erosion further accelerated the diminishing returns from agriculture, and city after city was abandoned across the densely packed south of the region. The minimal presence of human occupation over the last thousand years has allowed the tropical forests to expand and today they cover almost the entire region.

THE SLOW RISE IN COMPLEXITY

The climate began to change yet again 500 years ago, entering a three-century long period of intermittently cooler temperatures that persisted until about 200 years ago. The regional and local effects were strongly differentiated, and the lowest temperature and least rainfall occurred in different places and at different times. For example, the coldest century in Europe occurred some 200 years before North American conditions cooled, by which time warmer conditions had returned to Europe. Knowledge of building materials and material manipulation for manufacturing processes was widespread throughout Europe, the Mediterranean region and right across Asia. Building plans and specifications were commonly produced only for larger buildings, were quite standardised, and clearly descended from the systems developed thousands of years earlier. Buildings were still marked out on the ground with ropes as they had always been, and drawings were usually produced during the construction of buildings to resolve difficulties of fabrication and assembly of what were becoming increasingly more complicated details. Evidence suggests that few drawings were necessary, and those that were required were full scale 'working' drawings on plastered floors or wood panels.[50] In China, south-west Asia and the Mediterranean region each craft guild kept their own private sketchbooks with notes on the processes of construction, but European books or texts for the coordination of the many trades and fabrication processes for building construction were rare. Few European examples have survived, and those that have suggest that the cultural diffusion of information from China and from the descendants of the ancient systems of the Mediterranean and south-west Asia took place over centuries rather than decades. Mathematics, surveying instruments and drawings had arisen and developed with the emergence of systems of cities at least 5,000 years before, and had slowly evolved since then. The first systematic use of machines for the mass printing and dissemination of information were the woodcut and moveable character printing presses that were widely used in China several centuries before they appeared in Europe. Mechanical printing systems began to evolve very rapidly about 500 years ago in Europe, enabling the systematic 'mass' production and distribution of books, maps and manuals.

The population of the world had risen to 500 million people, an increase of two thirds over a period of 500 years. The increase is remarkable, as the combination of pandemics of plague that swept across Europe together with the sustained warfare of the expansion of the nomadic peoples of Asia through China to the

Mediterranean resulted in more than 100 million deaths. The plague, sometimes referred to as the 'Black Death', is thought to have originated in the widely distributed 'wild' populations of gerbils in the semi-arid region of Central Asia. The vector of transmission between rodents, and from rodents to humans, was the bite of a flea that had abandoned an infected host animal. There is a clear relationship between climate, cities and the dynamics of the plague. Both the host rodents and fleas greatly increase their numbers during warm springs and wet summers, initiating an acceleration of plague events.[51] Cities and settlements have always had large populations of rodents, in many cases thought to equal or exceed the number of humans, and once the transmission of the disease from 'wild' rodents to 'urban' rodents has occurred, the chances of human infection increase exponentially. When the outbreaks of plague in cities occurred, people fled to seek refuge in uninfected cities or settlements, spreading the disease further. The flow of people along the extensive multiple overland and maritime connections between Asia and Europe accelerated the spread into western Europe, where it is estimated that a third of the population died. The enormous expansion of agriculture in Europe was halted, as the population fell and energetic demands reduced, farms were abandoned and the forests began to grow again over what was once cultivated land.

In Asia, the nomadic people of the Asian steppes and deserts had greatly expanded their numbers during the ecologically favourable centuries of the 'Medieval Optimum'. As the steppes began to cool and dry again in the latitudes sensitive to monsoon variability,[52] crop failures and famine were widespread. Right across northern China ecological pressures on the greatly expanded populations induced yet further waves of migration to the south. In the semi-arid regions of the steppes, the social and military organisation of the nomadic system had increased in informational complexity, and the dispersed tribes were united under a single ruler or 'Khan'. Driven south into the more economically favourable territories they conquered all before them, including the imperial systems of China and Islam.

Within one generation the Mongol system extended from the Pacific coast of Russia, right through Asia and into Europe as far as the river Danube. It became the largest land-based system ever, covering 33 million square kilometres and with a total population of over 100 million people. However, the nomadic system had always either traded with or been predatory towards cities and settlements, and had not developed informational systems for the long-term occupation and regulation of their metabolism. Once the limit of territorial expansion had been reached, the Mongol nomadic system split into four semi-autonomous regional systems that were rapidly absorbed into the more complex systems of information of the territories they occupied. In consequence the process of acculturation modified the nomadic system. In China, the nomads adopted many of the cultural patterns of the imperial system, and were in turn transformed by them. The first city ever built by the steppe nomads, known as Dadu, or great city, conformed closely to the Chinese *Kao Gong Ji* model cities in plan and material construction, and is today part of Beijing. Travellers from the small dense cities of Europe, including Marco Polo, were astonished by the number of cities in China, the enormous areas enclosed within their walls, and the dense populations two or three times larger than that of any city in Europe. The imperial system of China progressively reduced overland trading contacts, recalled their large fleets and effectively closed its borders to the rest of the world for hundreds of years.

Further to the east, at Angkor on the flat floodplain of the Siem Reap River in Cambodia, the urban population had expanded to over a million people. The array of settlements was similar in many ways to that of the Maya, with many small cities without any obvious hierarchy. The polycentric system with multiple 'suburbs' extended over a land area of more than 1,000 square kilometres, integrated by an irrigation system of ponds, reservoirs and canals with built up banks to cope with variability of the monsoons.[53] The system had developed to the maximum level of complexity that could be supported by intensive irrigated rice agriculture. The extensive land clearance deforested the land and accelerated erosion, and the increasingly intensive agriculture required to support expanding populations over centuries depleted the nutrients in the soil. When the latitudinal shifts in the monsoons induced the prolonged cool and dry conditions, it led to accelerated agricultural failure, which ultimately caused widespread famine. The population declined rapidly, and much of the city and its multiple suburbs were abandoned.

In Europe 500 years ago the network of cities, towns and villages that exist today was substantially completed. As the population began to increase rapidly after the plague, the area of land needed for cultivation increased accordingly, reversing the growth of forests over abandoned agricultural land, and accelerating the deforestation of much of Europe. Most dwellings were built of wood, and construction in brick or stone required enormous quantities of strong timber as scaffolding, and the processes of transforming raw materials into even the most basic components of buildings, such as brick, ceramics and metal, all required timber or charcoal fuelled furnaces. It is thought that the largest quantities of all the timber cut from the forests were consumed as firewood for domestic cooking and heating. The development of professional navies and merchant fleets consumed the best quality timber such as oak, larch, ash and beech.

The population of the city of Venice, located between the Eastern Roman empire and the Islamic empire, is estimated to have been as large as 150,000 or so, at the time when the population of Rome had fallen below 50,000, and even the largest city of the Eastern Roman empire, Constantinople, had a central population of no more than 200,000. Venice evolved from Roman settlements on marshy islands at the mouth of the river Po, and sits on millions of oak and larch piles. Over the centuries the forests upriver of the city were cut down to supply the piles, the structural frames of many of the buildings, industrial processes and domestic heating, and for export around the Mediterranean. The rapid erosion of the cleared land and the riverbanks increased flooding and silt deposits in the lagoon.[54] Ships had been constructed in Venice, like other port cities in the western Mediterranean, for at least a thousand years before the building of the Arsenal. The Venice Arsenal was an extensive municipal shipyard within which the systematic fabrication of trading vessels and warships was organised. Craftsmen worked in teams – each specialised in one part of the sequence of construction – using standard pre-shaped timber components. What we now think of as the assembly line logic of industrial manufacturing originates in shipyards, and the shipyard systems were themselves descendants of the organisation of the shared assembly and fabrication of pit structures, dwellings and larger building constructions that had evolved over tens of thousands of years. The Venice Arsenal employed over 16,000 people on its production line 500 years ago, and is reputed to have completed one ship a day.

The form of the Venetian merchant ship or galley was a descendant of the Egyptian and Roman galleys, and still made use of oarsmen. The carrying capacity of ships had increased only marginally from the Roman galleys, but the speed, reliability in adverse weather conditions and the sheer number of ships greatly accelerated the flow of materials and manufactured artefacts through Venice and the Mediterranean region. The evolutionary development of ship design and construction was strongly coupled to a rise in the complexity of information and the emergence of new modes of representing and disseminating it. Venice was the centre for the first systematic mass production and dissemination of printed information, replacing handwritten manuscripts with books and charts of which thousands of copies could be produced in a single 'print run'. Developments in the forms of ships constructed in Portugal and other Atlantic cities made ships faster, sturdier and capable of a much greater range than the oared Venetian galleys. Construction systems for deep-water ships coevolved with the development of maps, charts and navigational instruments, and had a significant effect on the systems of cities in Europe, enabling their colonial expansion across the continents of the Americas and Africa. The emergence of three-masted sailing ships, with greatly increased sail areas and more sophisticated control systems that enabled them to sail closer to the wind, allowed longer voyages along the coast of Africa and around into the Indian Ocean, across the Atlantic to the Americas, and into the Pacific to complete the circumnavigation of the world. Changes to the form of sailing ships over the next three centuries included increases in size, speed, carrying capacity, and the development of armed ships with accurate gunnery and greatly extended range. Lisbon and Oporto, Amsterdam and Antwerp, Paris and London expanded rapidly to become the largest cities, each with extensive maritime systems through which materials from across the world flowed into Europe, and from where information flowed out.

Maritime systems continued to develop, with systematic mass production of great numbers of ever larger and faster sailing ships, more precise navigation, and professional navies. The capacity to move substantial numbers of people and material across the oceans enabled military excursions and the subsequent colonisation of the Americas. The indigenous people had not developed resistance to viruses that were common in Europe, such as smallpox and influenza, and these diseases spread rapidly through their populations with catastrophic consequences. The total population of North and South America was estimated to have been about 60 million people, similar to the maximum numbers in either the Roman or Han Chinese empires. The densest populations were the Aztecs and the Incas; they were able to support a high population density through intensively irrigated agricultural systems, complex information systems and social organisation. Within a century of the first contacts, however, the demographic collapse was complete, with the population reduced by 90 per cent.[55] In the absence of people, forests began to expand over the abandoned settlements and cultivated lands.

ENERGY, INFORMATION AND COMPLEXITY

A century ago the world population was calculated to have exceeded 1.6 billion (1,600 million), more than three times as many as the number of people alive in the world when the first Europeans made land falls in the Americas. As the existing networks of systems of cities in Asia, Europe and the Mediterranean were connected to each other by a greatly expanded maritime system to the Americas, new forms of fuel energy and information emerged and the interconnected global system was increased in complexity. Successive waves of migrating people flowed from Europe, particularly Spain, Portugal, England, France and the Netherlands. The expansion of settlements and cities in North and Central America accelerated and prolonged the flow over successive generations.

The energy resources of the systems of cities had not changed since they emerged between 5,000 and 6,000 years ago. Biomass in the form of wood and crop residues, human and animal muscles, flowing water and wind were the primary resources. Wood, and later charcoal, provided the source of heat for cooking, the heating of dwellings in winter and for the transformation of materials to be used for construction and manufacturing such as brick making, metallurgy and ceramics. Human and animal muscles were also used to drive water wheels and other mechanisms for lifting water. The lever, wedge, pulley systems, wheel and axle, and the endless screw provided amplification of muscle power in all these activities. River and sea-going craft driven by wind energy, usually supplemented by human muscles, were also in widespread use. Variations and developments in form, size, numbers and efficiency occurred in differing climatic regimes and ecologies, as did their recombination into more complex mechanisms and larger and more complex irrigation systems, manufacturing and construction processes. Nonetheless, the set of energy resources did not change until the expanding populations and consequent increase in demands for timber and charcoal were already surpassing the limits of supply in the extensively deforested territories of North America, Europe and Asia.

Fossil fuels contain more energy per unit of volume than wood and charcoal. The use of fossil fuels occurred first in Europe where localised and small-scale use of coal from surface outcrops is thought to have begun about 2,000 years ago, but it was not until 100 years ago that the burning of coal (and some oil) equalled the use of wood, charcoal and crop residues. Coal requires relatively little processing beyond the difficulties of extracting it from ground, but it did require a whole new infrastructure of increasingly rapid distribution systems that connected sources and cities, principally canals, railways and steam powered shipping, each with their own specialised buildings and artefacts, that made the fast transportation of coal and other bulk materials possible. The final elements in the new physical infrastructure were the power stations to burn the coal to generate electricity and the 'grid' or extended cable networks to distribute it. The full transition from local systems to national and continental scale systems had taken four generations[56] in Europe and North America, and in other parts of the world it took perhaps a generation or two longer. There are still some parts of the world where, either by circumstance or choice, wood and charcoal persist today as primary energy sources. Oil and gas have followed similar trajectories over time, each taking more than two generations to implement and deploy. All three energy sources are simultaneously in use today, augmented by hydroelectric and nuclear systems, but coal still supplies almost one third of all the energy used in the world.

The ability to extract and deploy energy from 'high density' fuels coevolved with an equally significant acceleration in the velocity of distribution of information, in the variety of its forms and in quantity. The full implementation and deployment of the newly emerged information networks had a similar multi-generation trajectory over time, and the new networks did not replace older distribution systems but added new velocity and greatly enlarged capacity. The forms of information had been greatly expanded over the previous century, with systematic studies of all natural phenomena leading to the development of new domains of knowledge and new disciplines. Naturalists, explorers and experimental investigators of all kinds gathered measurements, made surveys and analysed data statistics, refined instruments and made taxonomies that provided the foundation for new sciences. New forms of communication networks emerged, giving open access to information to many more people, as national postal services became interconnected across continents by railways and between continents by faster and more regular shipping. Newspapers, encyclopaedias, instruction manuals and books of all kinds were rapidly distributed across continents and oceans. Information encoded in electrical impulse, the dots and dashes of Morse code, was almost instantaneously transmitted along continental scale networks of cables by the telegraph, and telephone and radio had begun to expand from their initially small and localised use. Analog calculating machines such as the water-powered astronomical clock described in the *Book of Knowledge of Ingenious Mechanical Devices*[57] had been known in the Islamic system. Analytical engines and machines that could read data from cards patterned with holes, perform calculations and regulate other machine processes in manufacturing industries and for large data projects such as national census had evolved to become widespread 100 years ago.

New material processes were enabled by the phase change in energy and information systems. The construction materials for manufacturing artefacts of all kinds had changed little in more than 5,000 years: wood and other biological materials, brick, and stone and their derivatives. Bronze and iron artefacts and weapons had also been produced for more than 2,000 years. The systematic mass production of iron and steel coevolved with the new infrastructures of energy and information, each acting as positive feedback and intensifying the development of the others. Fuel and food energy, people and materials flowed in increasing volumes and accelerating velocity through the networks of the extended and increasingly connected metabolisms of the global set of systems of cities. The subsequent development of oil and gas, synthetic materials, television and digital computation, each with their respective infrastructures and networks has added complexity to the system, overlaying but not displacing the systems within which they emerged. They also followed similar trajectories over time, taking more than two generations to implement and deploy.

A hundred years ago the number of cities had rapidly increased in North America, and across the world there were at least 16 cities that had more than 1 million citizens. London was the largest at that time with more than 6 million citizens. London, New York, Paris, Berlin, Vienna, Tokyo, Beijing, St Petersburg and Moscow were each the centre of very large imperial systems with extensive land and maritime networks of connections to subsidiary cities and settlements. Europe was intensively urbanised, with more than half of the population living in urban areas. North America and Japan became similarly urbanised within one generation. Asia and Africa were predominantly rural, and remained so until very recently. In China today about one third of the population live in cities,[58] but in Europe and North America four out of every five people do. As the world population has grown exponentially, existing cities have expanded out over their adjacent territories, and new cities have been rapidly built. Over the last century, despite two periods of systematic warfare at a global scale, and several smaller scale but decade-long interregional conflicts, the global system has become increasingly connected over greater and greater distances. There are very few cities in the world today that could survive unchanged on disconnection from the global network, or its failure.

Ten years ago the world population had increased to 6 billion, an increase which had significantly more than trebled in just 90 years. The number of cities with over a million citizens had increased from 16 to more than 450, with uncounted numbers of smaller cities with their own subsidiary settlements. The geographical distribution of extremely large cities, commonly known as 'megacities', reveals the pattern of population growth and city expansion was accelerating most rapidly in Asia, India and South America. Tokyo, for example, had more than 35 million inhabitants at that time, more than half the number of people in either the Han or the Roman imperial systems but concentrated into a tiny fraction of their geographical area. Seoul, Manila, Delhi and Mumbai, Mexico City and São Paulo, and New York each had 20 million or more, and Shanghai, Guangzhou, and Beijing, Osaka, Jakarta, Calcutta, Karachi, Cairo and Los Angeles each had more than 15 million citizens. In some regions cities of varying sizes and densities have become so numerous that there are no distinct territories between them, and they have coalesced into one continuous regional scale urban configuration, commonly referred to as a 'megalopolis'.[59] The largest tend to be located on river deltas, such as the Yangtze River region in China that now has more than 80 million inhabitants. Many more are expected to emerge in Asia within the next generation, and the consolidation of already dense regions in Europe and North America is also likely to continue.

City forms almost everywhere have been modified by the increasing proportion of the physical infrastructures required for the mass movements of energy, information and materials, and people too move greater distances more frequently and at greater velocities than 100 years ago. Cities have become increasingly similar, convergent in the forms of their material and their metabolic organisation, with identical high velocity networks of energy and information that flow across continents and oceans. This is as true of motorcars and mobile phones as it is of clothes and computers, of skyscrapers, suburban homes and shopping malls, of cities, 'megacities' and the regional scale urban configurations of 'megalopolis'. As cities across the world have become increasingly interconnected, and new cities are rapidly built and connected, the complexity of the whole system increases in consequence. The increased size and connectivity enables increased flows between the systems of cities, but it also allows failures and perturbations to travel further and faster from their local origin.

THE ARCHITECTURE OF EMERGENCE

COMPLEXITY AND ECOLOGY

Humans, like all other life, have to extract energy from their environment to generate and maintain their forms, and to reproduce and propagate their descendants out into new territories and down through time. In consequence there are no ecological systems on the surface of the earth that have not been modified in some way by the effects of the extended metabolisms of human societies. The founding system of civilisation used fire to clear land and drive game, cut down trees for fuel and the construction of dwellings, and the extinction of megafauna on three continents induced changes in steppe grasslands, in cool forests and in the warmer grasslands. As human populations expanded across the surface of the earth, the gathering of grains altered the regime of natural selection and initiated genetic changes in wild cereals. These genetic changes, together with the domestication of animals, enabled the development of systematic agriculture. After cities emerged between 6,000 and 5,000 years ago, the increased quantities of energy and materials extracted from their environments began to substantially modify ecological systems over more extensive territories. Food and fuel energy and materials for construction and the manufacturing of artefacts flowed from networks of settlements to the cities. Information flowed back from the city to the settlements as data in the forms of accounts and encoded in transformed materials, such as bricks and ceramics, timber, artefacts, tools and implements. As the system of cities expanded and developed over time the flows became more complex, generating more complex social organisations in the cities, more kinds of and greater quantities of notation and calculation, and more specialists to process that information. As the number of specialised occupations grew, more intensive cultivation was needed to support them, generating extensive irrigation systems, and the modification of ecologically marginal territories was greatly increased. Over time ever more extensive and complex metabolic networks were developed, drawing energy and materials over regional and continental scale territories. The evolutionary development of the metabolic systems of cities has been episodic and irregular, with many periods of expansion to the critical limit of stability, and subsequent collapse and reorganisation. The emergence and development of the systems of cities is strongly coupled to extensive deforestation and the spread of savannahs, the extinction of animal and plant species, soils exhausted of their nutrients, silted river courses and accelerated erosion of the land across Asia, North Africa, Europe and America.

Human modifications to the surface of the earth and to the ecological systems that live upon it have altered the interactions between the surface of the earth and the atmosphere at local, regional, and global scales. The progressive deforestation over three continents and many thousands of years has reduced the transpiration of water up into the atmosphere and altered the storage of water in the soil. It also changed the albedo of the surface, allowing more heat energy to be absorbed by the land. Systematic intensive agriculture has further accelerated these modifications.[60] Additionally, the chemical composition of the atmosphere has been modified, by black carbon (soot) particulates from the burning of timber, charcoal, crop residues and fossil fuels which have added increasing amounts of carbon dioxide and other greenhouse gases to the atmosphere, enabling it to retain more heat energy.

The emergence and development of the coupled high density fossil fuel and equally high density information systems has enabled increasingly rapid acceleration in the rate of growth in human populations over the last two centuries. Half of all humans alive today live in cities, although the geographical pattern is uneven; in Europe and North America this figure is four out of every five people. Existing cities are expanding and new cities are being built, connected and integrated into the world system of cities. The flow of information and energy has accelerated accordingly, the population of the world is rapidly expanding and the complexity of the world system continues to increase. The energetic expense of complexity in the system continues to accelerate, with increasingly greater numbers of people in specialised roles to generate and process the flow of information, and in manufacturing, constructing and maintaining its physical infrastructure. The most densely populated regions of Asia, Europe and North America now consume biological materials at more than twice the rate at which the ecological systems of their own regions can regenerate. They are now dependent on the resources of other regions to meet the deficit in the flow of energy and materials required to support their preferred patterns of consumption.[61] In turn, the increased demands on other regions limits their capacity to expand their own populations. More than half of all the fuel energy consumed in the USA and Europe today is currently imported from other regions, and the dependence on energy imports in Asia is accelerating. There are many indicators that suggest that the system is close to the threshold of stability. Systems that have evolved close to their maximum capacity are poised at the critical threshold of stability and are consequently very sensitive to social, climatic and ecological changes. A local failure may trigger a cascade of failures that amplify each other right across the world and so trigger the collapse of the whole system.

THE ARCHITECTURE OF EMERGENCE

1   Data from *The World at Six Billion*, Population Division, Department of Economic and Social Affairs, United Nations Secretariat, 1999.

2   Smith, HJ, 'Did Climate Rock the Cradle?', *Science*, vol 312, no 5777, 2006, pp 1109.

3   Lomax, A and CM Arensberg, 'A Worldwide Evolutionary Classification of Cultures by Subsistence Systems', *Current Anthropology*, vol 18, 1977, pp 659–701.

4   The Sumerian king who ruled the city of Lagash, Southern Mesopotamia between 4,144 and 4,124 years ago. Statues of Gudea have also been found in Ur and Uruk.

5   Suter, CE, 'A New Edition of the Lagas II Royal Inscriptions including Gudea's Cylinders', *Journal of Cuneiform Studies*, vol 50, 1998, pp 67–75.

6   Kostov, S and D Cuff, *The Architect: Chapters In The History Of The Profession*, University of California Press (Berkeley), 2000, pp 7–10.

7   From the wedge-shaped mark that a reed stylus makes when pressed into clay, derived from the Latin word *cuneus*, meaning wedge.

8   In the collection of the Museum of Archaeology and Anthropology at the University of Pennsylvania.

9   Harrell, JA and VM Brown, 'The Oldest Surviving Topographical Map from Ancient Egypt (Turin Papyri 1879, 1899 and 1969)', *Journal of the American Research Center in Egypt*, vol 29, 1992, pp 81–105.

10 'From Knots to Narratives: reconstructing the art of historical record-keeping in the Andes from Spanish transcriptions of Inka Khipus', *Ethnohistory*, vol 45, 1988, pp 409–38; and Mann, CC, 'Unraveling Khipu's Secrets', *Science*, vol 309, 2005, pp 1008–9; and Mann, CC, *1491: new revelations of The Americas before Columbus*, Random House (New York), 2005, pp 345–9.

11 The process of evolutionary development from pictograms/logograms to phonetic alphabets is summarised in Diamond, J, Chapter 12, 'Blueprints and Borrowed Letters', in *Guns, Germs and Steel, A Short History of Everybody for the Last 13,000 Years*, Chatto & Windus (London), 1997; and the development and diaspora of the family of Indo-European languages from a common root is traced in Diamond, J, Chapter 15, 'Horses, Hittites and History', in *The Rise and Fall of the Third Chimpanzee*, Random House (New York), 1991; and a detailed comparison of human genetic evolution and linguistic evolution can be found in Chapter 5, 'Genes and Languages', in Cavalli-Sforza, LL, *Genes, Peoples and Languages*, The Penguin Press (London), 2000.

12 Hovgaard, W, 'The Arsenal in Piraeus and the Ancient Building Rules', *Isis*, vol 8, 1926, pp 12–20.

13 Frank, AG, 'Bronze Age World System Cycles [and Comments and Reply]', *Current Anthropology*, vol 34, 1993, pp 383–429.

14 Kininmonth, W, 'The Climate of Past Ages', in *Climate Change: a natural hazard*, Multi-science Publishing Company (Essex), 2004, pp 28–30.

15 deMenocal, PB, 'Cultural Responses to Climate Change during the Late Holocene', *Science*, vol 292, 2001, pp 667–73.

16 The meaning of the Latin word *imperium* is 'territory'.

17 The estimated population of the world 2,000 years ago was 300 million people, *The World at 6 Billion*, United Nations Population Division, 1999.

18 Chandler, T, *Four Thousand Years of Urban Growth: an historical census*, Edwin Mellen Press (Lampeter), 1987, pp 522–4.

19 Fulford, M, 'Economic Interdependence among Urban Communities of the Roman Mediterranean', *World Archaeology*, vol 19, 1987, pp 58–75.

20 Fulford, M, 'Territorial Expansion and the Roman Empire', *World Archaeology*, vol 23, 1992, pp 294–305.

21 Storey, GR, 'Regionaries-Type Insulae 2: architectural/residential units at Rome', *American Journal of Archaeology*, vol 106, 2002, pp 411–34.

22 Stanford University holds a complete digital copy of the surviving 1,186 fragments of the marble, available online at http://formaurbis.stanford.edu/index.html; the original marble pieces are held in Rome at the Museum of Roman Civilization.

23 Dilke, OAW, 'Illustrations from Roman Surveyors' Manuals', *Imago Mundi*, vol 21, 1967, pp 9–29.

24 Watkins, TH, 'Roman Legionary Fortresses and the Cities of Modern Europe', *Military Affairs*, vol 47, 1983, pp 15–25.

25 Tainter, J, TFH Allen and TW Hoekstra, 'Energy Transformations and Post-Normal Science', *Energy*, vol 31, 2006, pp 44–58.

26 Tainter, JA, 'Problem Solving: complexity, history, sustainability', *Population and Environment: A Journal of Interdisciplinary Studies*, vol 22, 2000, pp 3–41; and Tainter, JA, 'Social Complexity and Sustainability', *Ecological Complexity*, vol 3, 2006, pp 91–103.

27 Chandler, T, 'Four Thousand Years of Urban Growth: an historical census', Edwin Mellen Press (New York), 1987, pp 522–4.

28 Qin Shi Huang declared himself the first Emperor of China and died 11 years later (2,200 years ago in 210 BCE).

29 Now measured to cover more than 2 square kilometres or 2.18 million square metres in total.

30 Kiser, E and C Yong, 'War and Bureaucratization in Qin China: exploring an anomalous case', *American Sociological Review*, vol 68, 2003, pp 511–39.

31 Xu, Y, *The Chinese City in Space and Time: the development of urban form in Suzhou*, University of Hawaii Press (Honolulu), 2000, pp 29–39.

32 Shatzman-Steinhardt, N, 'Why Were Chang'an and Beijing so Different?', *The Journal of the Society of Architectural Historians*, vol 45, 1986, pp 339–57.

33 Trewarta, GT, 'Chinese Cities: origins and functions', *Annals of the Association of American Geographers*, vol 42, 1952, pp 69–93.

34 Ho, Ping-ti, 'Lo-yang, AD 495–534: a study of physical and socio-economic planning of a metropolitan area', *Harvard Journal of Asiatic Studies*, vol 26, 1966, pp 52–101.

35 Chang, Sen-Dou, 'Some Observations on the Morphology of Chinese Walled Cities', *Annals of the Association of American Geographers*, vol 60, 1970, pp 63–91.

36 World population 2,000 years ago was 300 million, 1,000 years ago 310 million, data from *The World at Six Billion*, Population Division, Department of Economic and Social Affairs, United Nations Secretariat, 1999.

37 Mann, ME, Z Zhang, MK Hughes, RS Bradley, SK Miller, S Rutherford and F Ni, 'Proxy-based Reconstructions of Hemispheric and Global Surface Temperature Variations over the Past Two Millennia', *Proceedings of the National Academy of Sciences*, vol 105, 2008, pp 13252–7.

38 Seager, R, N Graham, C Herweijer, AL Gordon, Y Kushnir and ER Cook, 'Blueprints for Medieval Hydroclimate', *Quaternary Science Reviews*, vol 26, 2007, pp 2322–36.

39 Lomax, A and CM Arensberg, 'A Worldwide Evolutionary Classification of Cultures by Subsistence Systems', *Current Anthropology*, vol 18, 1977, pp 659–701.

40 Sachs, JD, 'Blackouts and Cascading Failures', *Scientific American*, vol 300, 2009, pp 20–1.

41 Scheidel, W, 'From the "Great Convergence" to the "First Great Divergence": Roman and Qin-Han state formation and its aftermath', *Princeton/Stanford Working Papers in Classics*, 2007.

42 Bao, Y, A Braeuning, KR Johnson and Y Shi, 'General Characteristics of Temperature Variation in China During the Last Two Millennia', *Geophysical Research Letters*, vol 29, 2002, pp 1324.

43 Fang, J and Z Xie, 'Deforestation in Preindustrial China: the loess Plateau region as an example', *Chemosphere*, vol 29, 1994, pp 983–99.

44 Cheyette, F, 'The Origins of European Villages and the First European Expansion', *Journal of Economic History*, vol 37, 1977, pp 182–206.

45 Tainter, JA, 'Problem Solving', pp 3–41.

46 Hughes, JD, 'How the Ancients Viewed Deforestation', *Journal of Field Archaeology*, vol 10, 1983, pp 437–45.

47 Cook, ER, R Seager, MA Cane and DW Stahle, 'North American Drought: reconstructions, causes, and consequences', *Earth Science Reviews*, vol 81, 2007, pp 93–134.

48 Sanders, WT and D Webster, 'The Mesoamerican Urban Tradition', *American Anthropologist*, vol 90, 1988, pp 521–46.

49 Diamond, J, 'Collapse: how societies choose to fail or survive', Viking Press (New York), 2005, pp 157–77.

50 Ghazarian, A and R Ousterhout, 'A Muqarnas Drawing from Thirteenth-Century Armenia and the Use of Architectural Drawings during the Middle Ages', *Muqarnas*, vol 18, 2001, pp 141–54.

51 Stenseth NC, NI Samia, H Viljugrein, KL Kausrud, M Begon, S Davis, H Leirs, VM Dubyanskiy, J Esper, VS Ageyev, NL Klassovskiy, SB Pole and KS Chan, 'Plague Dynamics Are Driven by Climate Variation', *Proceedings of the National Academy of Sciences*, vol 103, 2006, pp 13110–15.

52 Jin, H, Z Su, L Sun, Z Sun, H Zhang and L Jin, 'Holocene Climatic Change in Hunshandake Desert', *Chinese Science Bulletin*, vol 49, 2004, pp 1730–5; and LP Zhu, PZ Zhang, WL Xia, BY Li and L Chen, '1400-year Cold/Warm Fluctuations Reflected by Environmental Magnetism of a Lake Sediment Core from the Chen Co, Southern Tibet, China', *Journal of Paleolimnology*, vol 29, 2003, pp 391–401.

53 Evans, DH, C Pottier, R Fletcher, S Hensley, I Tapley, A Milne and M Barbetti, 'A Comprehensive Archaeological Map of the World's Largest Preindustrial Settlement Complex at Angkor, Cambodia', *Proceedings of the National Academy of Sciences*, vol 104, 2007, pp 14277–82.

54 Appuhn, K, 'Inventing Nature: forests, forestry, and state power in Renaissance Venice', *The Journal of Modern History*, vol 72, 2000, pp 861–89.

55 Butzer, KW, 'The Americas Before and After 1492: an introduction to current geographical research', *Annals of the Association of American Geographers*, vol 82, 1992, pp 345–68; and Denevan, WM, 'The Pristine Myth: the landscape of the Americas in 1492', Current Geographical Research, *Annals of the Association of American Geographers*, vol 82, 1992, pp 369–85.

56 One human generation = 25 years.

57 Al-Jazari, 1206.

58 Lu, Q, JY Zhan and KW Lee, 'An Overview on the Urban-Rural Interaction in the Past 50 Years in China', *Chinese Geographical Science*, vol 11, 2001, pp 193–200.

59 From the Greek word meaning 'great city', the name of the first city founded in Arcadia about 2,500 years ago.

60 Robock, A and HF Graf, 'Effects of Pre-Industrial Human Activities on Climate', *Chemosphere*, vol 5, 1994, pp 1087–97.

61 Haberl, H, KH Erb, F Krausmann, V Gaube, A Bondeau, C Plutzar, S Gingrich, W Lucht and M Fischer-Kowalski, 'Quantifying and Mapping the Human Appropriation of Net Primary Production in Earth's Terrestrial Ecosystems', *Proceedings of the National Academy of Sciences*, vol 104, 2007, pp 12942–7.

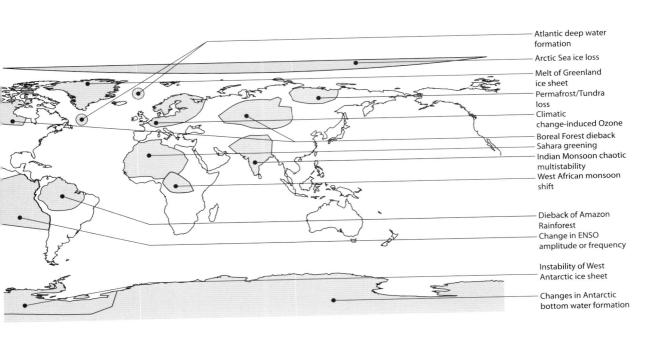

Atlantic deep water formation
Arctic Sea ice loss
Melt of Greenland ice sheet
Permafrost/Tundra loss
Climatic change-induced Ozone
Boreal Forest dieback
Sahara greening
Indian Monsoon chaotic multistability
West African monsoon shift
Dieback of Amazon Rainforest
Change in ENSO amplitude or frequency
Instability of West Antarctic ice sheet
Changes in Antarctic bottom water formation

9.1 Critical Thresholds

There are many continental scale ecological and climatic systems that are known to be sensitive to temperature changes, and that are close to their critical threshold and have begun to change now. As the world continues to warm, the transition of one or more system through its critical threshold will provide positive feedback that has the potential to initiate a cascade of changes in others. The large and multiple changes produced by transition through critical threshold are irreversible on millennia timescales.

THE ARCHITECTURE OF EMERGENCE

Emergence

All forms and all systems change over time, and the forms of nature and the cultural forms of civilisation are inextricably entwined. Humans emerged and evolved within nature, and all the forms of human culture have evolved and developed as part of nature and in turn have extensively modified the natural forms of the surface of the earth, the ecological systems of living forms that exist upon it, and the climate 'metasystem'. All the systems of the world, in nature and in civilisation, have tended to evolve until they are poised close to the critical threshold of stability. The outcomes of the collapse and reorganisation of the systems of civilisation have been the complete loss of social order and dispersal of the people by famine, disease, abandonment of cities and mass migration; a simplification into smaller and simpler assemblies or a reorganisation to a lower level of complexity; and the reordering of the cities, people and subsidiary systems into a more complex system with a higher flow of energy and information. The world is within the horizon of systemic change that will cascade through all the systems of nature and civilisation, and new forms will emerge.

The architecture of all the forms of nature, their arrangement of material in space and over time, emerges from the dynamic interaction of energy and material within complex systems. The systems of the climate, the oceans and atmosphere, and the surface of the land also interact with each other, with many exchanges of energy and materials at varying scales of time and space. All the forms of life on the surface of the earth, including humans, have also emerged from the process of complex systems that are coupled to the transmission of biologically encoded information over time. Living forms exist in varied populations, and where they organise themselves into social collectives, culture emerges. Culture provides another system for the transmission of information down through time, linked to, but distinct from, the biological system. Culturally produced forms exist within, and are modified by, all the other natural systems, and as their numbers have increased they in turn have accelerated or inhibited changes to those systems.

All forms change over time. The forms of clouds and storms, of mountains, rivers and deserts are not static things but are constantly being broken down and renewed. The forms of life come into being, flourish and die in each generation, and although these forms may persist through millennia they are also subject to change. Over time living forms change in response to changes in the climate, in the topography of the land and to changes in the ecological systems within which they and other living forms exist. The culturally produced forms of settlements and cities are also constantly being broken down and rebuilt, and in doing so they are changed. The patterns of energy, information and material that flow through all the forms of the world are subject to many oscillations and perturbations. The flow is modified by 'feedbacks', but occasionally there is such an amplification that the system collapses and is reorganised, and a new form emerges. The new form may be either simpler or more complex. An increase in complexity is usually coupled to an increase in the flow of energy and information through the system, and systems that collapse and revert to a simpler organisation are coupled to a reduced flow of energy and information. Over time, there has been a marked tendency of living systems and of cultural systems towards increasingly higher complexity.

CLIMATE, SURFACE AND LIFE

Climate distributes heat around the world by an intricate choreography of forms and behaviour and in doing so it modulates the exchange of energy and material between all other systems. In turn, climate is affected by the exchanges of energy and material between the ocean, the atmosphere, the land, by all living beings and by the extended metabolic systems of humans. The exchanges occur across multiple scales of dimension and time, so that interactions between the systems are complex and non-linear, subject to fluctuations and variations. These in turn affect the intensity of local weather, and modify the dynamics of the climate system through positive feedback that amplifies change, or through negative feedback that inhibits change. Some changes occur within timescales of hours and days, while other changes take place over decades, hundreds or thousands of years. The metasystem is delicately poised, with many different critical thresholds across multiple scales of space and time, so that a small stimulus at one scale may drive a great and rapid change at another.

The forms of the land emerge from the interaction of tectonic forces uplifting the land from below, and the climatic forces of weathering and erosion breaking down the tectonic forms into fragments and sediments that are carried away and deposited elsewhere. The regional and latitudinal patterns of the climate metasystem generate differentiated regimes of temperature, precipitation and wind, with a range of variation and perturbations in each regime. Weathering, erosion and deposition are produced by the climate; variations and changes to the climate change the behaviour, duration and force of each process. In turn, geomorphic processes also contribute to the generation of climate feedbacks: changes in the 'feedbacks' of surface albedo, increases in greenhouse gases, and aerosols from dessicated soils and deserts. Many landforms are poised at the critical threshold of change, so that small differences to the ratio or balance between force and resistance, energy and material, will precipitate a rapid change of form.

The emergence of new living forms and diverse species is also strongly coupled to the dynamics of climate and its effects on the surface of the earth. Before life emerged, the sun was weaker than it is today, and the chemistry of the atmosphere and the climate were very different. Cyanobacteria were the first photosynthetic forms of life to emerge; photosynthesis absorbs carbon dioxide and excretes oxygen. Over a billion years oxygen levels rose, the levels of heat-retaining greenhouse gases fell, and temperatures began to fall, precipitating the first ice age.

The smallest and simplest of living forms initiated significant changes to the climate, and in consequence to the forms of the surface of the earth. New regional climatic zones and new physical barriers arise from these dynamics, and these induce migrations, shifts in the range of the species, and isolation from the parent species. Exposure to new and different climatic regimes, topography and ecologies modified the regime of natural selection and new species emerged. All the forms of life exist within ecological and climatic regimes that are poised close to the critical threshold of change, and rapid changes have been a significant factor in all extinction and speciation events. Living forms affect the processes of the atmosphere and oceans, and the geomorphic systems of the surface of the earth.

INFORMATION AND METABOLISM IN LIVING FORMS

All living forms are composed of cells, and each cell carries within it the information for the development of the whole form. The genome encodes the programme for the self-assembly of descendants identical to itself, and so it is passed down through time from one generation to the next. The genome consists of only four different molecules, arranged into many long and complicated sequences, in turn arrayed in distinct modules and groups. One small subset of the genome acts as a feedback on the activation of all the other genes, accelerating or inhibiting growth in varying sequences and patterns. Many of the regulatory genes are similar across multiple species, incorporated into the system from their earliest ancestors. Changes arise in the genome by 'copy errors' and mutations that shuffle the sequences of genes or repeat some segments, which in turn produce changes to the physical form. No new molecules are needed, and the reconfiguration of existing sequences and repetition produces a higher complexity within the genome. As the regulatory genes control the sequence of growth, small changes to this set can produce variations in the size, shape and number of the repeating modules of the 'body plan' in the living form. Most changes do not offer any significant benefit or are harmful to the living form. Changes that are advantageous are preserved by natural selection, and over time produce better adaptations to changed ecological or climatic circumstances. Every living form emerges from two strongly coupled processes, operating over maximally differentiated time spans: the differential development of cells in the growth of an embryo to an adult form, and the evolution diversification of forms over time. Information is the critical vector between them. Complexity builds over time by a sequence of modifications to existing forms, and from small and simple forms to ever larger and more complex forms. The emergence of the general organisation or 'body plan' of vertebrates, and its subsequent modification into amphibians, reptiles, birds and mammals and eventually humans, occurred in this sequence.

Metabolism is the 'fire of life', the system of all living forms that captures energy and materials from their environment, transforms them and transports them in fluids to every cell, and excretes changed materials as waste back into the environment. It functions through surfaces and branching networks that exhibit identical mathematical parameters in all living forms, from the smallest microbes to giant sequoias, from mice to mammoths.

The metabolic processes of living forms produce changes in their environment, and these changes modify the local regime of natural selection. The organisation of whole ecological systems emerges from the multiple interactions between the metabolic processes of all the forms of life that coexist within it. Many living forms externalise some aspects of their metabolism by material constructions, often collectively arrayed and organised. Constructions such as burrows and nests lessen the load on individual metabolisms within the collective by smoothing out fluctuations in the external temperatures and humidity, storing food and providing strategic access to the home range.

The behavioural complexity of the social insects arises from the collective actions of multiple individuals, each of which has only a very small set of simple programmed behaviours. There is no 'central control, no decision making' individual or group. Each individual insect will have a slightly different threshold of sensitivity to temperature, humidity and chemical stimuli that triggers their actions, and a slightly differing degree of response to them. The collective constructions are permanent, usually centrally located, and their mobility patterns are determined by the spatial pattern of food sources within their range. The collective construction is constantly adjusted by adding or removing material, one grain at a time, to regulate constant temperature, humidity and the ratio of oxygen to carbon dioxide. The intelligent behaviour of the collective as a whole emerges from the interaction of millions of very simple individual actions.

The mobility pattern of the great apes also arises from the spatial pattern of distribution and the seasonality of food plants across the large territory of the group. Their material constructions are temporary, abandoned after a day or two. They are individual constructions, but closely grouped at night for defence. Information in the form of ecological knowledge of their home range, and the expertise needed for nest construction, tool making and use is socially acquired, passed down through the generations from adult to child. It is their cultural system for the transmission of information that modifies and extends the inherited and genetically conserved innate responses to environmental stimuli.

Social order, distributed intelligence and patterns of mobility emerge from the processes of externalised metabolisms. Children are born into an externalised metabolism modified by the ancestral population, and the genes that are linked to these traits are inherited and passed on to the next generation. Genes are transmitted between individuals, but the collective as a whole maintains the ecological inheritance of an extended metabolic system from one generation to the next. This changes the regime of natural selection in the favour of the most successful collectives, and it is their genes that will be conserved.

INFORMATION AND METABOLISM IN HUMAN FORMS

The evolution of human forms and their externalised and extended metabolic system is inseparable from the evolutionary development of their culture system for the transmission of information. Culture acts to transmit complex social and ecologically contextualised information down through the generations, and it has also tended to increase in complexity over time. In humans, like all other living forms, information and the ability to extract and process energy and materials from their environment are strongly coupled. The human form and culture coevolved during an extended period of extremely rapid variations in the climate and ecology, and the ability to adapt to a variety of climates and ecological conditions was genetically conserved. All people alive today are descendants of a small founding population of anatomically modern humans that emerged in east Africa about 135,000 years ago, and possibly from one woman within that population, the 'Mitochondrial Eve'. Ecological and social information, transmitted down through the generations by the cultural systems of humans, provided the 'programme' or set of instructions for the metabolic, spatial and social organisation of the founding system of civilisation. It enabled humans to regulate their collective metabolisms and thrive in a variety of climatic and ecological territories, to expand their numbers and flow across the surface of the earth.

The founding system of civilisation developed for tens of thousand of years, with gradually accelerating flow of information and energy that enabled expansion of their populations until the system reached its maximum capacity in many locations. Abrupt climate change induced ecological changes and famine, and the collapse of the founding system was precipitated. The flow of surviving migrants to the more ecologically favourable river valleys increased their population density, and cities emerged through a process of nucleation. In the more marginal ecological territories, nomadic systems emerged, and their interaction with cities provided another vector for the linking of cities and the flow of information over greater distances. Cities and their networks of settlements expanded and developed, strongly coupled to the dynamic changes of climate and ecology within which they were situated.

The integration of settlements, cities and colonies into larger and more complex hierarchical systems, linked by maritime and land-based nomadic systems, extended their collective metabolic systems over increasingly larger geographical areas. The flow of energy and materials intensified at a regional scale, and the quantity and complexity of information to regulate the flows acted as a positive feedback to the evolutionary development of more complex information systems. Information grew exponentially in the cities, and flowed out from the cities through the networks of settlements, to the colonies and their networks, and between systems of cities. Complex

THE ARCHITECTURE OF EMERGENCE

information systems arose to account for and to regulate the collection, storage and redistribution of food and fuel, the transformation of raw materials and the manufacture of artefacts and construction of ships and buildings. The acceleration in complexity enabled systems of cities to expand their populations beyond the metabolic constraints of their local and regional territories. Complexity consumes energy and generates information, and each increase in complexity required a further acceleration in the flow of energy and information. The increased demands on the system were met by intensification of production and by expansion over larger territories. Information and metabolism each provide a positive feedback on the development of the other, and on the growth of populations that in turn drove the system to expand yet further. The emergence of the imperial systems that extended their metabolic system over continental scale territories was driven by growth in the kinds of information and its quantity, and by the continual growth of population.

The massive expansion of maritime systems linked the networks of systems of cities in Eurasia and North Africa to the Americas, and moved increasingly large quantities of people, materials and information around the world. The interconnected global system slowly increased the velocity and quantity of flows in most parts of the world, and populations continued to grow. The global system increased in complexity, with rapid increases in populations driving metabolic demands that had begun to surpass the ecological resources of North America, Europe and Asia. The lands available for further territorial expansion were both limited and ecologically more marginal, and began to show rising costs and diminishing returns. Intensification of production to meet the accelerating demands was enabled by the emergence of new forms of information, and the consequent coevolution of new 'high density' energy and information systems. New domains of knowledge, new sciences, and information of all kinds accumulated and grew exponentially. The full transition of energy and information systems, from local to national and then continental scales, took four generations[1] in Europe and North America, and longer elsewhere. A second phase of information and energy development followed, with a somewhat shorter two to three generation deployment. Oil and gas, digital computation, analysis and imaging, each with increasingly interconnected manufacturing and distribution infrastructures drove yet further intensification of production, with greater and more rapid flows of energy and information across continents and oceans.

There are remarkable mathematical similarities in the metabolic distribution networks of living forms and the culturally produced networks for the distribution of information and energy of the global system. Although there is wide variation in their individual components and chemical processes, the metabolic branching networks of all living forms, from the smallest of microbes to the very largest blue whale, exhibit the same topological scaling properties. Networks for information distribution exhibit many similar parameters to the hierarchical branching metabolic networks of living forms,[2] and a great variety of other culturally produced networks also exhibit comparable 'scale free' power law characteristics. This is most likely to be produced by the way in which the systems grow. Both biological and cultural networks grow continuously by the addition of new nodes or hubs, but these new nodes preferentially attach to nodes that are already well connected. In consequence, the topology of the whole network has only few nodes with a high number of connections that link to all of the other nodes that have progressively smaller numbers of connections. Flow patterns are dominated by the highly connected nodes, through which the maximum volume and velocity of energy, information or material flow. These properties characterise the evolution of biological systems and culturally produced metabolic systems.[3] It is important, however, not to confuse the topology diagram with the physical reality. Physical infrastructures are generally massive, constructed from dense materials, with geometry and scale that do not resemble biological networks.

CIVILISATION, ECOLOGY AND CLIMATE

The emergence of cities from the founding system and their subsequent growth, and the subsequent development of the descendant systems of cities, land and maritime nomadic systems, imperial systems and the various phases of the global system were characterised by episodic and irregular expansions and contractions. All developed until they were operating close to the limit of their capacity to support their expanding populations, and to manage the complexity of flows of information, energy and materials through their increasingly extended metabolic systems. Over the last 10,000 years humans have increased their numbers from an estimated 5 million[4] people spread across the world to significantly more than 6 billion today. All human systems have modified ecological systems and the topography of the earth at a variety of spatial and temporal scales, and in doing so they have altered the exchanges between the surface of the earth and the atmosphere. The dynamic thermal processes of the atmosphere are changed, and in consequence the climatic regimes, ecological system and topography of the surface of earth are altered in turn. In the last 100 years the growth of the population has been exponential,[5] and it is widely thought that the total will reach 9 billion within two generations.[6] It is uncertain that the extended metabolism of the world system can be further accelerated to extract sufficient fuel and food energy, materials and water to support 9 billion people.

The megafauna[7] were driven to extinction on all continents by human predation and by the additional indirect stress on their habitats induced by human occupation. Land clearance by fire promoted the spread of grasslands, replacing the mature forest.[8] The gathering of wild grains, nuts, fruit and tubers over tens of thousands of years modified the regime of natural selection to the benefit of those plants and trees favoured by humans. Over tens of thousands of years preferential selection had an impact on the genetic diversity of the ecology,[9] and initiated the genetic changes for the subsequent domestication of wheat, barley, rice, millet and maize. Agriculture has rearranged the trophic processes of ecological systems, modifying the flow of food energy exclusively to support human needs. Humans harvest the primary production of the products of photosynthesis, and this changes the flow of the whole trophic web of ecological systems and in consequence the variation, distribution and population density of the species. Water flow and the carbon exchange between plants and the atmosphere have also been modified.[10] The clearance of forests for agriculture, and the cutting down of trees for fuel and construction over many thousands of years has resulted in the progressive deforestation over three continents, reducing the transpiration of water up into the atmosphere and altering the storage of water in the soil. It has accelerated the spread of savannah grasslands, and the elimination of tree roots has exposed the land to drought and erosion. It has also changed the albedo of the surface. Systematic intensive agriculture has further accelerated these modifications,[11] and contributed to the alteration of river flows and their courses and the silting of deltas. Fuel for domestic uses and for the transformation of materials in manufacturing has added carbon dioxide and other greenhouse gases to the atmosphere, together with soot or black carbon particulates, enabling it to retain more heat energy.

Anatomically modern humans evolved in an extended period of multiple climatic and ecological changes. There have been several major episodes of abrupt change and multiple smaller oscillations since then, many with a very rapid onset of a decade or two. Non-linear perturbations and variations in the monsoon belt tend to induce abrupt cooling in the Atlantic Ocean, and changes to the timing and geographical distribution of rainfall. Changes to the vegetation cover of the land surfaces by human clearance of the forests and woodlands have acted as positive feedback to the changes in temperatures and in the global pattern of precipitation that have varied in duration from decades to several centuries. In many episodes of climatic and ecological changes the agricultural capacity of soils already exhausted by intensive cultivation and overgrazing was further reduced. Energetic returns of extended metabolic systems were diminished, populations declined, and prolonged famines and warfare induced waves of migration and abandonment.

Climate change is strongly coupled to the emergence of all of the cultural systems of civilisation, to their subsequent evolutionary diversifications and developments, expansions and contractions, and to their eventual collapse and reorganisation.

CRITICAL THRESHOLDS

All systems that develop over time pass through a number of changes. The most frequent changes are small, and large changes from which new forms emerge are far less frequent. The form of a hill, sand dune or accumulated snow, for example, is a balance between the resistance of the grains and the force of gravity; that balance between forces produces the angle of the slope. If more mass accumulates, for example, by 'saltating' sand grains, or by fresh snowfall higher up the slope, the slope will be in a state of 'self organised criticality',[12] poised close to the threshold of change. The addition of more grain may be enough to cause the form to change. The change may be small, just a few grains slipping down the slope, or more rarely it may be large, a catastrophic collapse over a large area. There may be more than one 'variable' that can induce change, for example, when water infiltrates the slope or it absorbs the energy of vibrations from earthquakes. Many other landforms develop to this condition, poised close to instability.[13] Critical thresholds are those where the effect produced by a small change in one or more variables, such as the addition of a few grains of material, is disproportionately large or 'non-linear', producing a rapid and substantial collapse and a subsequent cascade of other changes, or a reorganisation from which new forms emerge. Unlike singular and small changes, the large and multiple changes produced by transition through critical threshold are irreversible. There are many continental scale ecological and climatic systems that are known to be sensitive to temperature changes and are either close to their critical threshold and change now, or very soon will be as the world continues to warm.[14] The transition of one or more of them through their critical threshold will provide positive feedback that has the potential to initiate a cascade of changes in others.

The Arctic summer sea ice, diminished by warmer air close to the surface, has a temperature threshold between 0.5° and 2° Celsius of global warming, and the timescale of complete transition through the threshold to an ice-free Arctic sea is thought to be very rapid, perhaps less than 10 years. There are many measured observations that suggest this threshold is very close. Transition will amplify warming and accelerate changes in the ecological systems of the high latitudes. The great ice sheets have such enormous volumes of ice that their complete transitions are widely thought to be slow, although there are many observations that strongly suggest that these transitions have begun, and are proceeding more rapidly than had been anticipated. The Greenland ice sheet has a temperature threshold between 1° and 2° Celsius of global warming, with a much longer timescale of complete transition of more than three centuries. When the transition is completed sea level will be 7 metres higher than it is today. The West Antarctic ice sheet has a temperature threshold of 3° Celsius or more of global warming, with a similar timescale of complete transition of more than three centuries. Complete transition will add a further sea level rise of 5 metres.

The Atlantic thermohaline overturning circulation is sensitive to increased freshwater entering the North Atlantic from the melting ice, with a temperature threshold of 3° Celsius or more of global warming. The reduction and eventual failure of the circulation will significantly shift the converge zones of the atmospheric circulation, inducing larger shifts to the existing climatic regimes across the Northern Hemisphere. The timescale of complete transition is thought to be about 100 years. The El Niño–Southern Oscillation is also similarly sensitive to temperatures of 3° Celsius or more of global warming, and will be greatly amplified after complete transition of about 100 years. The effects will be prolonged and see intense droughts in South-East Asia and other regions in similar latitudes. The monsoon belt has always been prone to abrupt changes, typically taking only one or two years for transition through its critical threshold, and the effects are prolonged droughts across much of Asia. Changes in the albedo of the surface of the Indian subcontinent are thought to be a trigger, but the history of rapid changes suggests that there are other variables that can drive this particular system through its critical threshold.

The forests of the world are conventionally thought to be sensitive to a temperature threshold of 3° Celsius or more of global warming, with a timescale for complete transition of less than 50 years. The shrinkage of spatial extent of the rainforests, including the Amazon, will diminish the transpiration of water and so decrease rainfall, change the albedo of the surface, induce the loss of other living species, and modify the exchange of oxygen and carbon dioxide between the atmosphere and the surface. The boreal forests are also thought to have a similar temperature sensitivity and a 50 year timescale for complete transition to a new form of ecological system such as grassland and shrubs. However, there are multiple variables that can increase that sensitivity and accelerate the transition to complete change of form, including drought, insect and viral infestations, and human predation. Other systems, particularly the tundra and permafrost, are observed and measured to be already in transition to new forms. It is not known how long the complete transitions will take, but the conventional assumption of 100 years now appears to be optimistic.

The increase in temperature observed in recent decades over Alaska provides a canonical example of the transition of a whole ecological system through a cascade of critical thresholds. The warming of the atmosphere has caused the snow to melt earlier in the spring, reduced the extent of sea ice, and increased the duration and depth of the summer melting of permafrost. Each effect provides a positive feedback that adds more warming to the atmosphere and amplifies the other effects. Substantial changes are now observed in the expansion of wetlands, changes to the flora and fauna of the tundra, in the general advance to the north of the tree line of forests, and the significant increases in the frequency and spatial extent of insect infestations over large areas of southern and central Alaska. One beetle, the spruce bark beetle, completed its life cycle in one year rather than in the two years that it took to do so in colder conditions. Spruce forests were already weakened by nine successive years of drought, and so highly vulnerable to the massive increase in insect infestations. Over large areas of south and central Alaska the spruce forests have died off, and the dead trees provide excellent fuel for wild fires, now increased in frequency and spatial extent.[15] As the forests die back in the south and central areas of Alaska, shrubs and grasses replace them, and that in turn produces changes in the species of birds and animals that can live within the ecological system, and the density of their populations.

CLIMATE CHANGE

There have been many changes to the climate system in the past, at a variety of spatial and temporal scales. The climate is changing now and will continue to do so, although there are many uncertainties about the pace and the amplitude of the changes to come. Evidence from the past, and computational models and simulations that are based on that historical data, indicate that there are a large number of subsidiary systems that are close to or approaching their critical threshold. However, it is clear from current observations and measurements that the pace and amplitude of changes has been far more rapid than predicted. It is widely thought that there will continue to be an increase in the emission of greenhouse gases from the burning of fossil fuels in the coming decades, although it is not clear how big that increase will be. Even if it were possible to immediately eliminate any further increases, and to begin to make steady reductions in the quantity of gases emitted, the atmosphere will still retain the gases that have already been emitted, and so the world will continue to warm for many centuries.[16] Evidence from the past suggests that the sensitivity of the climate to greenhouse gases may be variable rather than static, so that changes amplify exponentially as the climate warms. The metasystem is delicately poised, with many different critical thresholds across multiple scales of distance and time, so that a small stimulus at one scale may drive a great and rapid change at another.

In the last decade the differing projections of the amplitude of future surface warming above the current average world temperatures by the end of this century were synthesised in the report by the Intergovernmental Panel on Climate Change (IPPC), with a range of estimates of an increase from below 2° Celsius to above 6° Celsius.[17] The climate simulations were run for different emission scenarios, either assuming that human activities would continue unchanged (the 'business-as-usual' scenario), or aimed at the stabilisation of emissions at a particular level, but with no probabilities attached to any of the scenarios. The higher projections were based on the assumption that the current failure to make any reductions at all in the emission of greenhouse gases will continue, and that emissions will continue to increase as the human population increases and fast feedbacks trigger a cascade of changes. Low estimates were based on the assumption that emissions will continue to rise only for the next decade or less, and then they will be reduced each year by 3 per cent. The middle of this range is based on the premise that emissions will continue to rise for one generation or 25 years before 'stabilising', and that steady reductions of 2 to 3 per cent per year will be achieved thereafter. There is an inherent optimism even in this projection, as it is based on the assumptions that there will be widespread coordination of effective actions across the world, that future technical advances will make the 'stabilisation' and subsequent reductions in emissions possible in only one generation. However, despite the many initiatives and commitments to reducing emissions, there continues to be a steady increase in emissions of between 2 and 3 per cent each year and a consequent rise in the quantity of heat-retaining greenhouse gases in the atmosphere. On this evidence it is reasonable to assume that a large swing from a steady 3 per cent increase to a steady 3 per cent decrease in emissions in such a short time is extremely unlikely.

The projections from the 'MIT Integrated Global System Model' forecast that the median surface warming in 2091 to 2100 will be between 4.1° Celsius and 5.1° Celsius.[18] The projections are 'probabilistic' rather than the scenario base adopted by the IPPC (a more formal mathematical approach to uncertainties), and the model has a higher resolution, and a more detailed representation of human activities across the world than any previous models. Furthermore, the model includes known fast and slow 'feedbacks' that inhibit or accelerate the processes of the climate metasystem, and the cascading effects of successive transitions through different critical thresholds. Significantly, the projections specifically exclude assumptions of future reductions in emissions by international policy changes, but do include mathematical models of irregular regional expansions and contractions of human activities abstracted from historical evidence.

As the percentage of carbon dioxide, nitrous oxide, methane and black carbon in the atmosphere continues to increase, so more heat energy can be absorbed and retained by the atmosphere, and the whole hydrological cycle will be accelerated. Evaporation will increase, and the patterns of atmospheric circulation, winds and precipitation will shift. More heat in the atmosphere will warm the surface below – a positive feedback that will continually increase the temperature of the atmosphere. The mid range projection of 4.6° Celsius global temperature increase will not be the end point of the warming, and it is far from certain that the convention of a century-long timescale is accurate. The evidence from the past shows that large climate changes have frequently occurred far more rapidly. It has long been thought that the thermal inertia of the oceans and the great ice sheets of Greenland and Antarctica would delay the onset of the effects of the current warming by centuries. However, the accumulation of evidence from ice cores, tree rings, corals and sedimentary deposits in lakes and oceans, indicates many episodes of abrupt climate changes in the past, including some with a rapid onset of between three years to a decade.[19] Positive feedbacks from the dynamical processes of the land, oceans and ice sheets, and from the effects of the extended metabolism of civilisation, interact with and accelerate each other. Positive feedbacks accelerate warming[20] and can induce very large and rapid fluctuations in the climate metasystem.[21]

The increase of surface air temperatures is conventionally expressed as an average across the world, but the pattern is differentiated, with smaller temperature rises near to the equator, much larger rises nearer the poles, and more rapid increases over the interior of continents than over the oceans. Temperature increases are also much greater, and more rapid, at the high altitudes in the mountain ranges of all latitudes. The observed shrinking of the permafrost region in recent years is well documented, and extensive areas of Canada, Alaska and Siberia will have increasingly unstable soils as the melt accelerates. The release of carbon dioxide and methane from the newly warmed ground will add yet more greenhouse gases to the atmosphere, providing another positive feedback. The increased air temperature in the Arctic region in recent years[22] has progressively reduced the geographical area and the thickness of sea ice, with increasingly large areas of open water in recent summers. Winter, spring and autumn temperatures in recent years have also been much warmer than the general pattern of the 20th century, with earlier melting in the spring and later formation of sea ice in the autumn and winter.[23] Right across the Northern Hemisphere snowfall will continue to decrease in the coming decades, and the flow of freshwater into the Arctic Ocean from the melting glaciers will accelerate further.

The great ice sheets are now melting at a faster rate than was ever anticipated, and the subsequent increase in albedo change generates a strong positive feedback that will further accelerate the ice melt until the physical stability of the ice sheets is undermined. Once this critical threshold is reached, rapid disintegration and break up will follow. It has long been recognised that a global temperature increase of just 3° Celsius will eventually lead to the elimination of the Greenland ice sheet, and up to 7 metres of sea level rise,[24] but the pace of recent changes in the ice sheets and in glaciers suggests that the predicted rise in sea level during this century has been substantially underestimated. It is now thought that if all the positive feedbacks continue to accelerate, sea level rise of up to 2 metres could occur by the end of the century, although a 1 to 1.5 metre rise is currently considered to be more likely.[25]

The very large river delta regions of Asia, including the Huang He, Changjiang (Yangtze), Pearl, Red, Mekong, Chao Phraya, Irrawaddy, Ganges-Brahmaputra, and Indus rivers have a total area of almost one million square kilometres, all of which is likely to be completely inundated within this century. Across the world almost all of the largest cities are located on rivers and coastal plains, with extensive land areas and infrastructure at or below 2 metres elevation, including London, Venice, New York, Boston, Miami, New Orleans, Los Angeles, Mumbai, Shanghai, Tokyo, Lagos and Capetown. All are highly vulnerable to sea level rise, and to the increased intensity and frequency of large storm surges in a warming world. Rising sea levels will disrupt the flow of freshwater in river deltas and the salt water will contaminate estuaries and groundwater. Increased salinisation will reduce the freshwater available for regional ecological systems, for agriculture and for cities.

As the glaciers continue to shrink, and snowfalls lessen, the quantity of freshwater they supply to river systems is reduced. The glaciers and snow packs of the mid latitude mountain ranges along the Pacific coast of North and South America, of the Alps, Pyrenees and Himalayas, and in New Zealand have all been in retreat for several decades, and the observed changes in ice melting and water run-off will accelerate further during the coming century. The major river systems that they supply will have increasingly early peak flows in winter and spring and greatly reduced summer flows when the demand for agricultural irrigation and drinking water is at its greatest.[26] The inevitable outcome is that these rivers will have little or no flow in the summer months, and by mid century it is anticipated that in many locations there will be complete failure of all river systems and lakes that are fed by mountain glaciers and snow packs.

As the world continues to warm in the coming decades, it is anticipated that the additional heat energy retained in the atmosphere will induce further and more pronounced changes in the mid latitudes 'inter-tropical convergence' zones. This is where warm, moist air rises up into the atmospheric convection cells, and they will shift substantially towards the poles in both hemispheres. Changes in the geographical distribution, variation and intensity of rainfall and monsoons around the world will follow, with complex regional and local outcomes. The intensity and frequency of extreme rainfall and storm events will further increase in regions that are already experiencing extreme rainfall events, including the west coast of India, north-east India, the Bay of Bengal and Bangladesh. There will also be an intensification of drought in the latitudinal band of deserts, which will expand their geographical area substantially, accelerating the observed drying out and desertification in these latitudes.[27] The most severe and prolonged droughts will occur in the south-western region of North America,[28] in the central region of South America, in South Africa and southern Australia, in the northern and western Mediterranean region and in the Sahara. In Europe, the reduction of snowfall in the Alps and the earlier melting of the snow will initially increase the flow of the Rhine and other rivers dramatically in the spring, with risks of widespread flooding across Germany and Holland, but it will also substantially reduce water flow by more than half in the summer months. On the Mediterranean side of the Alps, the land will become increasingly arid from the lack of water and very high temperatures, and desertification will accelerate. Forests will die back in Europe and Asia, and the northern tree line will shift much further into the high latitudes that are currently semiarid savannahs or tundra. In North and South America there will be extensive loss of forest areas as temperatures rise and freshwater diminishes.[29] Agricultural cultivation, particularly wheat, rice and maize, will become increasingly difficult and likely to fail in all tropical regions, where crops are already close to their thermal threshold. As temperatures continue to rise, lack of water will also affect cultivation in the more temperate mid-latitudes, where it is anticipated that crop yields will eventually fall after an initial increase. Forests will shrink back and become increasing vulnerable to fire and pests as droughts become more intense and frequent in subtropical and southern temperate latitudes, especially in the western United States, northern China, southern Europe, the Mediterranean and Australia. Fuel, charcoal and other forest products that are essential for a significant fraction of the world's rural populations will be rapidly diminished. Many forest ecological systems have been affected by climate changes in recent decades, and those effects will be accelerated as the climate continues to warm.

COLLAPSE AND REORGANISATION

Despite their many variations, there are some common characteristics that all the systems of civilisation have exhibited when close to their particular critical threshold, and so vulnerable to change. These include accelerating informational complexity, rising energetic costs of the information and processes that collect and regulate the flow of energy and material over extended distances, small but increasingly frequent oscillations between expansion and contraction, diminishing returns and rising costs, expanding populations and disproportionate and inequitable distribution of consumption. Climatic and ecological changes have often initiated decline, and the responses to diminishing returns and decline have included warfare to capture or defend resources, inappropriate intensification of agricultural and energetic resources already at maximum capacity, planned simplification, and abandonment and mass migrations. These processes have usually occurred over the course of a single human generation, but some persisted over several generations.

It is clear that the current metabolic system of the world, with its accelerating informational complexity, extreme velocity and volumes of fuel and food energy flowing across continents and oceans, and high but inequitable energy and material consumption, exhibits similar characteristics. Despite the high density flow of information and the high proportion of the population engaged in regulating and administering the energy and material flows, the global system is now highly vulnerable to disruption and perturbation. Further intensification of flows through the extended metabolism, sometimes referred to as 'continuing economic growth', is incompatible with the significant reductions in agricultural returns of food and fuel energy that are anticipated as the climate changes over the next decades. It follows that if the predicted increase in the population of the world, from significantly more than 6 billion today to over 9 billion in the next three decades, were to come about it would precipitate the catastrophic collapse of the system. A decade ago there were 450 cities in the world with a population of 1 million or more. An additional 3 billion people will require the equivalent of 3,000 new cities of that size to be built within one generation. The quantities of materials required, and the energy required to transform and manipulate those materials and construct the cities are immense. The supply of food and fuel energy to support an additional population half the size again of the world's existing population cannot be met by the current metabolic system that is already operating close to its maximum capacity.

The outcomes of the collapse of cultural systems in the past have been strikingly similar to the collapse and reorganisation of natural complex systems; the complete loss of social order and dispersal of the people by famine, disease, abandonment of cities and mass migration; a regrouping of the cities and settlements within the extended systems into smaller and simpler assemblies with reduced connections to other local and regional systems or a reorganisation to a lower level of complexity; and the reordering of the cities, people and subsidiary systems into a more integrated assembly or more complex reorganisation with a higher flow of energy and information. If it is so that the world system is now poised close to its critical threshold of stability, and if it is

THE ARCHITECTURE OF EMERGENCE

so that the climate changes currently under way cannot be inhibited by significant reduction in emissions within the next decade, then it follows that changes will cascade through all the systems of nature and civilisation. Although the scale of the world system is currently at least one order of magnitude greater than the largest imperial system of the past,[30] there are sufficient similarities to suggest the delineation of three principal modes of transition through the critical thresholds of nature and civilisation from which new forms will emerge.

DISPERSAL AND ABANDONMENT

If the present course is continued, the quantities of resources invested in the intensification of flows of energy, information and materials through the system will necessarily increase as the population rises. Emissions will be accelerated by the intensification of the system and resources will be further depleted. The inequitable differentiation of resources and consumption within nations and between them will continue, the existing social and commercial institutions will be maintained and populations will continue to expand exponentially. Thousands of new cities need be built, but are likely to be significantly underfunded, and in consequence poorly constructed and inadequately serviced as resources become increasingly scarce. The widespread failure to recognise the necessity for a timescale of two generations and massive resource commitment for continental scale deployment and activation of new energy systems will continue to inhibit the funding of research and development. Similarly, there is a widespread failure to recognise that the first regional scale transitions to new ecological systems have already commenced and are likely to be completed within two generations. Significant reductions in agricultural returns and freshwater will accelerate rapidly over the next generation, and it is very likely that the differentiated and inequitable distribution will lead to widespread social unrest and famine in the most ecologically stressed regions. In these regions construction of new buildings and cities will cease altogether, and it is likely that within one generation large territories will be abandoned. Mass migration into territories that are less stressed is likely to be resisted by closed borders and by arms. In the less stressed regions, despite rapidly diminishing ecological resources, intensification will have to be continued. This will provide positive feedback that will amplify and accelerate climate and ecological changes.

The transoceanic and intercontinental flow of energy, materials and people is likely to be significantly diminished, and countries and regions that import a high percentage of their food and fuel energy from outside their borders will be greatly stressed. As the climatic and ecological transitions accelerate, widespread social unrest, famine, and sporadic but massive incursions will lead continental scale systems with substantial agricultural and energy resources within their borders to seal their boundaries entirely. It is likely that their own diminished resources will make it increasingly difficult to feed and fuel their own system, and they are likely to cease transoceanic and intercontinental flows altogether. Sealed within their own borders they may well allow the depredations of famine and disease to reduce their populations in order to husband their resources. Rising sea level, famine and disease will eventually lead to the widespread abandonment of delta cities, and the mass dispersals of people will further stress immediately adjacent territories. The smaller systems and aggregations of small systems will be weakened by mass famine and increasingly limited resources and will then rapidly decline and effectively cease to exist as distinct entities.

Widespread abandonment of cities in significantly stressed territories will follow, but the lack of energy resources, insufficient land for subsistence agriculture and the sealed borders of larger systems will rapidly reduce the population in these territories. Isolated 'refugia' will certainly continue at a variety of scales and in locations where the climatic and ecological changes are broadly favourable or at least endurable, but the world population will inevitably be significantly reduced. Within four generations the extended metabolic system of civilisation that now extends across the world will have shrunk back to a few strictly contained metabolic systems with defined boundaries and restricted connections to other systems. The first climatic and ecological transitions will then be completed and changes will have begun to cascade rapidly through both natural and cultural systems. New forms of ecological system will have emerged in the high and mid latitudes, the deserts will be expanding and sea level will have risen. Some 'refugia' may gradually decay and decline as their existing energy, agricultural and information systems fail over time. It is likely, however, that the majority of 'refugia' cities and their localised metabolic systems will have already begun to change, rebuilding themselves slowly cell by cell as resources allow, and new forms of metabolic system based on local resources will emerge. New building and ultimately new city forms will emerge over multiple generations. It is likely that the warming of the climate will continue over the next millennia, and the evolution of the forms and metabolic systems of settlements, cities and systems of cities that are viable in those new conditions from the small base of isolated 'refugia' into an integrated new world system is likely to occur at best very slowly, if at all.

SIMPLIFICATION

If it is so that a worldwide consensus does eventually emerge that the present course cannot be continued and that consumption of all kinds should be reduced, it is likely to take a whole human generation to do so. Similarly, a widespread agreement to limit the expansion of the population is also likely to take a generation to become effective, and in the meantime population growth will continue but at a slower rate than is currently predicted. The quantities of resources invested in the intensification of flows of energy, information and materials through the system will be slowly reduced, although the increase in population will inhibit the reduction of flows for at least one generation. Some elements within all societies may never abandon their commitment to high energy systems, expansion and increasing and inequitable consumption. Those elements will eventually be coerced, or overtaken by events, but their resistance to change will be effective for at least one generation. Emissions will continue to increase throughout the next generation but at a slower rate, and it is likely that emissions will only begin to significantly diminish after two generations have passed. The inequitable differentiation of resources and consumption within nations and between them will be minimally moderated by the gradual reduction in consumption, and existing social and commercial institutions will slowly be reduced and transformed to align with the new consensus. Research and development of new sources of energy will continue to be minimally funded, but will slowly increase as recognition of the two generation timescale and resource commitment necessary for continental scale deployment and activation of new energy systems becomes widespread. Deployment of solar energy systems and other energy sources that do not emit greenhouse gases and black carbon particles may provide one third of all fuel energy within two generations, and two thirds within three generations.

Significant reductions in agricultural returns and freshwater will accelerate rapidly over the next two generations, and the expanded populations will reduce surplus capacity everywhere. Despite willingness to assist others, it is likely that there will be insufficient surplus to ameliorate the famine and widespread social distress in the most ecologically stressed regions. In these regions construction of new buildings and cities will cease altogether, and city after city will be abandoned. Mass migration into territories that are less ecologically stressed will be restricted, but not completely resisted until the numbers threaten to overwhelm their own capacity. Ultimately there will be too many migrants and borders are likely to be closed. Reduced consumption everywhere will begin to reduce transoceanic and intercontinental flows within two generations, but it is the shortage of fuel and food supplies for the expanded population that is most likely to significantly reduce them. As the climatic and ecological transitions accelerate, widespread social unrest, famine, and sporadic but massive incursions will increase the necessity for smaller systems and assemblies of smaller systems to close their borders and defend what resources they have to sustain their populations at a low level of consumption. The majority of small systems are currently located within regions that have a high dependency on fuel and food imports from across the world, and widespread abandonment of their cities will follow the significantly diminished flow within two generations. If transoceanic and intercontinental flows do eventually cease altogether, the majority of the population in ecologically distressed territories will attempt to migrate or will succumb to famine.

Rising sea level, famine and disease will lead to the widespread abandonment of delta cities, and the mass dispersals of peoples will further stress immediately adjacent territories. Continental scale systems with expanded populations and diminished resources will only be able to accept large numbers of migrants by further reducing consumption. Within their own territories the migration from cities to smaller more rural cities and settlements will accelerate over two generations, and within three generations even the largest cities are very likely to have significantly reduced populations. Societal commitment to reducing the population will inevitably be reinforced by coercion and closed borders, and will only begin to be significantly effective within three generations. The new forms of ecological system in the high and mid latitudes, and the expanding deserts and rising sea level will produce significant stress on the emerging reconfiguration of the larger systems. Local and regional scale patches will decline and fail as their local ecological systems change and further reduce agricultural returns. Famine will further reduce the population. Within four generations the reduced population will be widely dispersed in localised systems of small cities and settlements, with the major fraction of their food and fuel energy extracted from their local environment. Connections to other systems will be maintained at a minimal level. Over multiple generations the reconfiguration of agricultural and low energy systems will be refined and fully deployed, regional connections will slowly intensify and a low energy and low density agrarian system with new forms of buildings and cities and a network topology adapted to the new forms of ecological system and climatic regime will emerge.

HIGHER COMPLEXITY

If it is so that civilisation will transit through multiple critical thresholds to higher complexity, those elements within all societies that are unwilling or unable to abandon their commitment to inequitable consumption will have to be bypassed within the next generation. The flows of energy, information and materials through the system will have to be accelerated. Despite the widespread consensus that there is insufficient capacity in the world metabolic system to successfully transit through the multiple critical thresholds, population growth is likely to continue unabated, necessitating extensive building of new cities and increased density in some existing cities. The increase of emissions caused by the expansion of populations, the mass construction of new cities and the intensification of energy, information and material flows will be amplified by the ecological transitions induced by climate change, and initiate the cascade of multiple transitions in all ecological systems. Thereafter, widespread observation that the impending cascade of transitions through all the systems of nature and civilisation is under way and accelerating will lead to societal commitment to the redesign and reconfiguration of the world's metabolic system.

The development of new sources of energy that do not emit greenhouse gases and black carbon particles will require the investment of a significant fraction of the global economy, as will the accelerated flow of information. The widespread deployment of new energy systems in suitable areas to supply half of all the fuel energy of the world is likely to take two complete generations, and full deployment in those territories is unlikely to be achieved before three generations have passed. Voluntary commitment to limiting the expansion of the population may begin to slow the rate of expansion within one generation, but will have to be reinforced by strong societal commitment with some coercion if the world population is to be stabilised within two generations. Emissions will thus continue to increase, and are unlikely to begin to diminish until the deployment of new energy systems has reached half of all energy generation. Investment in information, both research and distribution systems, is likely to continue at current levels and is only likely to increase when the first regional scale ecological transitions begin to significantly diminish agricultural returns and reduce freshwater supplies, and all resources become scarce. The wide dissemination of free information to all parts of the world will then begin to have a significant impact on all energy and material transformations, and the transition to a truly 'distributed intelligence' world system will be accelerated. The first regional scale transitions to new ecological systems are likely to be completed within the next two generations, and severe famines in ecologically stressed regions will lead to widespread social unrest in those territories. In those circumstances the construction of new buildings and cities will rapidly diminish and ultimately cease altogether. In city after city the generation-long process of abandonment and mass migrations will commence.

Completed ecological transitions of the high and mid latitudes, expanded deserts and rising sea level will produce significant stress on all systems, and there will be multiple local and some regional failures everywhere. However, high density energy and information systems will help to ameliorate a significant fraction of the difficulties in providing food and fuel that all systems will experience. Systemic agricultural failure and the depredations of famine and disease in regions that have not adapted their systems will induce widespread abandonment of their cities in favour of small subsistence level rural systems where there is available territory, and mass migrations will increase the stresses elsewhere. There is very likely to be a significant reduction in the world population within four generations.

Higher complexity in all systems is characterised by increased differentiation and increased connections, in conjunction with an accelerated flow of energy. In the systems of civilisation the accelerated flow of energy has always been coupled to increased quantities and kinds of information and to greater transformation and flow of materials. In each of the newly emerged and reconfigured ecological systems, new forms of cities will begin to emerge within two generations, and be widely proliferated within four generations. Continental flows of energy and material are likely to be intensified as intelligent inhabited infrastructures that unite and service ecological systems rather than divide them come on-line. Transoceanic flows are only likely to be significantly reduced within three generations if the flow of information accelerates and begins to reduce the necessity to move transformed materials over great distances.

In the high latitudes where the tundra and permafrost will have completed transition to boreal forests and grassland, new large but low density cities will emerge that are organised as intelligent ecological infrastructures that capture methane and sequester carbon, fix nitrogen, collect and purify water, and produce agriculture materials that are symbiotically integrated with the regional ecological system. Surface farming of methane released by the melting permafrost will provide a substantial high-density energy source for systems of cities above the soft terrain right across the high latitudes, incorporating large-scale intensive agricultural systems. These city systems will be morphologically and topologically very different from cities today, most likely configured with multiple small nuclei within networks of inhabited energy and agricultural infrastructures.

In the mid latitudes new agricultural infrastructures will be inhabited more densely and large urban densely inhabited systems will be gradually transformed as their populations decline, but these transformations will be very slow over multiple generations. Cities and metabolic systems everywhere will be more differentiated in scale, intensively but selectively connected in new network topologies that are symbiotically configured to the flows in their local and regional ecological systems. Within three generations rising sea level will have a profound effect on river delta cities and densely inhabited low-lying coastal territories. Some delta cities will gradually be transformed to highly engineered and intelligent polders, substantially reconfigured above and below sea level as marine ecological machines that capture energy and have extensive breeding and husbandry of marine life. However, where such transformations fail from lack of investment and political will, rising sea levels, famine and disease will induce widespread abandonment of most if not all delta cities and many coastal territories, and the mass dispersals of peoples will further stress immediately adjacent inland territories.

Desert cities will be gradually transformed into inhabited energy infrastructures, with vast arrays of solar energy systems generating constant supplies of high-density energy that can be transmitted across continental scale distances through intelligent electrical grids.

It is clear that the world is within the horizon of a systemic change, and that transitions through multiple critical thresholds will cascade through all the systems of nature and civilisation. New forms will emerge down through all the generations to come, and they will develop with new connections between them as they proliferate across the surface of the earth.

1 One human generation = 25 years.

2 Moses, ME, S Forrest, AL Davis, MA Lodder and JH Brown, 'Scaling Theory for Information Networks', *Journal of The Royal Society Interface*, vol 5, no 29, 2008, pp 1469–80.

3 Barabási, AL and R Albert, 'Emergence of Scaling in Random Networks', *Science*, vol 286, 1999, pp 509–12; and Jeong, H, B Tombor, R Albert, ZN Oltvai and AL Barabási, 'The Large-Scale Organization of Metabolic Networks', *Nature*, vol 407, 2000, pp 651–4.

4 Data from *The World at Six Billion*, Population Division, Department of Economic and Social Affairs, United Nations Secretariat, 1999.

5 The larger the number gets, the faster it grows.

6 By 2050. The US Census Bureau International Data Base, April 2009.

7 Animals weighing more than 44 kilograms are generally referred to as 'megafauna' – but the mammoths and mastodons weighed over 1,000 kilograms.

8 Hope, G, 'Early Fire and Forest Change in the Baliem Valley, Irian Jaya, Indonesia', *Journal of Biogeography*, vol 25, 1998, pp 453–61.

9 Ledig, FT, 'Human Impacts on Genetic Diversity in Forest Ecosystems', *Oikos*, vol 63, 1992, pp 87–108.

10 Foley, JA, C Monfreda, N Ramankutty and D Zaks, 'Our Share of the Planetary Pie', *Proceedings of the National Academy of Sciences*, vol 104, 2007, pp 12585–6.

11 Robock, A and HF Graf, 'Effects of Pre-Industrial Human Activities on Climate', *Chemosphere*, vol 5, 1994, pp 1087–97.

12 Bak, P, C Tang and K Weisenfeld, 'Self-Organized Criticality: an explanation of the 1/f noise', *Physical Review Letters*, vol 59, 1987, pp 381–4. Presents the first argument that unconstrained dynamical systems naturally evolve into a self-organised critical state.

13 Schumm, SA, 'Geomorphic Thresholds: the concept and its applications', *Transactions of the Institute of British Geographers*, New Series vol 4, 1979, pp 485–515.

14 Lenton, TM, H Held, E Kriegler, JW Hall, W Lucht, S Rahmstorf and HJ Schellnhuber, 'Tipping Elements in the Earth's Climate System', *Proceedings of the National Academy of Sciences*, vol 105, no 6, 2008, pp 1786–93.

15 'Thresholds of Climate Change in Ecosystems', US Climate Change Science Program and the Subcommittee on Global Change Research, 2009, pp 4, 32–6.

16 'There is high agreement and much evidence that with current climate change mitigation policies and related sustainable development practices, global GHG emissions will continue to grow over the next few decades'; and 'Both past and future anthropogenic CO_2 emissions will continue to contribute to warming and sea level rise for more than a thousand years'. *Climate Change 2007 Synthesis Report*, Intergovernmental Panel on Climate Change, 2008.

17 '… the best estimate for the low scenario is 1.8°C (likely range is 1.1°C to 2.9°C), and the best estimate for the high scenario is 4.0°C (likely range is 2.4°C to 6.4°C).' *Climate Change 2007 Synthesis Report*, Intergovernmental Panel on Climate Change, 2008.

18 Sokolov, AP, PH Stone, CE Forest, R Prinn, MC Sarofim, M Webster, S Paltsev, CA Schlosser, D Kicklighter, S Dutkiewicz, J Reilly, C Wang, B Felzer and HD Jacoby, 'Probabilistic Forecast for 21st Century Climate Based on Uncertainties in Emissions (without Policy) and Climate Parameters', *MIT Joint Program on the Science and Policy of Global Change*, 2009.

19 Jones, PD, KR Briffa, TP Barnett and SFB Tett, 'High-Resolution Palaeoclimatic Records for the Last Millennium: interpretation, integration and comparison with General Circulation Model control-run temperatures', *The Holocene*, vol 8, 1998, pp 455–71; and Mann, ME, RS Bradley and MK Hughes, 'Global-Scale Temperature Patterns and Climate Forcing over the Past Six Centuries', *Nature*, vol 392, 1998, pp 779–87; and Mann, ME, RS Bradley and MK Hughes, 'Northern Hemisphere Temperatures during the Past Millennium: inferences, uncertainties and limitations', *Geophysical Research Letters*, vol 26, 1999, pp 759–62.

20 Cox, PM, RA Betts, CD Jones, SA Spall and J Totterdell, 'Acceleration of Global Warming due to Carbon-Cycle Feedbacks in a Coupled Climate Model', *Nature*, vol 408, 2000, pp184–7.

21 Hansen, James, Makiko Sato, Pushker Kharecha, Gary Russell, David W Lea and Mark Siddall, 'Climate Change and Trace Gases', *Philosophical Transactions of the Royal Society* of London *A*, vol 365, 2007, pp 1925–54.

22 'Arctic Report 2008 – Atmosphere', *US National Oceanic and Atmospheric Administration*, http://www.arctic.noaa.gov/reportcard/atmosphere.html.

23 Overland, JE, M Wang, and S Salo, 'The Recent Arctic Warm Period', *Tellus*, vol 60A, 2008, pp 589–97.

24 *Climate Change 2007 Synthesis Report*, Intergovernmental Panel on Climate Change, 2008.

25 Pfeffer, WT, JT Harper and S O'Neel, 'Kinematic Constraints on Glacier Contributions to 21st-Century Sea-Level Rise', *Science*, vol 321, 2008, pp 1340–3.

26 Barnett, TP, JC Adam and DP Lettenmaier, 'Potential Impacts of a Warming Climate on Water Availability in Snow-Dominated Regions', *Nature*, vol 438, 2005, pp 303–9.

27 'Globally, the area of land classified as very dry has more than doubled since 1970', *Climate Change 2007 Synthesis Report*, Intergovernmental Panel on Climate Change, 2008.

28 Cook, ER, R Seager, MA Cane and DW Stahle, 'North American Drought: reconstructions, causes, and consequences', *Earth Science Reviews*, vol 81, 2007, pp 93–134.

29 Scholze, M, W Knorr, NW Arnell and CI Prentice, 'A Climate-Change Risk Analysis for World Ecosystems', *Proceedings of the National Academy of Sciences*, vol 103, 2006, pp 13116–20.

30 In 1938 the British Empire is though to have had a population of over 500 million or half a billion. In 2009 the world population is thought to be rapidly approaching 7 billion.

SELECT BIBLIOGRAPHY

Full bibliographic details are provided in the footnotes of each chapter. This small selection provides an outline of processes of the complex systems from which all forms emerge, develop and proliferate, collapse and reorganise in an endless sequence.

Chapter 1. Nature and Civilisation

Anderson, GM, *Thermodynamics of Natural Systems*, Cambridge University Press (Cambridge), 2005.

Bak, Per, Chao Tang and Kurt Weisenfeld, 'Self-Organized Criticality: an explanation of the 1/f noise', *Physical Review Letters* 59, 1987

Camazine, S, J-L Deneubourg, N Franks, J Sneyd, G Theraulaz and E Bonabeau, *Self-Organization in Biological Systems*, Princeton Studies in Complexity, Princeton University Press (Princeton), 2001

Cowan, GA, D Pines, D Meltzer (eds), *Complexity: metaphors, models and reality*, Santa Fe Institute Studies in the Sciences of Complexity, Advanced Book Program, Perseus Books (Reading, MA), 1994

Darwin, Charles, *On the Origin of Species by Means of Natural Selection, or the Preservation of Favoured Races in the Struggle for Life*, John Murray (London), 1859

Thompson, D'Arcy Wentworth, *On Growth And Form* (first published 1917), Cambridge University Press (Cambridge), 1961

Whitehead, Alfred North, *The Concept of Nature*, Cambridge University Press (Cambridge), 1920

Chapter 2. Climate and the Forms of the Atmosphere

Barry, RG and AM Carleton, *Synoptic and Dynamic Climatology*, Routledge (London and New York), 2001

Gribbin, J and M Gribbin, *FitzRoy: the remarkable story of Darwin's captain and the invention of the weather forecast*, Yale University Press (Yale), 2004

Hansen, James, Makiko Sato, Pushker Kharecha, Gary Russell, David Lea and Mark Siddall, 'Climate Change and Trace Gases', *Philosophical Transactions of the Royal Society of London A*, vol 365, 2007, pp 2117–31

Chapter 3. Surface and the Forms of the Land

Bak, Per, Chao Tang and Kurt Weisenfeld 'Self-Organized Criticality: an explanation of the 1/f noise', *Physical Review Letters*, vol 59, 1987, pp 381–4

Büdel, J, *Climatic Geomorphology*, Princeton University Press (Princeton), 1982, first published as *Klima-geomorphologie*, Gebrüder Bornträger (Berlin), 1977

Bull, WB, *Geomorphic Responses to Climatic Change*, The Blackburn Press (New Jersey), 1991

Phillips, JD, 'Sources of Nonlinear Complexity in Geomorphic Systems', *Progress in Physical Geography*, vol 27, 2003, pp 1–23

Schumm, SA, 'Geomorphic Thresholds: the concept and its applications', *Transactions of the Institute of British Geographers*, New Series, vol 4, 1979, pp 485–515

Chapter 4. Living Forms

Carroll, SB, *Endless Forms Most Beautiful, the new science of EvoDevo and the making of the animal kingdom*, Weidenfeld and Nicolson (London), 2006

Carroll SB, 'Homeotic Genes and the Evolution of Arthropods and Chordates', *Nature*, vol 376, 1995, pp 479–85

Cavalier-Smith, T, 'Cell Evolution and Earth History: stasis and revolution', *Philosophical Transactions of the Royal Society B*, 2006

Davies, JA, *Mechanisms of Morphogenesis, the creation of biological form*, Elsevier Academic Press (Burlington, MA), 2005

Gould, Stephen Jay, *The Structure of Evolutionary Theory*, Harvard University Press (Cambridge, MA), 2002

Harold, FM, *The Way of the Cell: molecules, organisms and the order of life*, Oxford University Press (New York), 2001

Chapter 5. The Forms of Metabolism

Gould, JL and CG Gould, *Animal Architects: building and the evolution of intelligence*, Basic Books (New York), 2007

Morowitz, HJ, *Energy Flow in Biology: biological organization as a problem in thermal physics*, Academic Press (New York), 1968

Niklas, KJ, *Plant Allometry*, University of Chicago Press (Chicago), 1994

Price, CA, BJ Enquist and VM Savage, 'A General Model for Allometric Covariation in Botanical Form and Function', *Proceedings of the National Academy of Sciences*, vol 104, no 32, August 2007, pp 1304–9

West GB, JH Brown and BJ Enquist, 'A General Model for the Origin of Allometric Scaling Laws in Biology', *Science*, vol 276, 1997, pp 122–6

Whitfield, J, *In the Beat of a Heart: life, energy, and the unity of nature*, Joseph Henry Press (New York), 2006

Chapter 6. Humans – Anatomical and Cultural Forms

Cavalli-Sforza, LL, *Genes, People and Languages*, North Point Press (New York), 2000

Lahr, M and R Foley, 'Towards a Theory of Modern Human Origins: geography, demography, and diversity in recent human evolution', *Yearbook of Physical Anthropology*, vol 41, 1998, pp 137–76

Odling-Smee, FJ, KN Laland and MW Feldman, *Niche Construction, The Neglected Process in Evolution*, Princeton University Press (Princeton), 2003

Chapter 7. City Forms

Brooks, N, 'Cultural Responses to Aridity in the Middle Holocene and Increased Social Complexity', *Quaternary International*, vol 151, 2006, pp 29–49

Roberts, N, *The Holocene, An Environmental History* (second edition), Blackwell Publishing (Oxford), 1998, pp 7, 62–3, 115–6

Chapter 8. Forms of Information, Energy and Material

Scheidel, W, 'From the "Great Convergence" to the "First Great Divergence": Roman and Qin-Han state formation and its aftermath', *Princeton/Stanford Working Papers in Classics*, 2007

Smil, V, *Energy in Nature and Society, General Energetics of Complex Systems*, The MIT Press, 2008

Tainter, JA, *The Collapse of Complex Societies*, Cambridge University Press (Cambridge), 1990

Chapter 9. Emergence

Hansen, James, Makiko Sato, Pushker Kharecha, Gary Russell, David W Lea and Mark Siddall, 'Climate Change and Trace Gases', *Philosophical Transactions of the Royal Society of London A*, vol 365, 2007, pp 1925–54

Jeong, H, B Tombor, R Albert, ZN Oltvai and AL Barabási, 'The Large-Scale Organization of Metabolic Networks', *Nature*, vol 407, 2000, pp 651–4

Lenton, TM, H Held, E Kriegler, JW Hall, W Lucht, S Rahmstorf and HJ Schellnhuber, 'Tipping Elements in the Earth's Climate System', *Proceedings of the National Academy of Sciences*, vol 105, no 6, 2008, pp 1786–93

Sokolov, AP, PH Stone, CE Forest, R Prinn, MC Sarofim, M Webster, S Paltsev, CA Schlosser, D Kicklighter, S Dutkiewicz, J Reilly, C Wang, B Felzer and HD Jacoby, 'Probabilistic Forecast for 21st Century Climate Based on Uncertainties in Emissions (without Policy) and Climate Parameters', *MIT Joint Program on the Science and Policy of Global Change*, 2009, pp 5175–5204

INDEX

PHOTO CREDITS

Boiling Water, page 10
Alfred Pasieka/Science photo Library

Eroded Mountain, page 13
Bernhard Edmaier/ Science photo Library

Eroded Canyon, page 15
Keith Kent /Science photo Library

Coral, page 17
Mary Beth Angelo/ Science photo Library

Mutation, page 21
Eye of Science/ Science photo Library

Primate Skulls, page 23
D. Roberts/ Science photo Library

Mammoth Bones, page 24
Ria Novosti/Science photo Library

Information, page 25
Science Source/ Science photo Library

Branching, page 28
Cristina Pedrazzini/ Science photo Library

Abandoned City, page 35
George Steinmaetz/ Science photo Library

Urbanisation of the World, page 38
NOAA /Science photo Library